SIMPSONS™ COMICS
GAME ON!

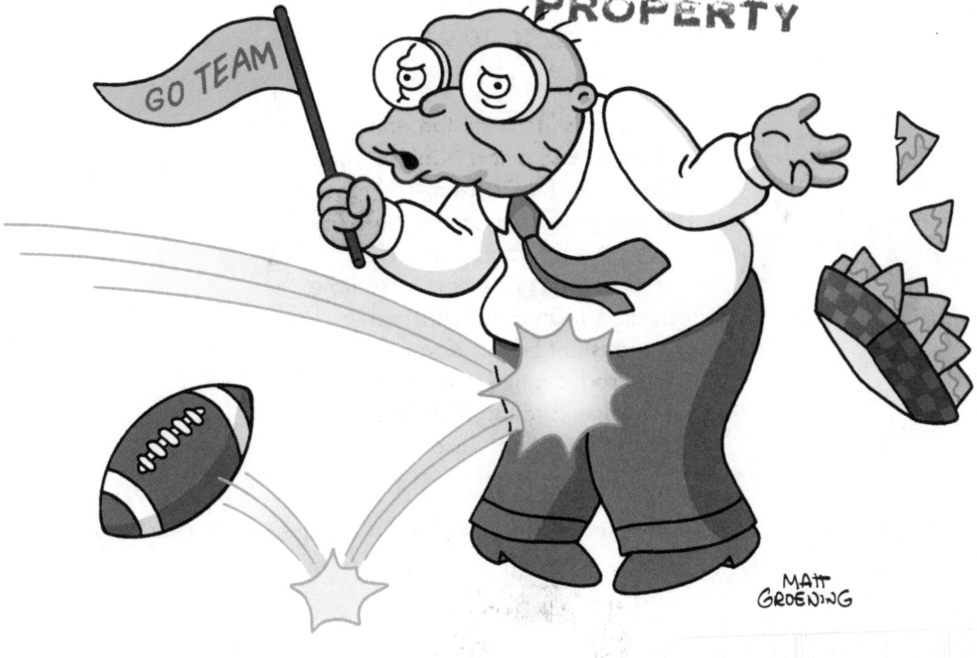
GO TEAM
MATT GROENING

HARPER DESIGN
An Imprint of HarperCollinsPublishers

SIMPSONS COMICS GAME ON!

Simpsons Comics #121, 122, 123, 124, 125

Copyright © 2018 by
Bongo Entertainment, Inc. All rights reserved.
No part of this book may be used or reproduced in any manner whatsoever
without written permission except in the case of brief quotations
embodied in critical articles and reviews. For information address
HarperCollins Publishers,
195 Broadway, New York, New York 10007.

FIRST EDITION

ISBN 978-0-06-269251-1
Library of Congress Control Number 2017936299
18 19 20 21 22 TC 10 9 8 7 6 5 4 3 2 1

Publisher: Matt Groening
Creative Director: Nathan Kane
Managing Editor: Terry Delegeane
Director of Operations: Robert Zaugh
Art Director: Jason Ho
Assistant Art Director: Mike Rote
Production Manager: Christopher Ungar
Assistant Editor: Karen Bates
Production: Art Villanueva
Administration: Ruth Waytz
Legal Guardian: Susan A. Grode

Printed by TC Transcontinental, Beauceville, QC, Canada. 12/04/2017

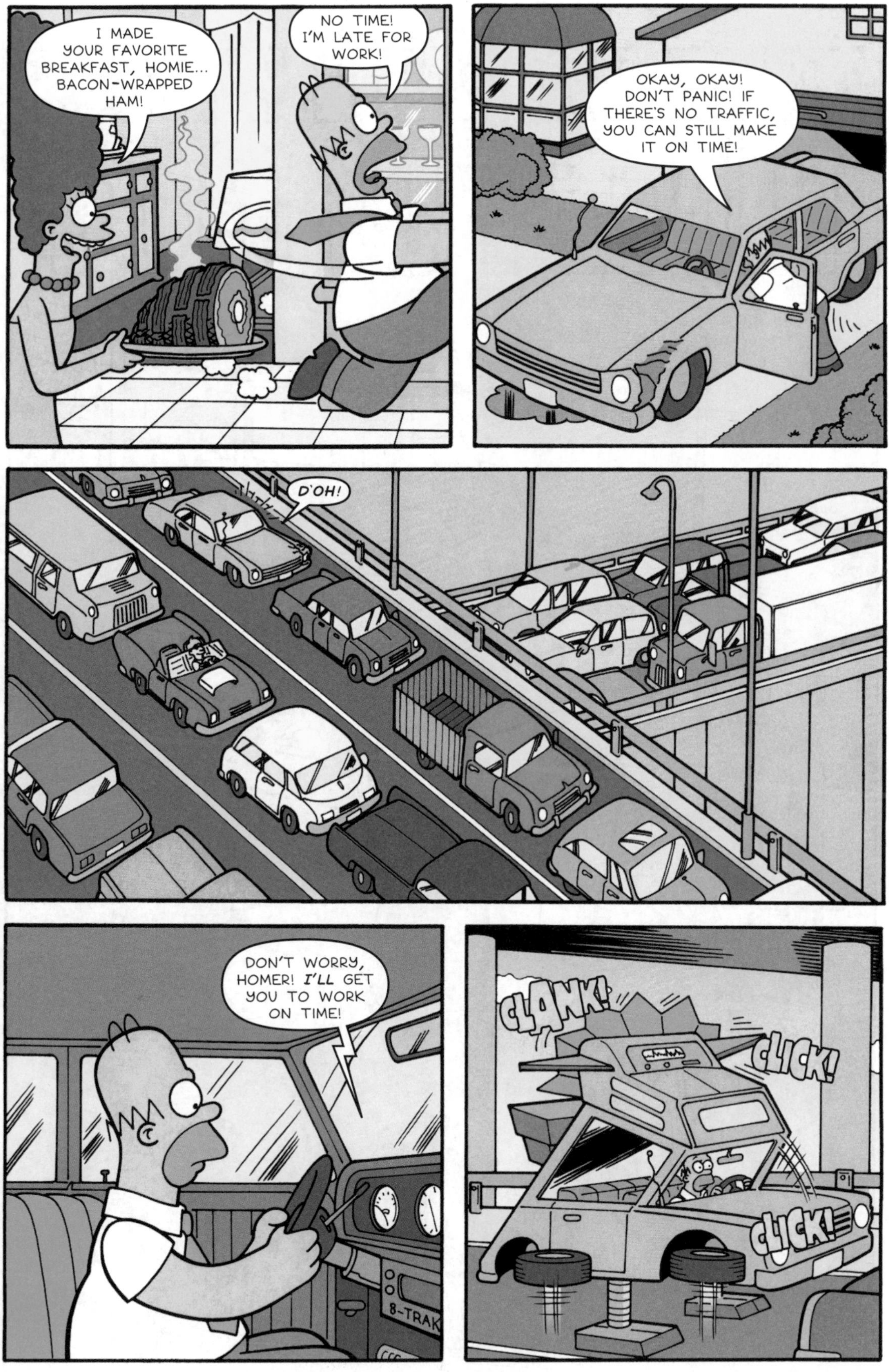
I MADE YOUR FAVORITE BREAKFAST, HOMIE... BACON-WRAPPED HAM!
NO TIME! I'M LATE FOR WORK!
OKAY, OKAY! DON'T PANIC! IF THERE'S NO TRAFFIC, YOU CAN STILL MAKE IT ON TIME!
D'OH!
DON'T WORRY, HOMER! *I'LL* GET YOU TO WORK ON TIME!
8-TRAK
CLANK!
CLICK!
CLICK!

MATT GROENING presents

THE TOWN THAT TIME FORGOT

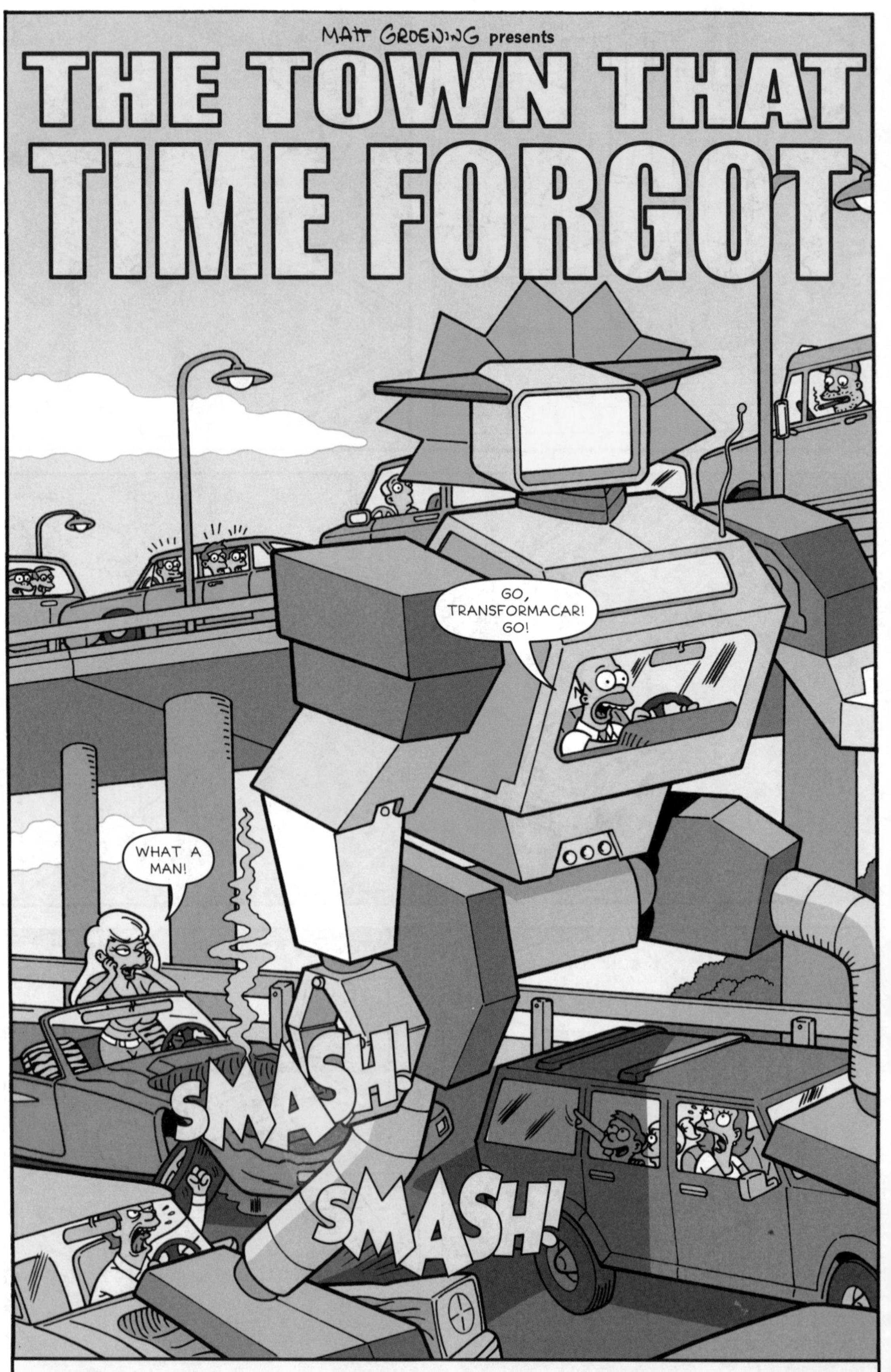
GO, TRANSFORMACAR! GO!
WHAT A MAN!
SMASH!
SMASH!

IAN BOOTHBY SCRIPT **PHIL ORTIZ** PENCILS **MIKE DECARLO** INKS **ART VILLANUEVA** COLORS **KAREN BATES** LETTERS **BILL MORRISON** EDITOR

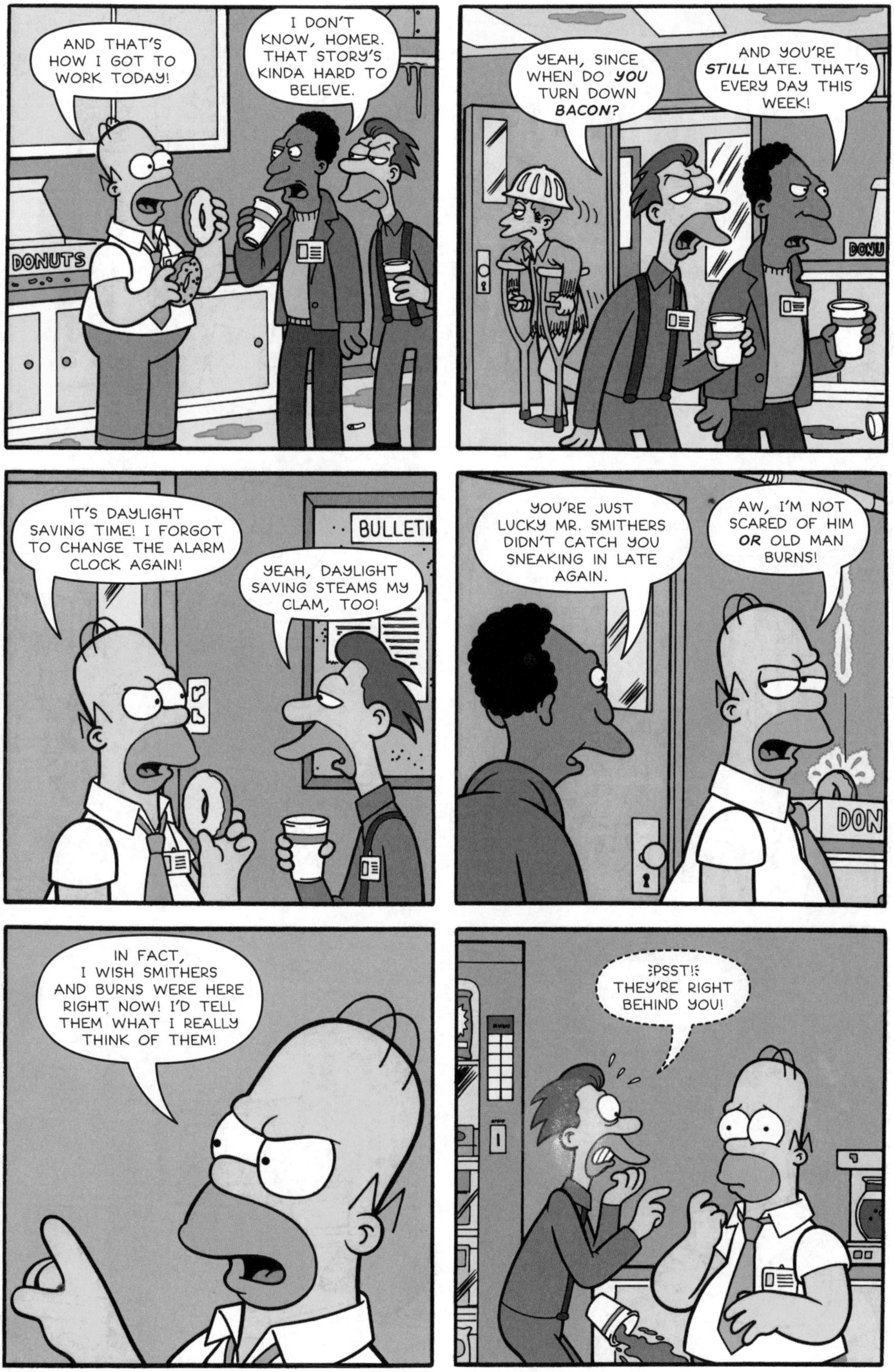
AND THAT'S HOW I GOT TO WORK TODAY!
I DON'T KNOW, HOMER. THAT STORY'S KINDA HARD TO BELIEVE.
DONUTS
YEAH, SINCE WHEN DO YOU TURN DOWN BACON?
AND YOU'RE STILL LATE. THAT'S EVERY DAY THIS WEEK!
DONU
IT'S DAYLIGHT SAVING TIME! I FORGOT TO CHANGE THE ALARM CLOCK AGAIN!
YEAH, DAYLIGHT SAVING STEAMS MY CLAM, TOO!
BULLETI
YOU'RE JUST LUCKY MR. SMITHERS DIDN'T CATCH YOU SNEAKING IN LATE AGAIN.
AW, I'M NOT SCARED OF HIM OR OLD MAN BURNS!
DON
IN FACT, I WISH SMITHERS AND BURNS WERE HERE RIGHT NOW! I'D TELL THEM WHAT I REALLY THINK OF THEM!
PSST! THEY'RE RIGHT BEHIND YOU!

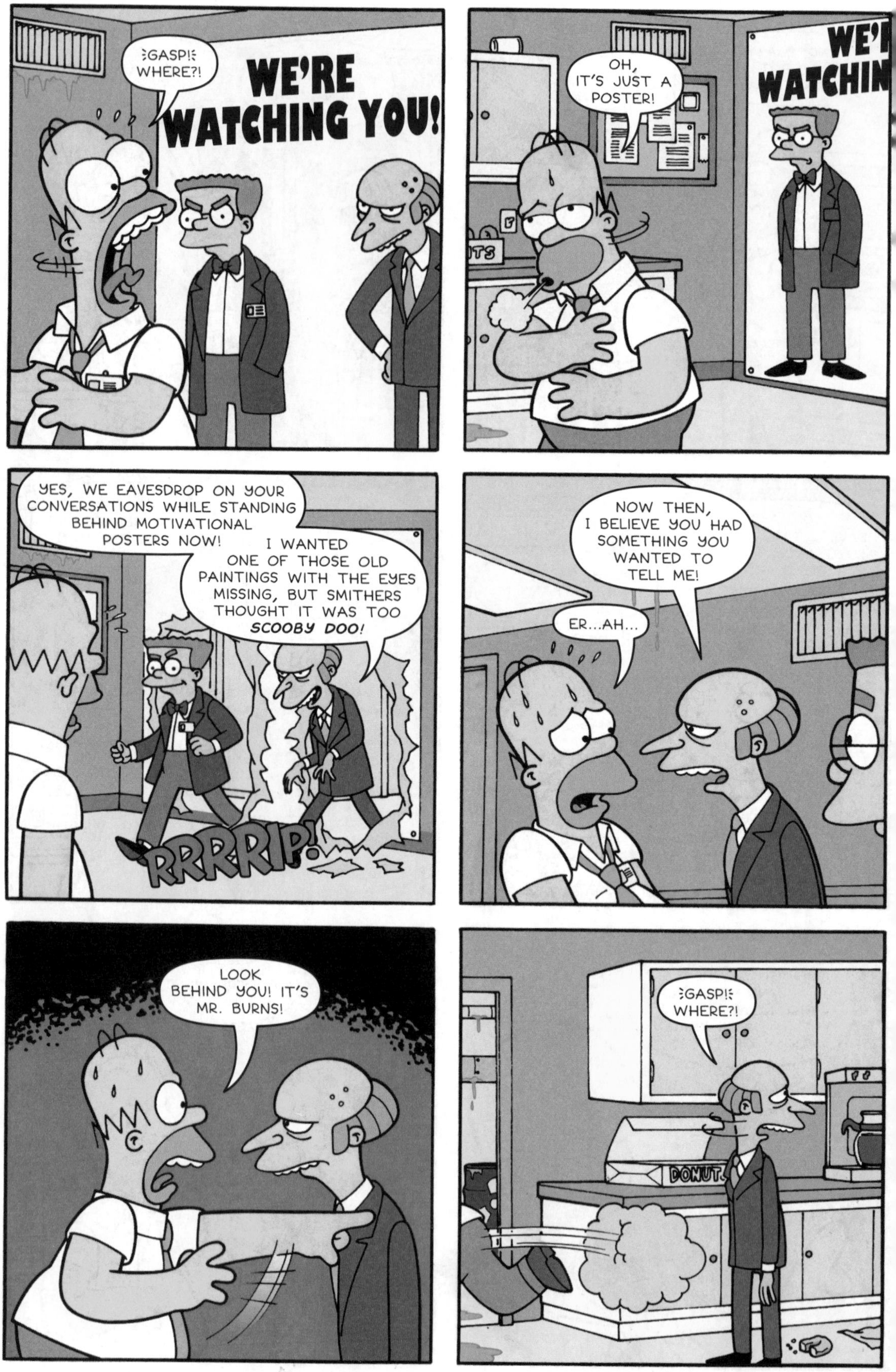

⁝GASP!⁝ WHERE?!
WE'RE WATCHING YOU!
OH, IT'S JUST A POSTER!
WE'R WATCHIN
YES, WE EAVESDROP ON YOUR CONVERSATIONS WHILE STANDING BEHIND MOTIVATIONAL POSTERS NOW!
I WANTED ONE OF THOSE OLD PAINTINGS WITH THE EYES MISSING, BUT SMITHERS THOUGHT IT WAS TOO SCOOBY DOO!
RRRRIP!
NOW THEN, I BELIEVE YOU HAD SOMETHING YOU WANTED TO TELL ME!
ER...AH...
LOOK BEHIND YOU! IT'S MR. BURNS!
⁝GASP!⁝ WHERE?!
DONUTS

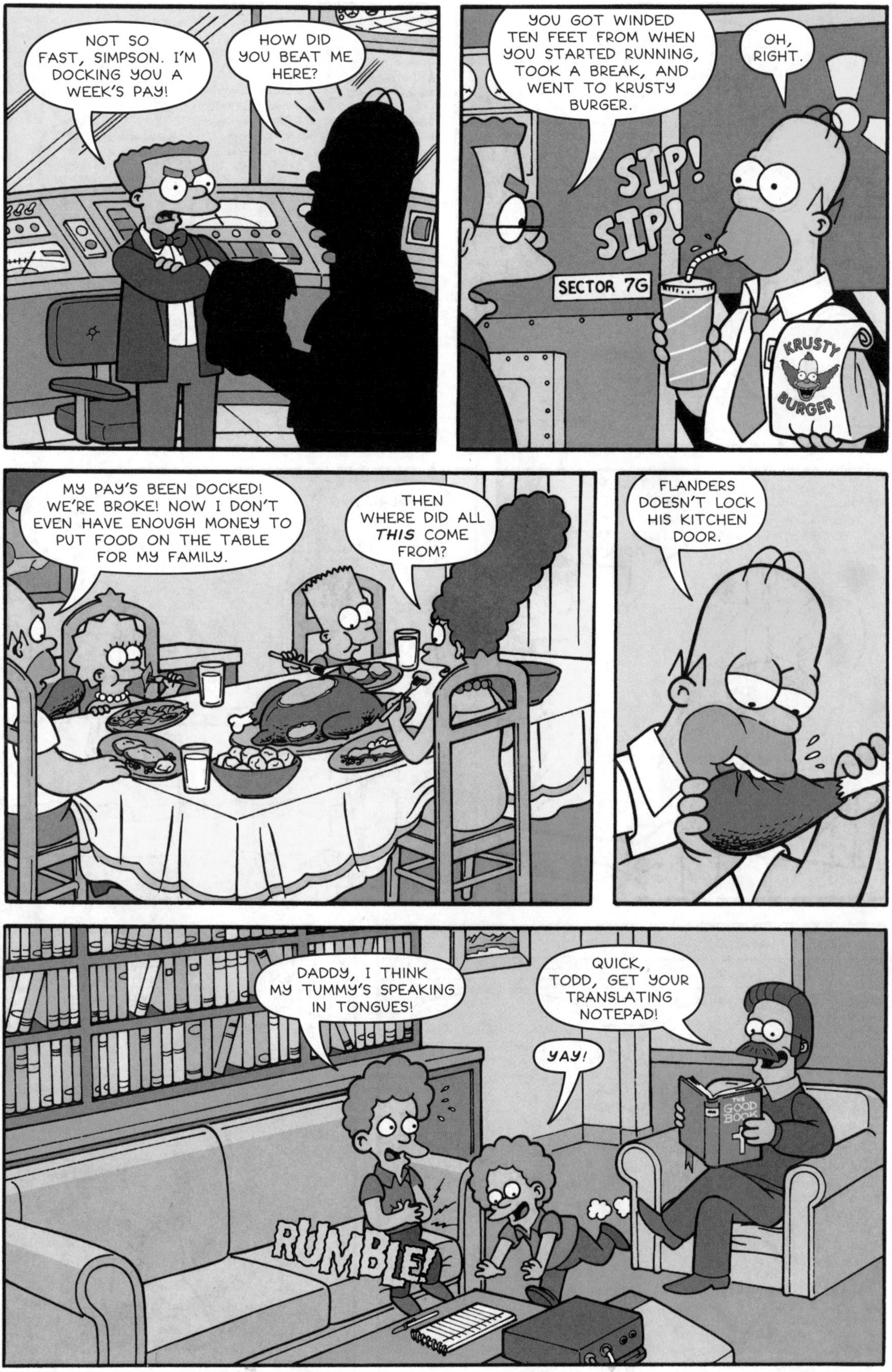
NOT SO FAST, SIMPSON. I'M DOCKING YOU A WEEK'S PAY!
HOW DID YOU BEAT ME HERE?
YOU GOT WINDED TEN FEET FROM WHEN YOU STARTED RUNNING, TOOK A BREAK, AND WENT TO KRUSTY BURGER.
OH, RIGHT.
SIP! SIP!
SECTOR 7G
KRUSTY BURGER
MY PAY'S BEEN DOCKED! WE'RE BROKE! NOW I DON'T EVEN HAVE ENOUGH MONEY TO PUT FOOD ON THE TABLE FOR MY FAMILY.
THEN WHERE DID ALL *THIS* COME FROM?
FLANDERS DOESN'T LOCK HIS KITCHEN DOOR.
DADDY, I THINK MY TUMMY'S SPEAKING IN TONGUES!
QUICK, TODD, GET YOUR TRANSLATING NOTEPAD!
YAY!
THE GOOD BOOK
RUMBLE!

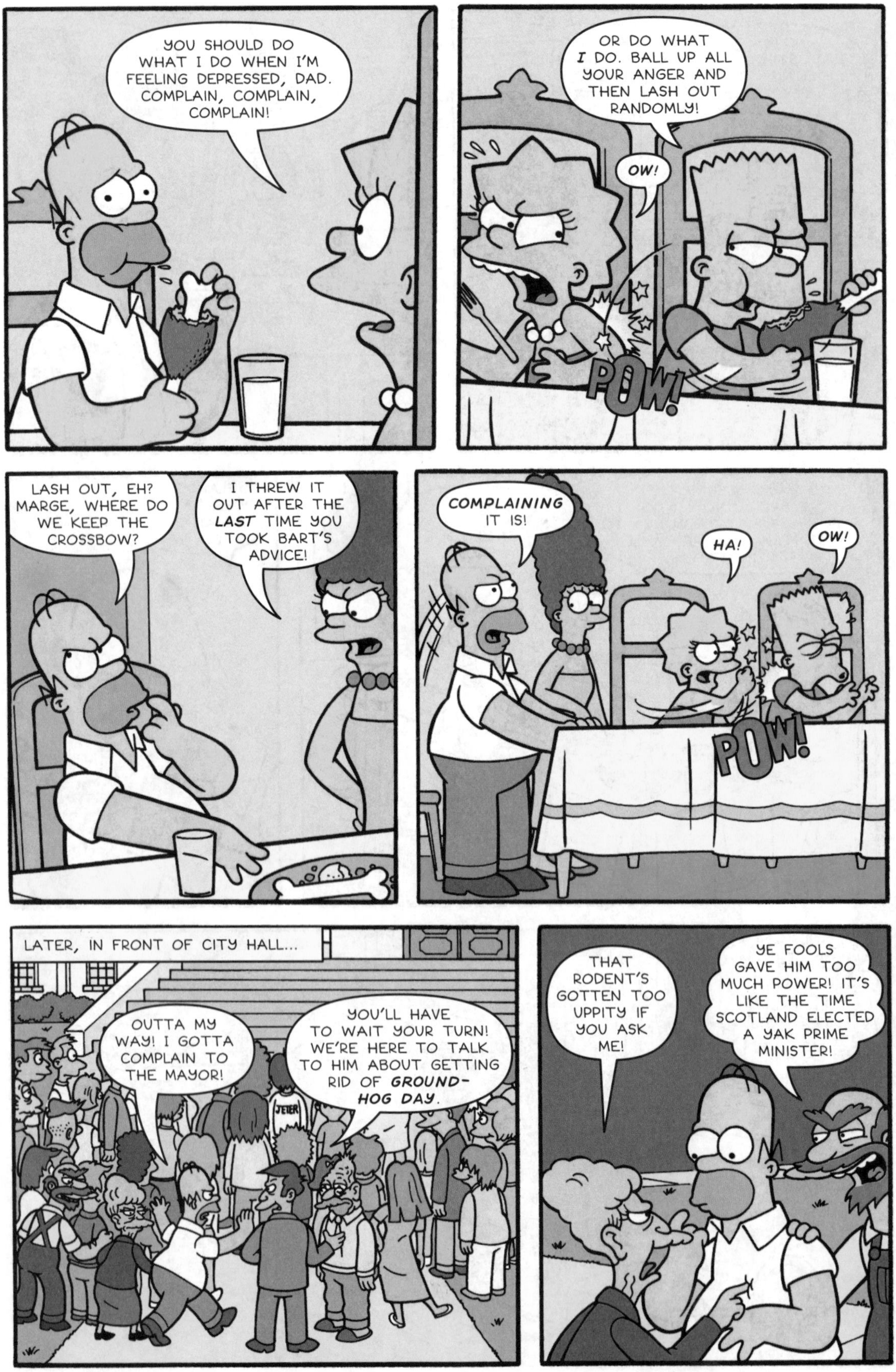

YOU SHOULD DO WHAT I DO WHEN I'M FEELING DEPRESSED, DAD. COMPLAIN, COMPLAIN, COMPLAIN!
OR DO WHAT I DO. BALL UP ALL YOUR ANGER AND THEN LASH OUT RANDOMLY!
OW!
POW!
LASH OUT, EH? MARGE, WHERE DO WE KEEP THE CROSSBOW?
I THREW IT OUT AFTER THE LAST TIME YOU TOOK BART'S ADVICE!
COMPLAINING IT IS!
HA!
OW!
POW!
LATER, IN FRONT OF CITY HALL...
OUTTA MY WAY! I GOTTA COMPLAIN TO THE MAYOR!
YOU'LL HAVE TO WAIT YOUR TURN! WE'RE HERE TO TALK TO HIM ABOUT GETTING RID OF GROUND-HOG DAY.
JETER
THAT RODENT'S GOTTEN TOO UPPITY IF YOU ASK ME!
YE FOOLS GAVE HIM TOO MUCH POWER! IT'S LIKE THE TIME SCOTLAND ELECTED A YAK PRIME MINISTER!

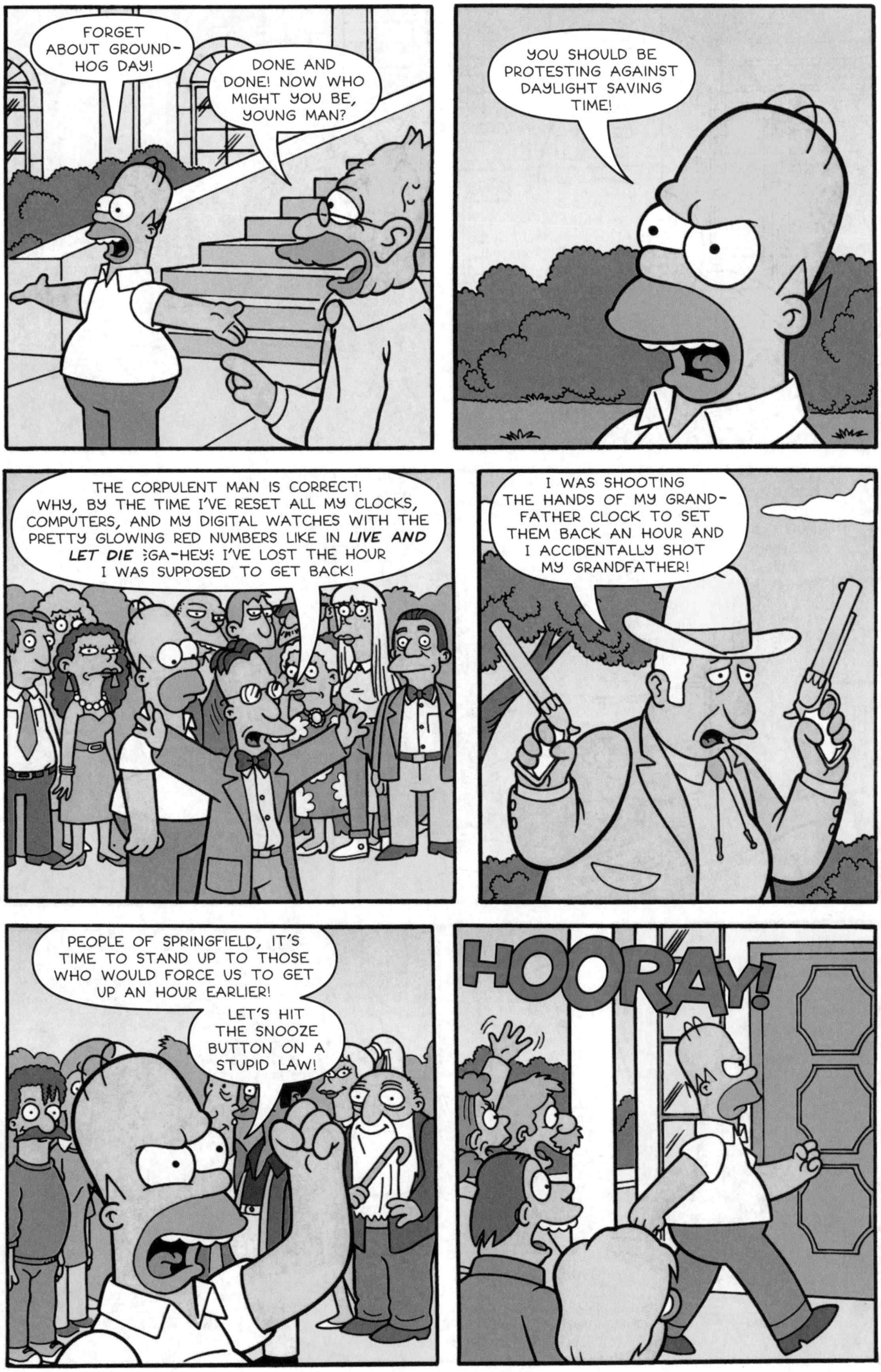

FORGET ABOUT GROUND-HOG DAY!
DONE AND DONE! NOW WHO MIGHT YOU BE, YOUNG MAN?
YOU SHOULD BE PROTESTING AGAINST DAYLIGHT SAVING TIME!
THE CORPULENT MAN IS CORRECT! WHY, BY THE TIME I'VE RESET ALL MY CLOCKS, COMPUTERS, AND MY DIGITAL WATCHES WITH THE PRETTY GLOWING RED NUMBERS LIKE IN *LIVE AND LET DIE* :GA-HEY: I'VE LOST THE HOUR I WAS SUPPOSED TO GET BACK!
I WAS SHOOTING THE HANDS OF MY GRAND-FATHER CLOCK TO SET THEM BACK AN HOUR AND I ACCIDENTALLY SHOT MY GRANDFATHER!
PEOPLE OF SPRINGFIELD, IT'S TIME TO STAND UP TO THOSE WHO WOULD FORCE US TO GET UP AN HOUR EARLIER!
LET'S HIT THE SNOOZE BUTTON ON A STUPID LAW!
HOORAY!

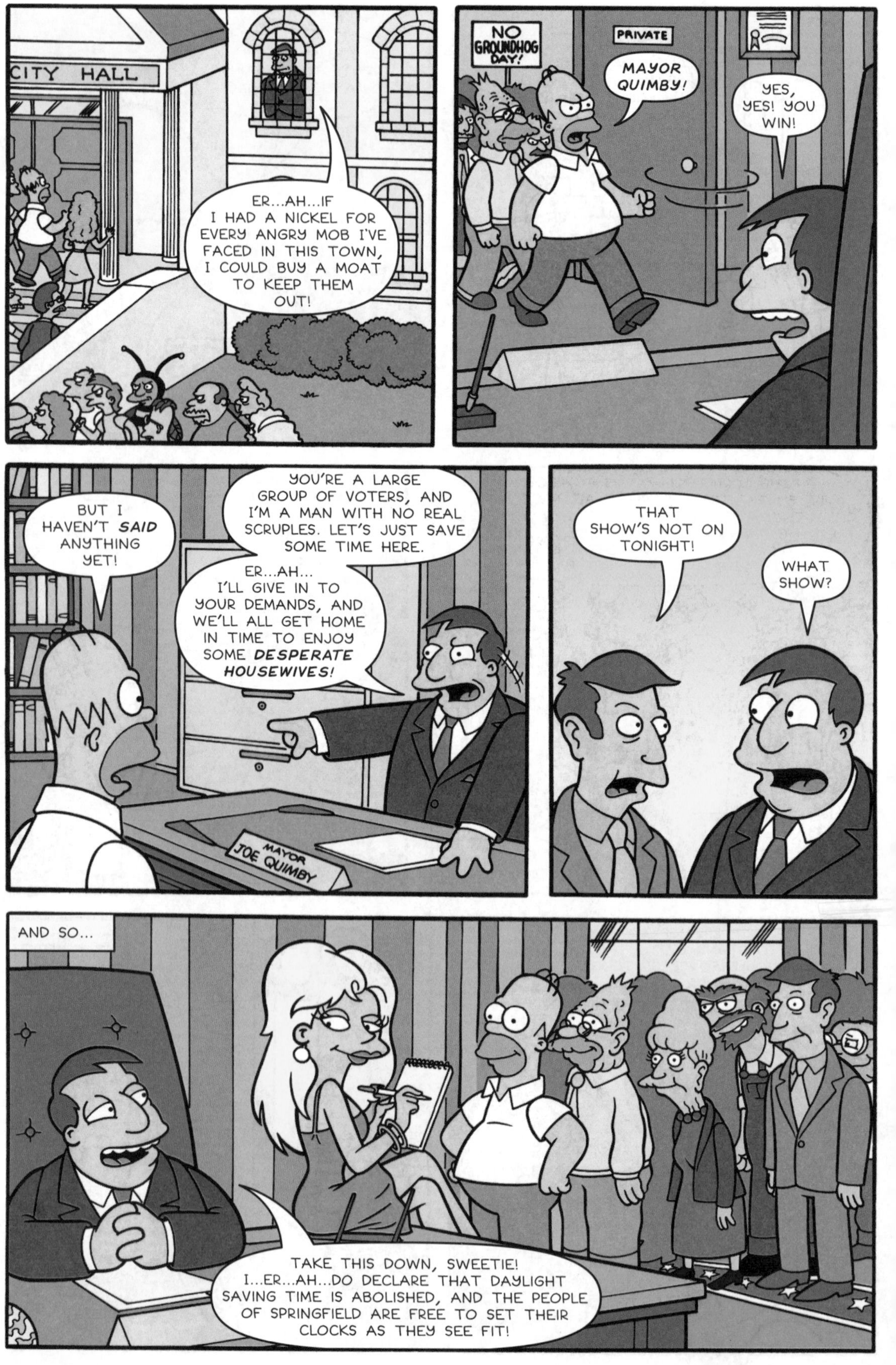
CITY HALL
ER...AH...IF I HAD A NICKEL FOR EVERY ANGRY MOB I'VE FACED IN THIS TOWN, I COULD BUY A MOAT TO KEEP THEM OUT!
NO GROUNDHOG DAY!
PRIVATE
MAYOR QUIMBY!
YES, YES! YOU WIN!
BUT I HAVEN'T **SAID** ANYTHING YET!
YOU'RE A LARGE GROUP OF VOTERS, AND I'M A MAN WITH NO REAL SCRUPLES. LET'S JUST SAVE SOME TIME HERE.
ER...AH... I'LL GIVE IN TO YOUR DEMANDS, AND WE'LL ALL GET HOME IN TIME TO ENJOY SOME ***DESPERATE HOUSEWIVES!***
MAYOR JOE QUIMBY
THAT SHOW'S NOT ON TONIGHT!
WHAT SHOW?
AND SO...
TAKE THIS DOWN, SWEETIE! I...ER...AH...DO DECLARE THAT DAYLIGHT SAVING TIME IS ABOLISHED, AND THE PEOPLE OF SPRINGFIELD ARE FREE TO SET THEIR CLOCKS AS THEY SEE FIT!

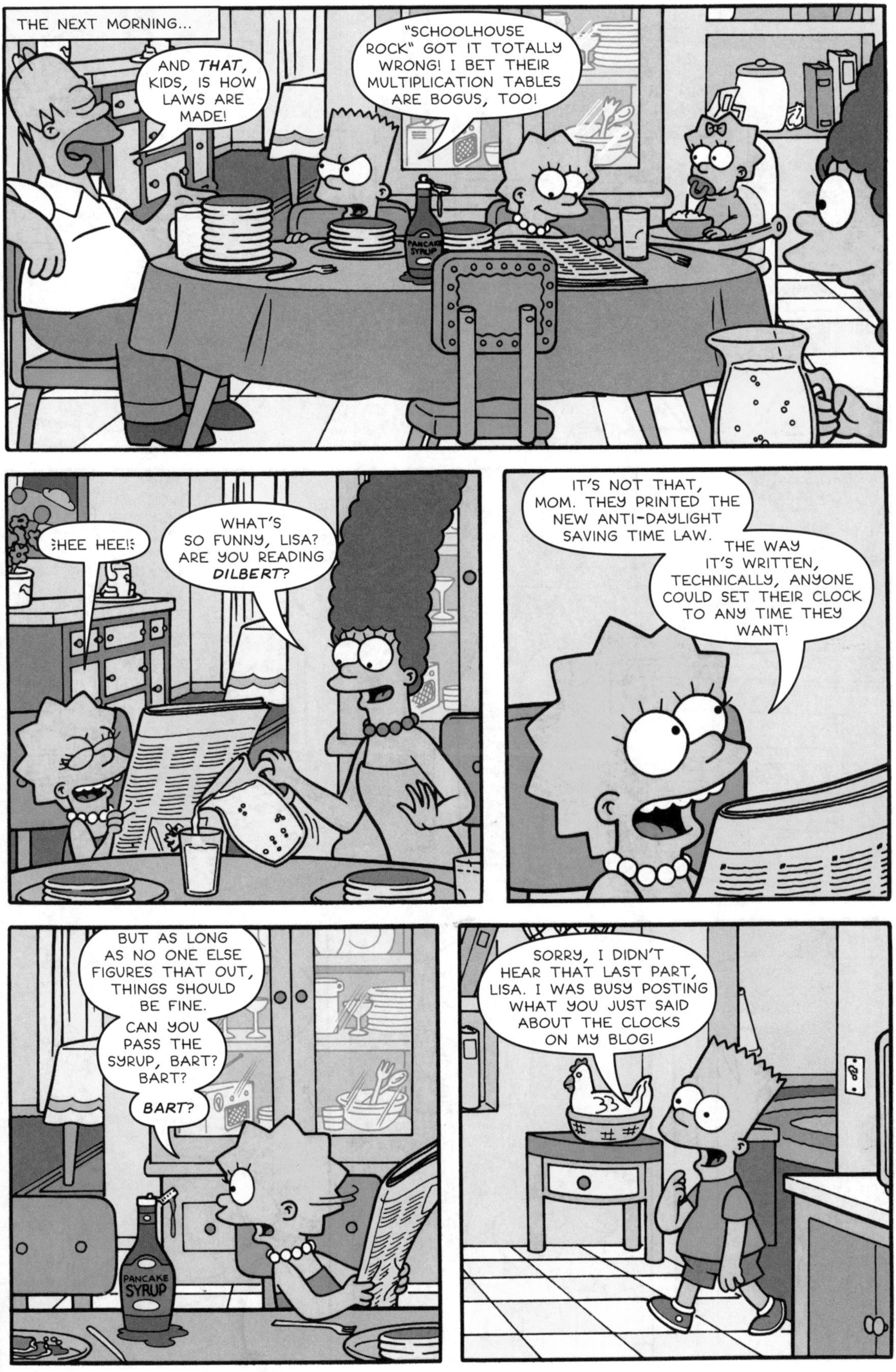

THE NEXT MORNING...
AND *THAT*, KIDS, IS HOW LAWS ARE MADE!
"SCHOOLHOUSE ROCK" GOT IT TOTALLY WRONG! I BET THEIR MULTIPLICATION TABLES ARE BOGUS, TOO!
PANCAKE SYRUP
HEE HEE!
WHAT'S SO FUNNY, LISA? ARE YOU READING *DILBERT*?
IT'S NOT THAT, MOM. THEY PRINTED THE NEW ANTI-DAYLIGHT SAVING TIME LAW.
THE WAY IT'S WRITTEN, TECHNICALLY, ANYONE COULD SET THEIR CLOCK TO ANY TIME THEY WANT!
BUT AS LONG AS NO ONE ELSE FIGURES THAT OUT, THINGS SHOULD BE FINE.
CAN YOU PASS THE SYRUP, BART? BART?
BART?
PANCAKE SYRUP
SORRY, I DIDN'T HEAR THAT LAST PART, LISA. I WAS BUSY POSTING WHAT YOU JUST SAID ABOUT THE CLOCKS ON MY BLOG!

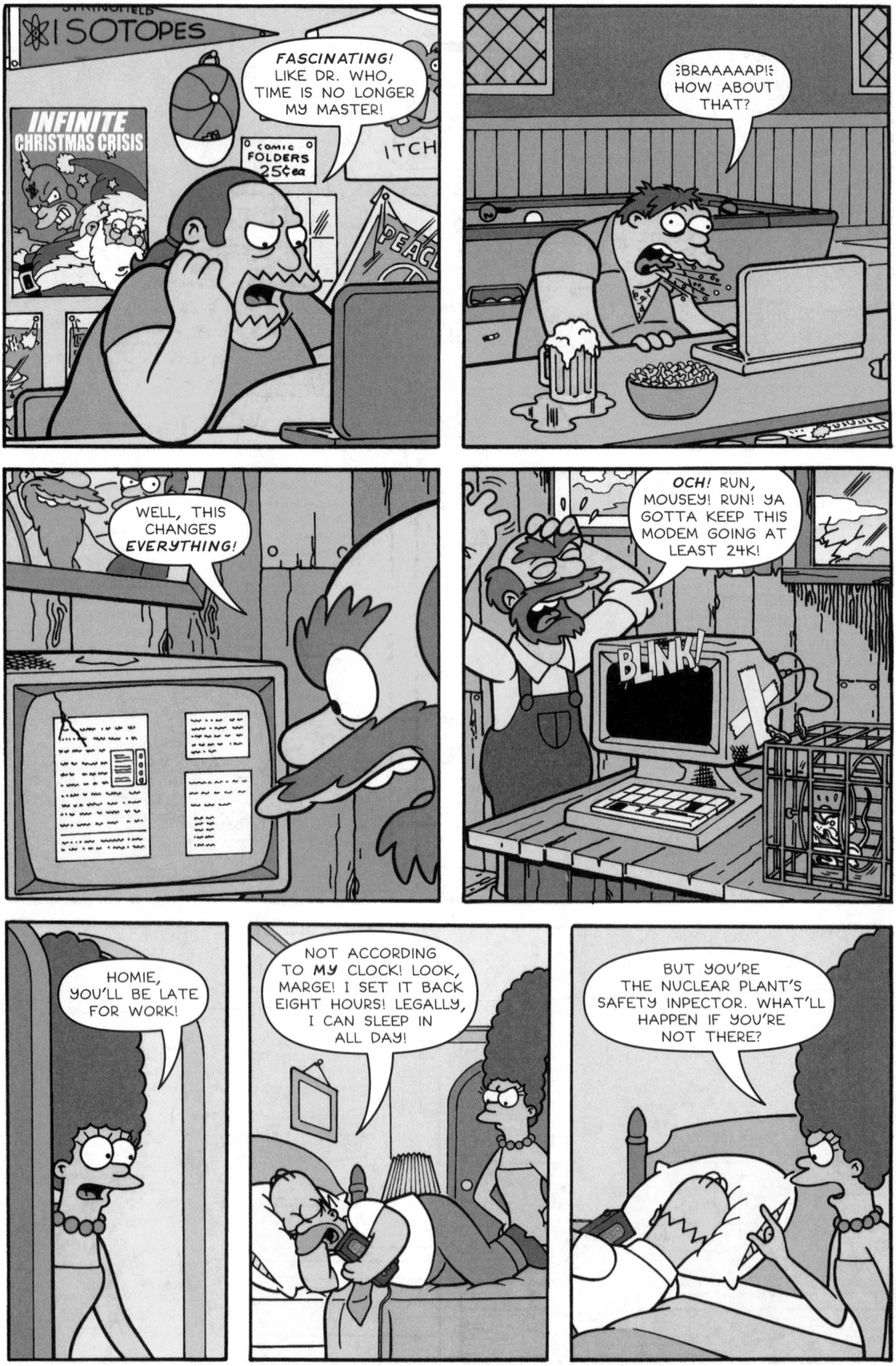

ISOTOPES
INFINITE CHRISTMAS CRISIS
COMIC FOLDERS 25¢ea
ITCH
FASCINATING! LIKE DR. WHO, TIME IS NO LONGER MY MASTER!
BRAAAAAP! HOW ABOUT THAT?
WELL, THIS CHANGES EVERYTHING!
OCH! RUN, MOUSEY! RUN! YA GOTTA KEEP THIS MODEM GOING AT LEAST 24K!
BLINK!
HOMIE, YOU'LL BE LATE FOR WORK!
NOT ACCORDING TO MY CLOCK! LOOK, MARGE! I SET IT BACK EIGHT HOURS! LEGALLY, I CAN SLEEP IN ALL DAY!
BUT YOU'RE THE NUCLEAR PLANT'S SAFETY INPECTOR. WHAT'LL HAPPEN IF YOU'RE NOT THERE?

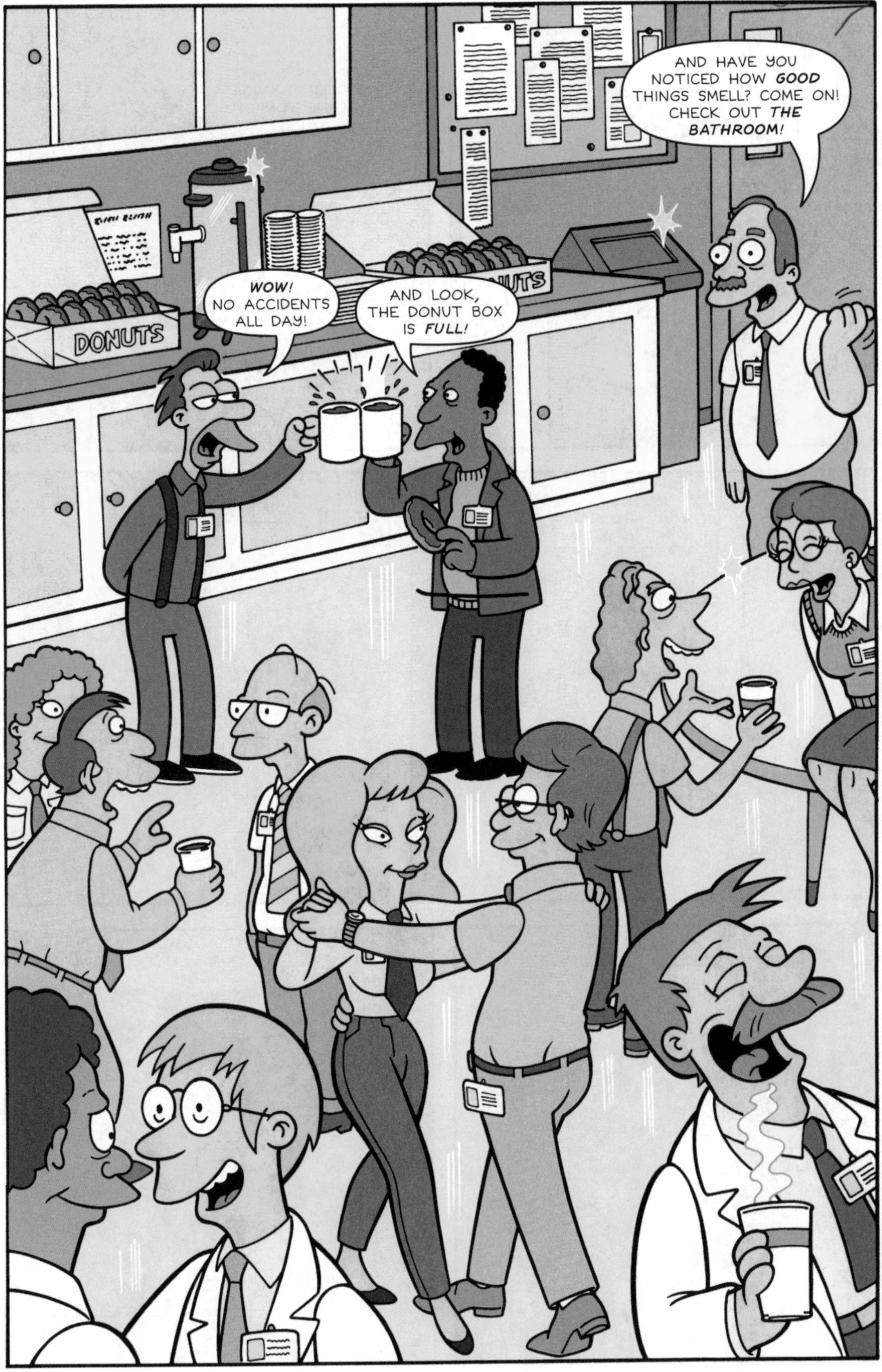
WOW! NO ACCIDENTS ALL DAY!
AND LOOK, THE DONUT BOX IS FULL!
AND HAVE YOU NOTICED HOW GOOD THINGS SMELL? COME ON! CHECK OUT THE BATHROOM!
DONUTS
DONUTS

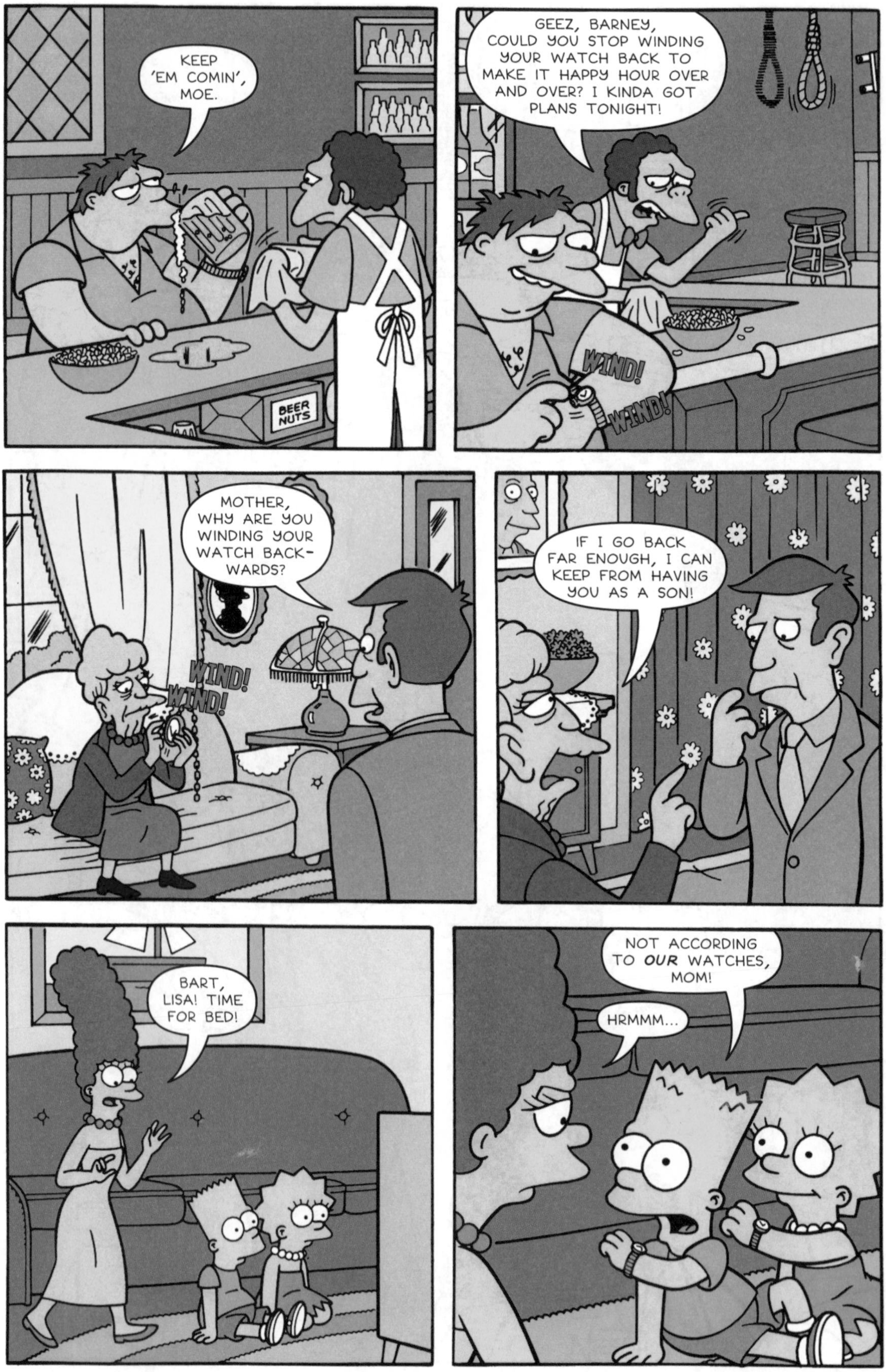
KEEP 'EM COMIN', MOE.
GEEZ, BARNEY, COULD YOU STOP WINDING YOUR WATCH BACK TO MAKE IT HAPPY HOUR OVER AND OVER? I KINDA GOT PLANS TONIGHT!
WIND!
WIND!
BEER NUTS
MOTHER, WHY ARE YOU WINDING YOUR WATCH BACK-WARDS?
WIND!
WIND!
IF I GO BACK FAR ENOUGH, I CAN KEEP FROM HAVING YOU AS A SON!
BART, LISA! TIME FOR BED!
NOT ACCORDING TO ***OUR*** WATCHES, MOM!
HRMMM...

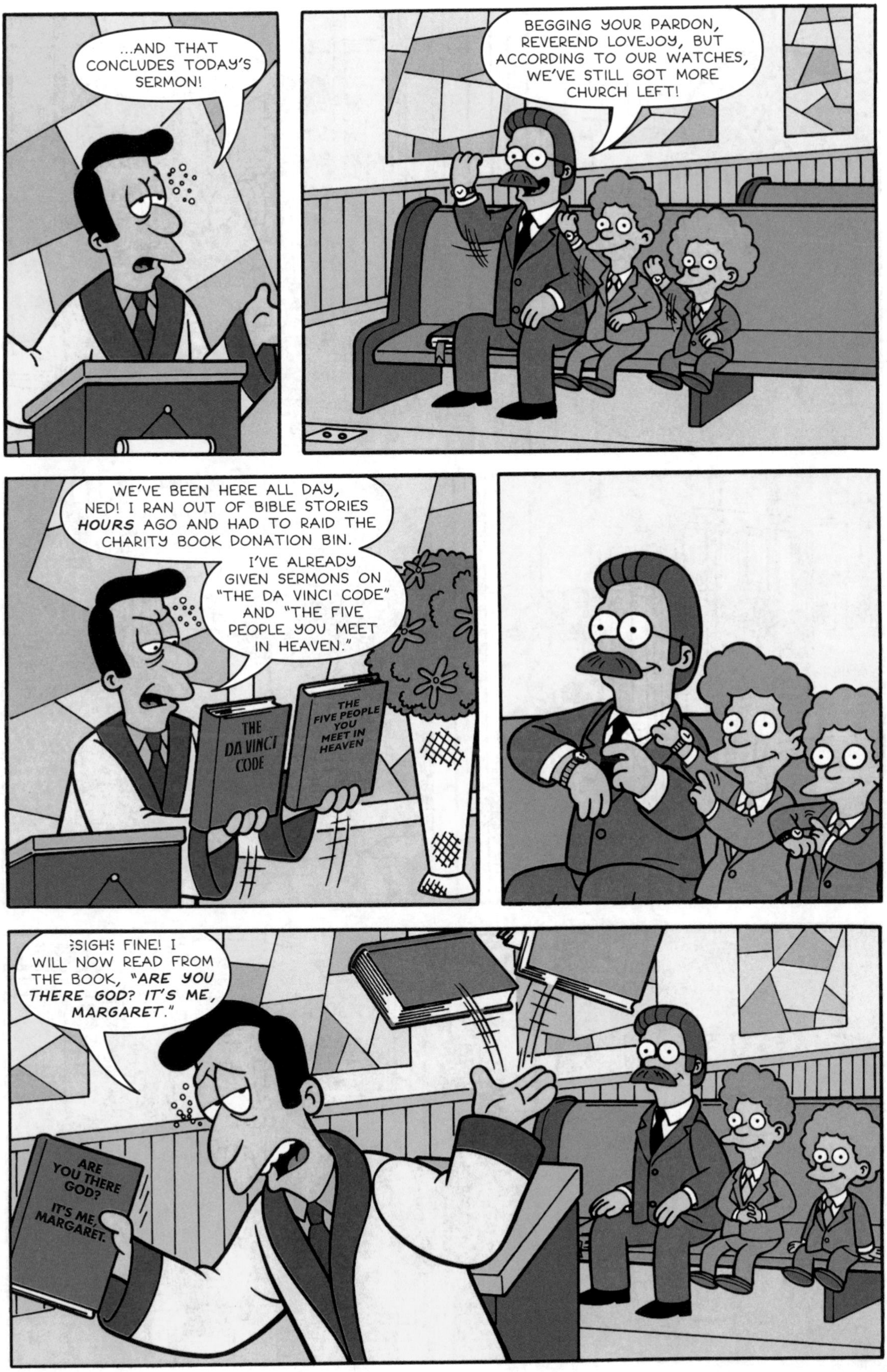
...AND THAT CONCLUDES TODAY'S SERMON!
BEGGING YOUR PARDON, REVEREND LOVEJOY, BUT ACCORDING TO OUR WATCHES, WE'VE STILL GOT MORE CHURCH LEFT!
WE'VE BEEN HERE ALL DAY, NED! I RAN OUT OF BIBLE STORIES **HOURS** AGO AND HAD TO RAID THE CHARITY BOOK DONATION BIN.
I'VE ALREADY GIVEN SERMONS ON "THE DA VINCI CODE" AND "THE FIVE PEOPLE YOU MEET IN HEAVEN."
THE DA VINCI CODE
THE FIVE PEOPLE YOU MEET IN HEAVEN
:SIGH: FINE! I WILL NOW READ FROM THE BOOK, "***ARE YOU THERE GOD? IT'S ME, MARGARET***."
ARE YOU THERE GOD? IT'S ME, MARGARET.

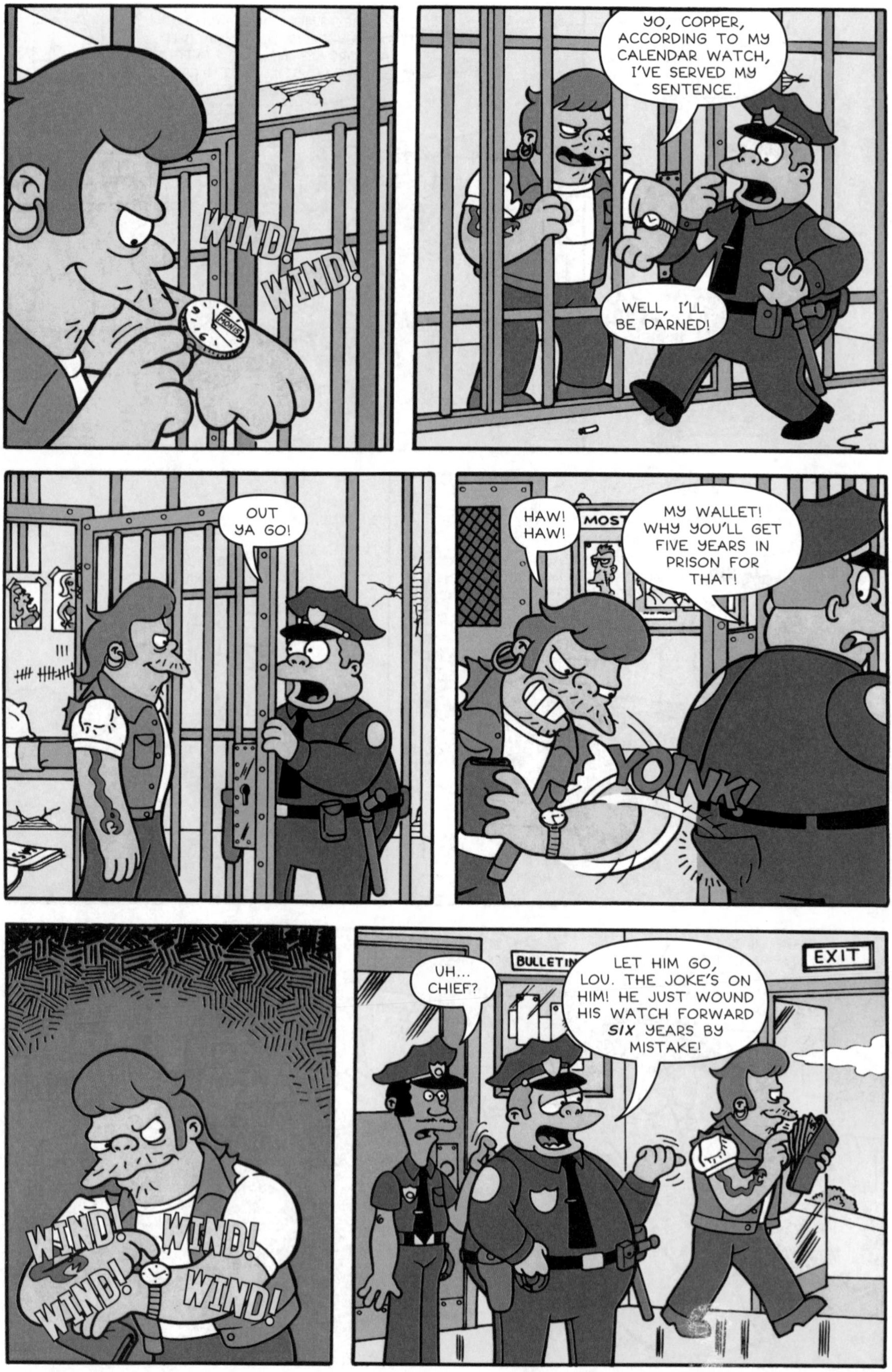
WIND! WIND!
MONIS
YO, COPPER, ACCORDING TO MY CALENDAR WATCH, I'VE SERVED MY SENTENCE.
WELL, I'LL BE DARNED!
OUT YA GO!
HAW! HAW!
MY WALLET! WHY YOU'LL GET FIVE YEARS IN PRISON FOR THAT!
YOINK!
WIND! WIND! WIND! WIND!
UH... CHIEF?
LET HIM GO, LOU. THE JOKE'S ON HIM! HE JUST WOUND HIS WATCH FORWARD SIX YEARS BY MISTAKE!
BULLETIN
EXIT

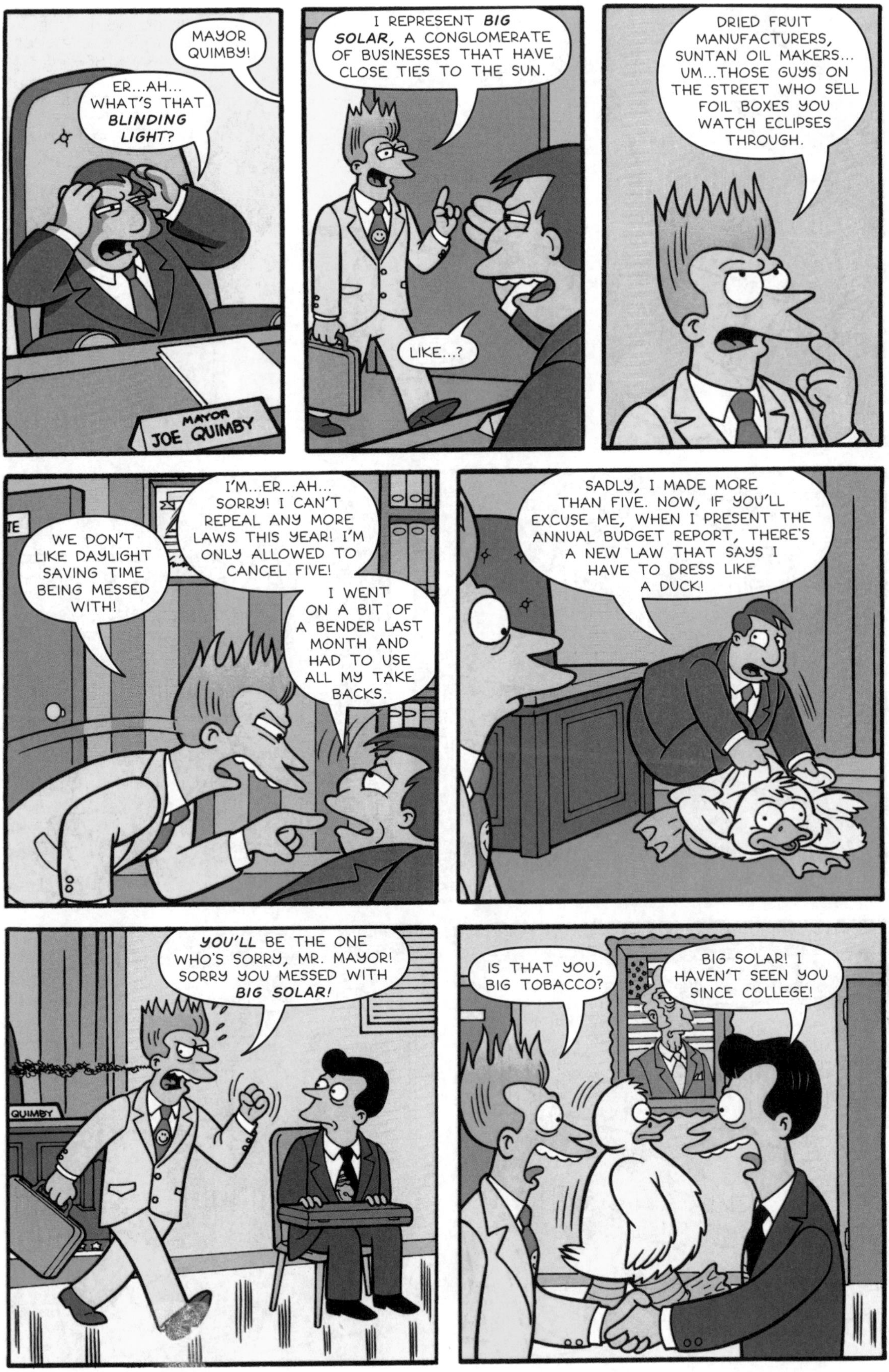
MAYOR QUIMBY!
ER...AH... WHAT'S THAT BLINDING LIGHT?
MAYOR JOE QUIMBY
I REPRESENT BIG SOLAR, A CONGLOMERATE OF BUSINESSES THAT HAVE CLOSE TIES TO THE SUN.
LIKE...?
DRIED FRUIT MANUFACTURERS, SUNTAN OIL MAKERS... UM...THOSE GUYS ON THE STREET WHO SELL FOIL BOXES YOU WATCH ECLIPSES THROUGH.
WE DON'T LIKE DAYLIGHT SAVING TIME BEING MESSED WITH!
I'M...ER...AH... SORRY! I CAN'T REPEAL ANY MORE LAWS THIS YEAR! I'M ONLY ALLOWED TO CANCEL FIVE!
I WENT ON A BIT OF A BENDER LAST MONTH AND HAD TO USE ALL MY TAKE BACKS.
SADLY, I MADE MORE THAN FIVE. NOW, IF YOU'LL EXCUSE ME, WHEN I PRESENT THE ANNUAL BUDGET REPORT, THERE'S A NEW LAW THAT SAYS I HAVE TO DRESS LIKE A DUCK!
YOU'LL BE THE ONE WHO'S SORRY, MR. MAYOR! SORRY YOU MESSED WITH BIG SOLAR!
QUIMBY
IS THAT YOU, BIG TOBACCO?
BIG SOLAR! I HAVEN'T SEEN YOU SINCE COLLEGE!

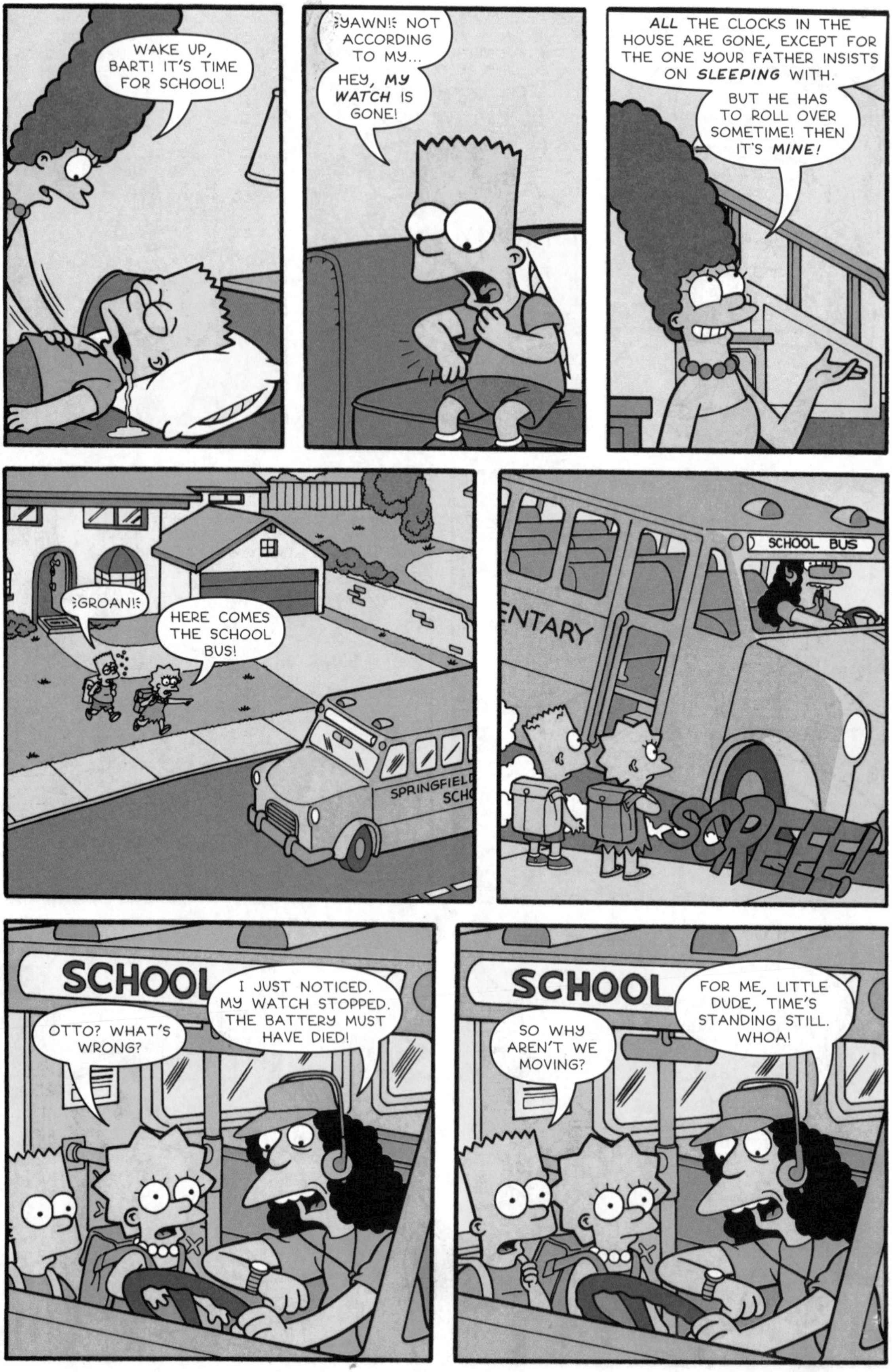
WAKE UP, BART! IT'S TIME FOR SCHOOL!
¦YAWN!¦ NOT ACCORDING TO MY...
HEY, MY WATCH IS GONE!
ALL THE CLOCKS IN THE HOUSE ARE GONE, EXCEPT FOR THE ONE YOUR FATHER INSISTS ON SLEEPING WITH.
BUT HE HAS TO ROLL OVER SOMETIME! THEN IT'S MINE!
¦GROAN!¦
HERE COMES THE SCHOOL BUS!
SPRINGFIELD SCHO
SCHOOL BUS
NTARY
SCREEE!
SCHOOL
OTTO? WHAT'S WRONG?
I JUST NOTICED. MY WATCH STOPPED. THE BATTERY MUST HAVE DIED!
SCHOOL
SO WHY AREN'T WE MOVING?
FOR ME, LITTLE DUDE, TIME'S STANDING STILL. WHOA!

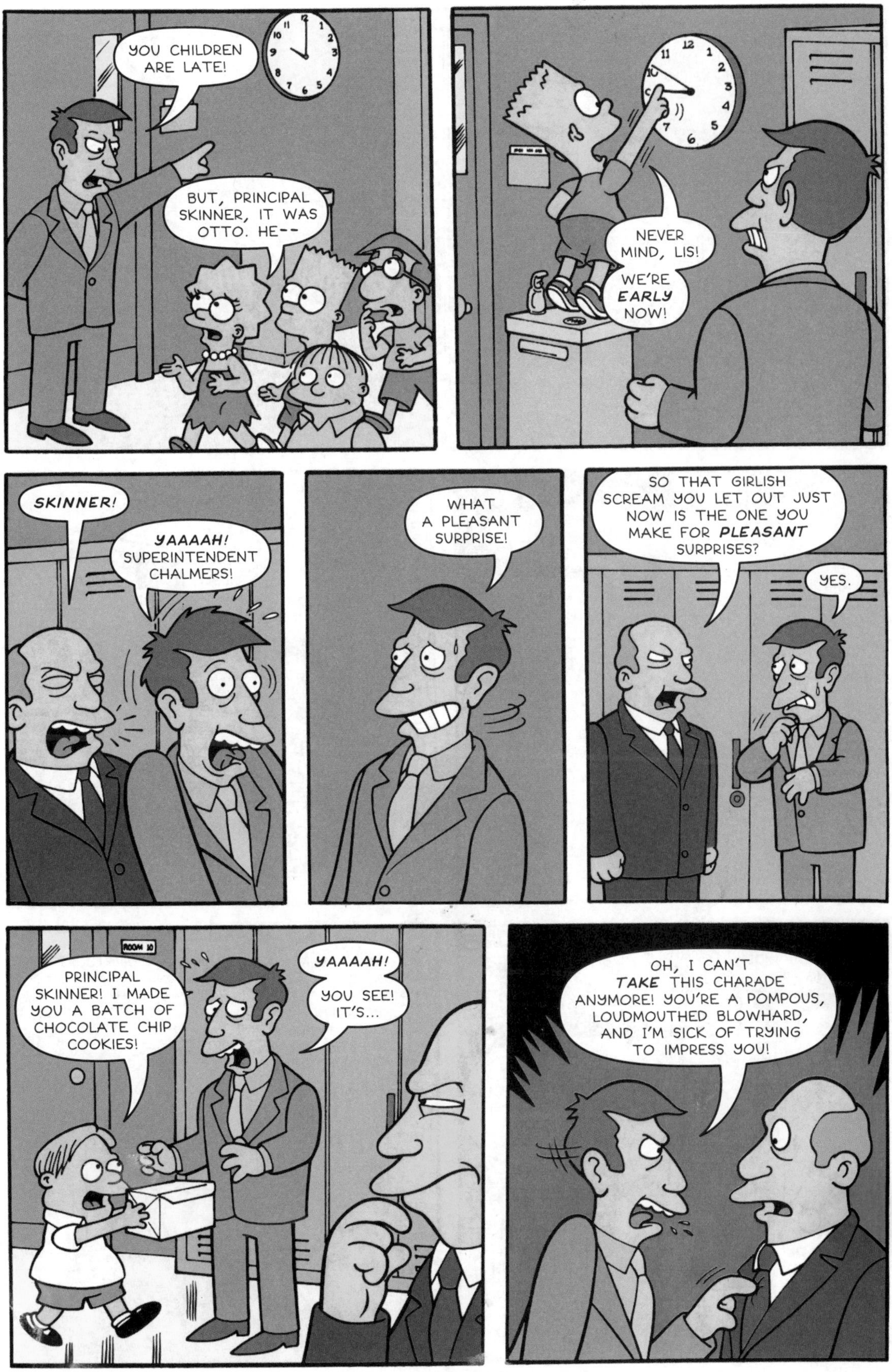
YOU CHILDREN ARE LATE!
BUT, PRINCIPAL SKINNER, IT WAS OTTO. HE--
NEVER MIND, LIS!
WE'RE *EARLY* NOW!
SKINNER!
YAAAAH! SUPERINTENDENT CHALMERS!
WHAT A PLEASANT SURPRISE!
SO THAT GIRLISH SCREAM YOU LET OUT JUST NOW IS THE ONE YOU MAKE FOR *PLEASANT* SURPRISES?
YES.
ROOM 10
PRINCIPAL SKINNER! I MADE YOU A BATCH OF CHOCOLATE CHIP COOKIES!
YAAAAH!
YOU SEE! IT'S...
OH, I CAN'T *TAKE* THIS CHARADE ANYMORE! YOU'RE A POMPOUS, LOUDMOUTHED BLOWHARD, AND I'M SICK OF TRYING TO IMPRESS YOU!

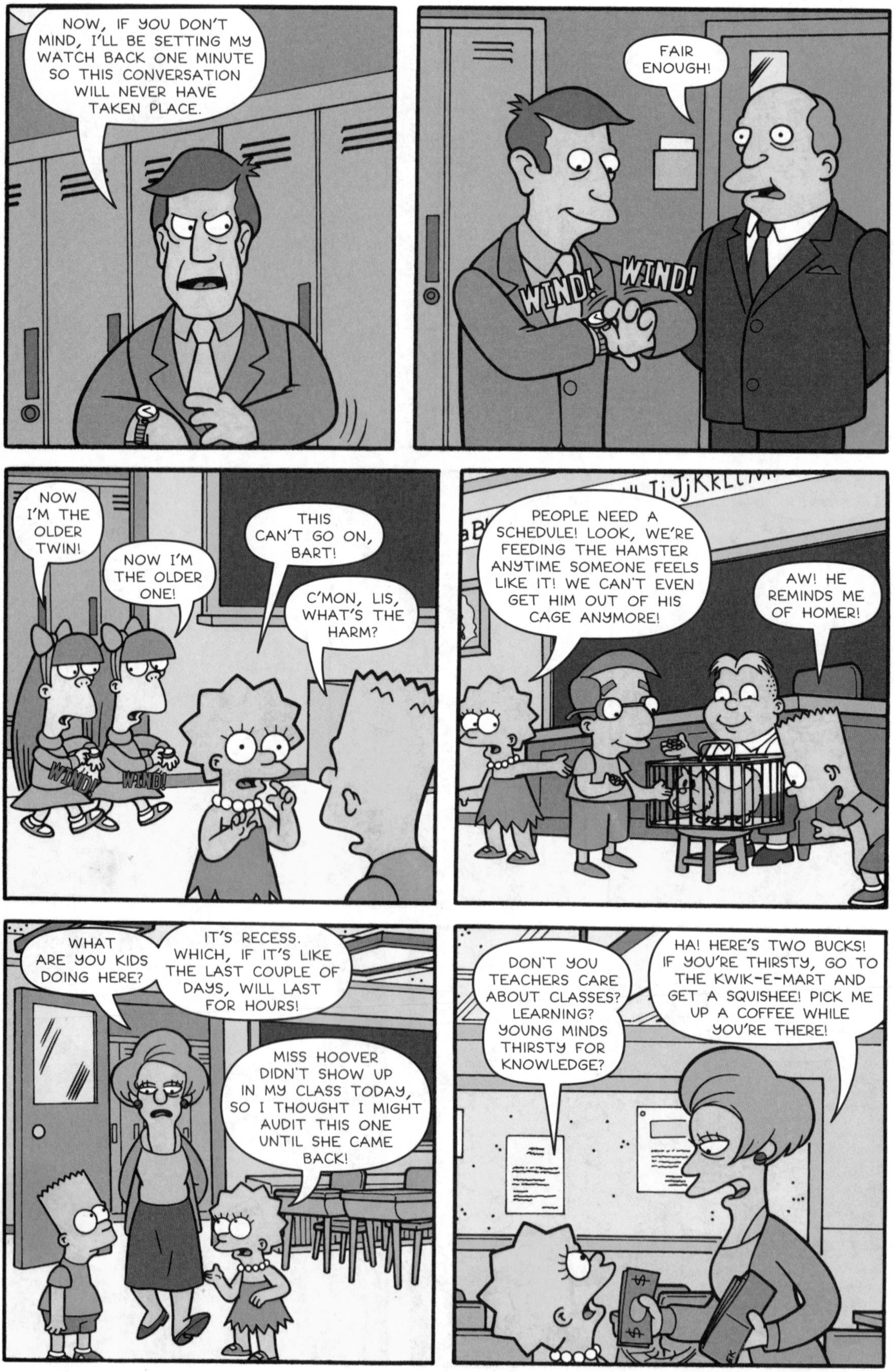
NOW, IF YOU DON'T MIND, I'LL BE SETTING MY WATCH BACK ONE MINUTE SO THIS CONVERSATION WILL NEVER HAVE TAKEN PLACE.
FAIR ENOUGH!
WIND!
WIND!
NOW I'M THE OLDER TWIN!
NOW I'M THE OLDER ONE!
WIND!
WIND!
THIS CAN'T GO ON, BART!
C'MON, LIS, WHAT'S THE HARM?
PEOPLE NEED A SCHEDULE! LOOK, WE'RE FEEDING THE HAMSTER ANYTIME SOMEONE FEELS LIKE IT! WE CAN'T EVEN GET HIM OUT OF HIS CAGE ANYMORE!
AW! HE REMINDS ME OF HOMER!
WHAT ARE YOU KIDS DOING HERE?
IT'S RECESS. WHICH, IF IT'S LIKE THE LAST COUPLE OF DAYS, WILL LAST FOR HOURS!
MISS HOOVER DIDN'T SHOW UP IN MY CLASS TODAY, SO I THOUGHT I MIGHT AUDIT THIS ONE UNTIL SHE CAME BACK!
DON'T YOU TEACHERS CARE ABOUT CLASSES? LEARNING? YOUNG MINDS THIRSTY FOR KNOWLEDGE?
HA! HERE'S TWO BUCKS! IF YOU'RE THIRSTY, GO TO THE KWIK-E-MART AND GET A SQUISHEE! PICK ME UP A COFFEE WHILE YOU'RE THERE!

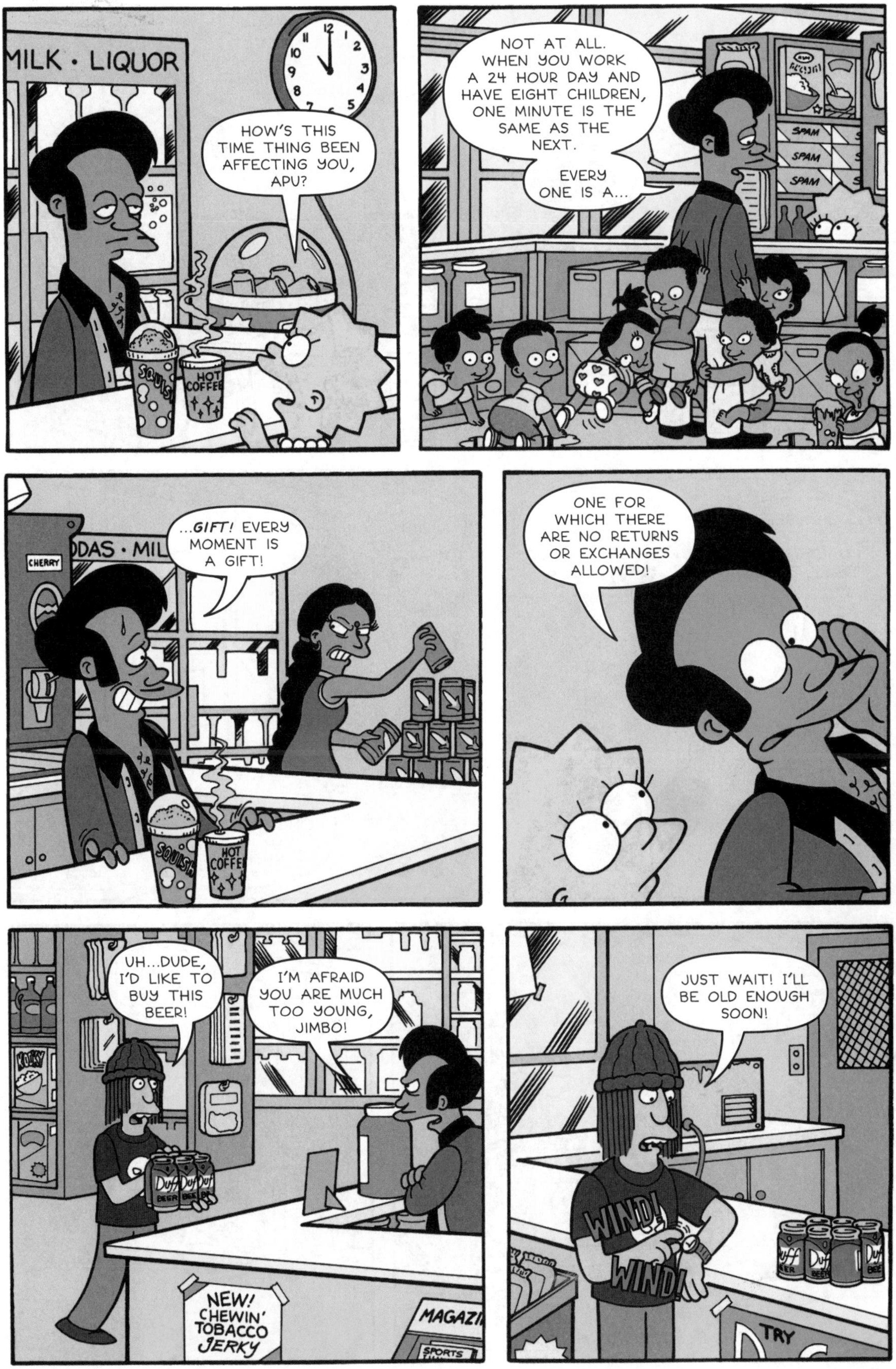
MILK • LIQUOR
HOW'S THIS TIME THING BEEN AFFECTING YOU, APU?
HOT COFFEE
NOT AT ALL. WHEN YOU WORK A 24 HOUR DAY AND HAVE EIGHT CHILDREN, ONE MINUTE IS THE SAME AS THE NEXT.
EVERY ONE IS A...
SPAM
SPAM
SPAM
CHERRY
...*GIFT!* EVERY MOMENT IS A GIFT!
HOT COFFEE
ONE FOR WHICH THERE ARE NO RETURNS OR EXCHANGES ALLOWED!
UH...DUDE, I'D LIKE TO BUY THIS BEER!
I'M AFRAID YOU ARE MUCH TOO YOUNG, JIMBO!
NEW! CHEWIN' TOBACCO JERKY
MAGAZI
SPORTS
JUST WAIT! I'LL BE OLD ENOUGH SOON!
WIND! WIND!
TRY

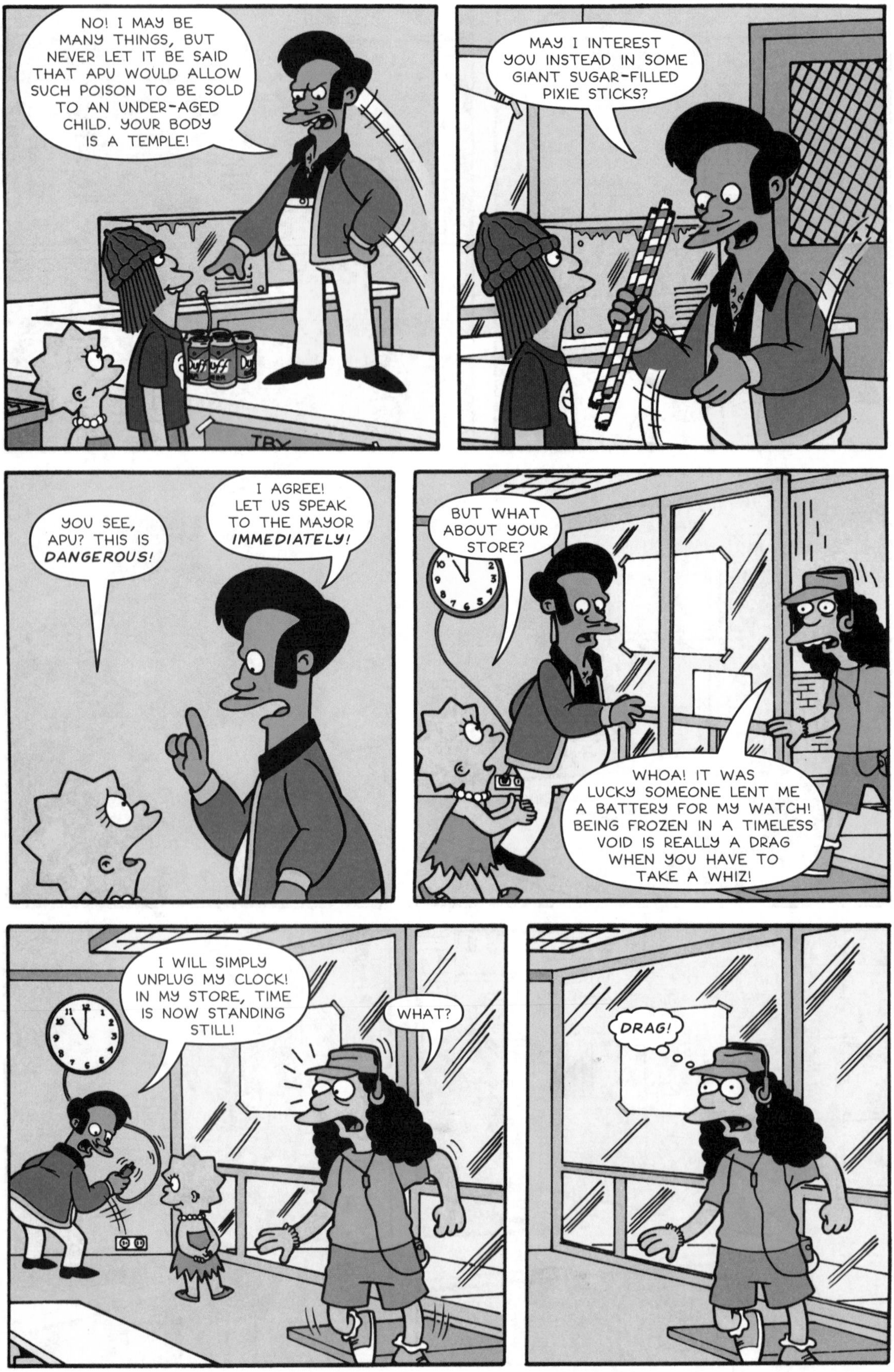
NO! I MAY BE MANY THINGS, BUT NEVER LET IT BE SAID THAT APU WOULD ALLOW SUCH POISON TO BE SOLD TO AN UNDER-AGED CHILD. YOUR BODY IS A TEMPLE!
MAY I INTEREST YOU INSTEAD IN SOME GIANT SUGAR-FILLED PIXIE STICKS?
YOU SEE, APU? THIS IS *DANGEROUS*!
I AGREE! LET US SPEAK TO THE MAYOR *IMMEDIATELY*!
BUT WHAT ABOUT YOUR STORE?
WHOA! IT WAS LUCKY SOMEONE LENT ME A BATTERY FOR MY WATCH! BEING FROZEN IN A TIMELESS VOID IS REALLY A DRAG WHEN YOU HAVE TO TAKE A WHIZ!
I WILL SIMPLY UNPLUG MY CLOCK! IN MY STORE, TIME IS NOW STANDING STILL!
WHAT?
DRAG!

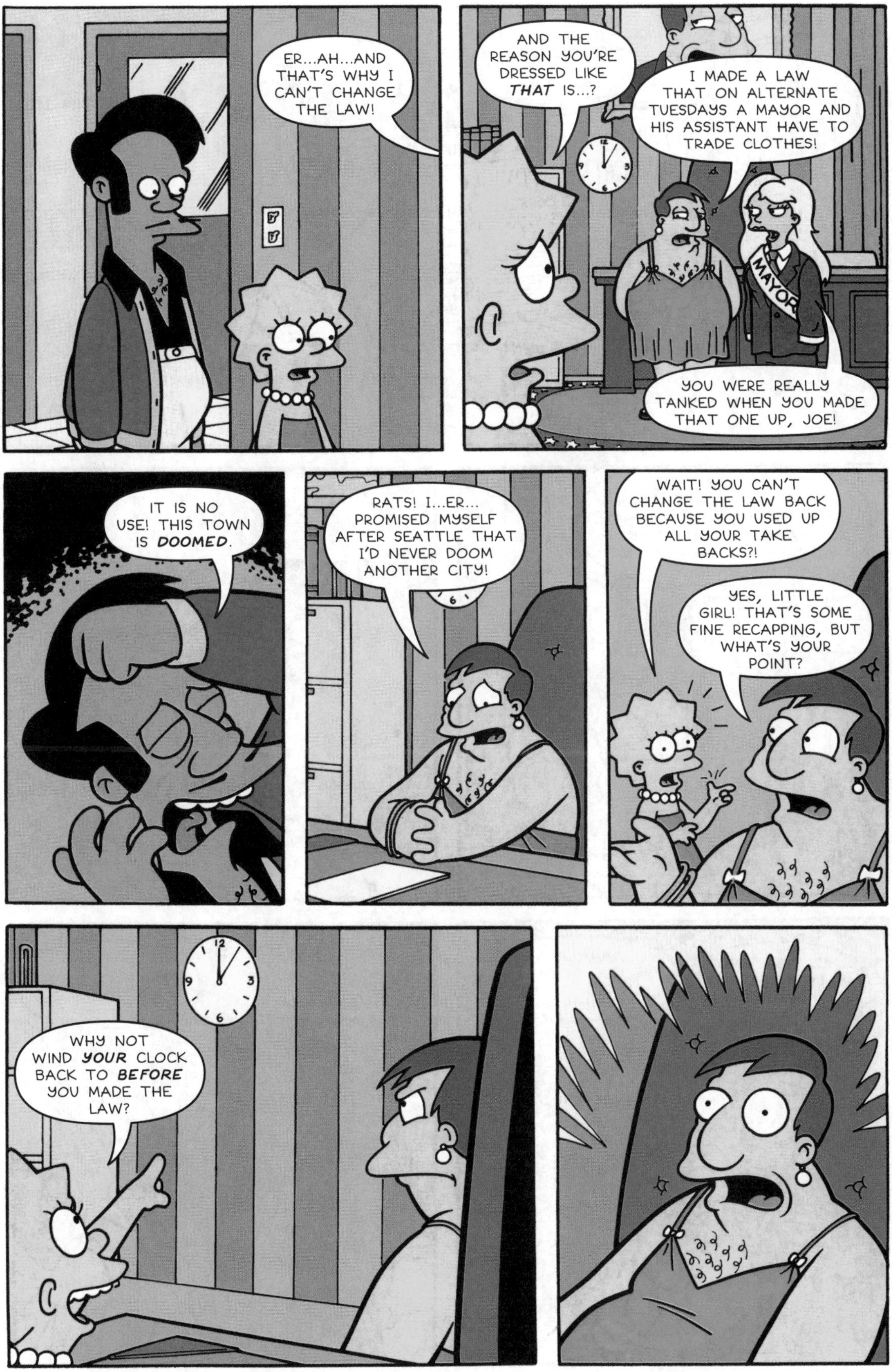
ER...AH...AND THAT'S WHY I CAN'T CHANGE THE LAW!
AND THE REASON YOU'RE DRESSED LIKE ***THAT*** IS...?
I MADE A LAW THAT ON ALTERNATE TUESDAYS A MAYOR AND HIS ASSISTANT HAVE TO TRADE CLOTHES!
MAYOR
YOU WERE REALLY TANKED WHEN YOU MADE THAT ONE UP, JOE!
IT IS NO USE! THIS TOWN IS ***DOOMED***.
RATS! I...ER... PROMISED MYSELF AFTER SEATTLE THAT I'D NEVER DOOM ANOTHER CITY!
WAIT! YOU CAN'T CHANGE THE LAW BACK BECAUSE YOU USED UP ALL YOUR TAKE BACKS?!
YES, LITTLE GIRL! THAT'S SOME FINE RECAPPING, BUT WHAT'S YOUR POINT?
WHY NOT WIND ***YOUR*** CLOCK BACK TO ***BEFORE*** YOU MADE THE LAW?

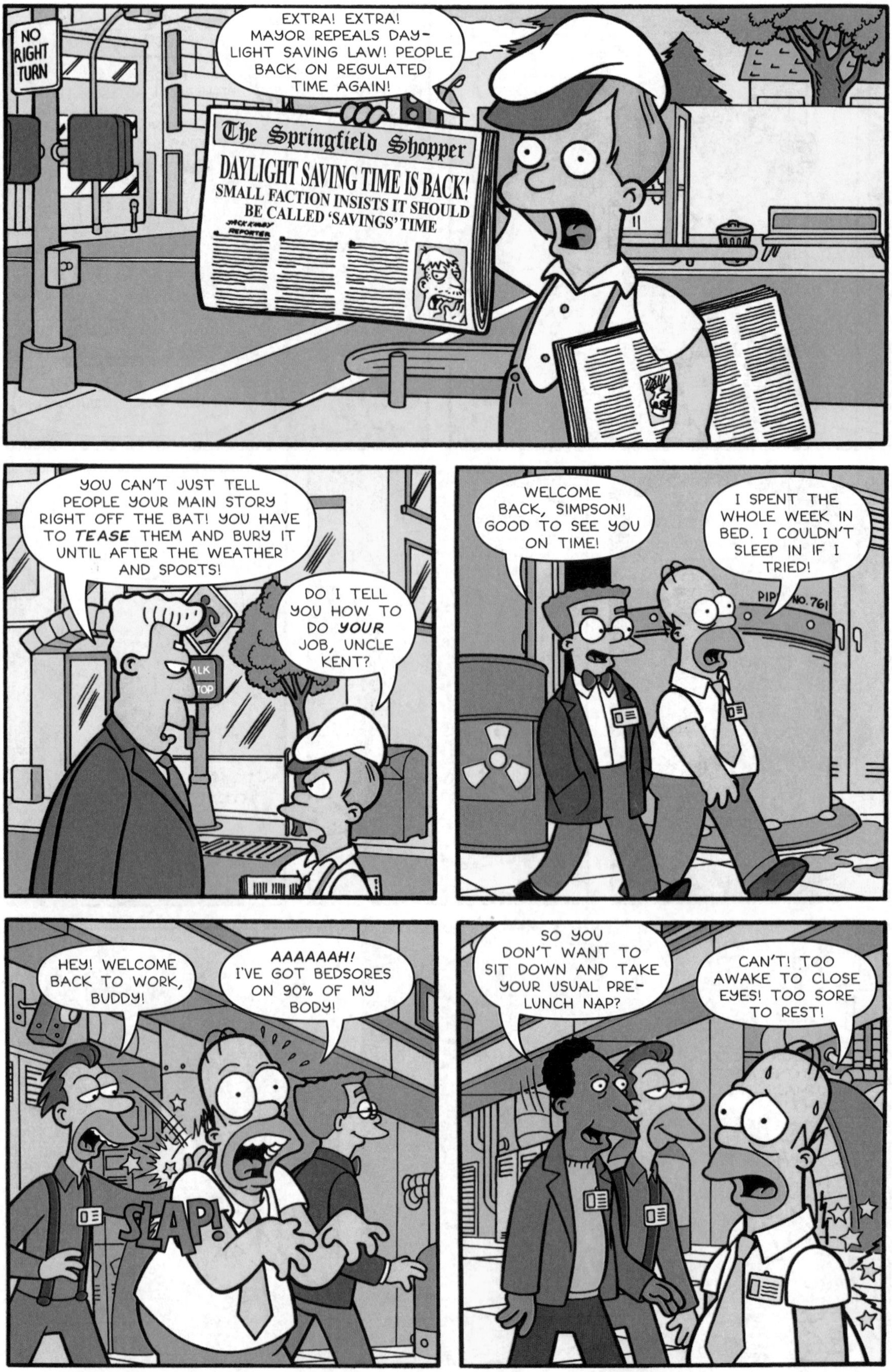
NO RIGHT TURN
EXTRA! EXTRA! MAYOR REPEALS DAY-LIGHT SAVING LAW! PEOPLE BACK ON REGULATED TIME AGAIN!
The Springfield Shopper
DAYLIGHT SAVING TIME IS BACK!
SMALL FACTION INSISTS IT SHOULD BE CALLED 'SAVINGS' TIME
YOU CAN'T JUST TELL PEOPLE YOUR MAIN STORY RIGHT OFF THE BAT! YOU HAVE TO *TEASE* THEM AND BURY IT UNTIL AFTER THE WEATHER AND SPORTS!
DO I TELL YOU HOW TO DO ***YOUR*** JOB, UNCLE KENT?
WELCOME BACK, SIMPSON! GOOD TO SEE YOU ON TIME!
I SPENT THE WHOLE WEEK IN BED. I COULDN'T SLEEP IN IF I TRIED!
HEY! WELCOME BACK TO WORK, BUDDY!
SLAP!
AAAAAAH! I'VE GOT BEDSORES ON 90% OF MY BODY!
SO YOU DON'T WANT TO SIT DOWN AND TAKE YOUR USUAL PRE-LUNCH NAP?
CAN'T! TOO AWAKE TO CLOSE EYES! TOO SORE TO REST!

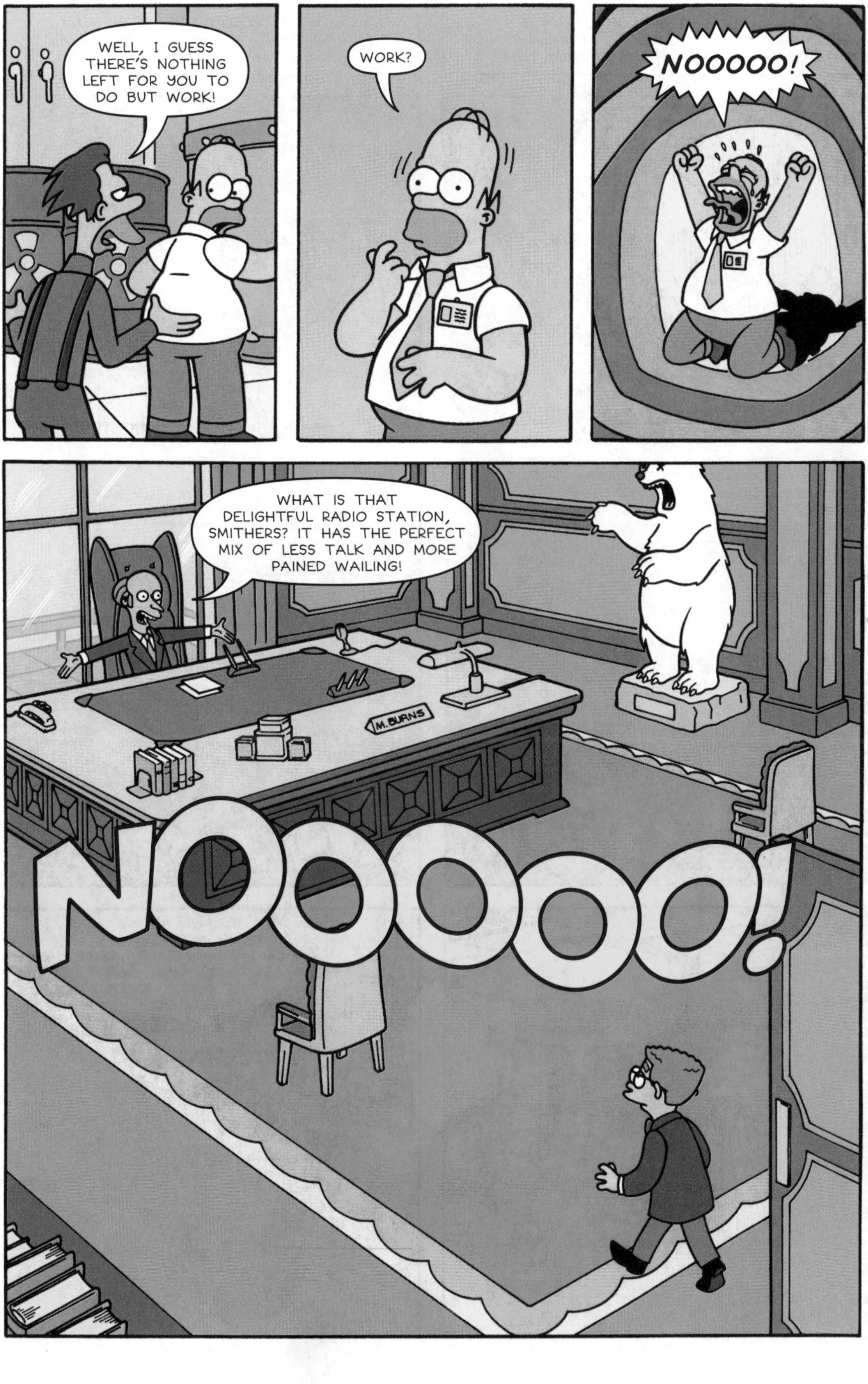
WELL, I GUESS THERE'S NOTHING LEFT FOR YOU TO DO BUT WORK!
WORK?
NOOOOO!
WHAT IS THAT DELIGHTFUL RADIO STATION, SMITHERS? IT HAS THE PERFECT MIX OF LESS TALK AND MORE PAINED WAILING!
M. BURNS
NOOOOO!

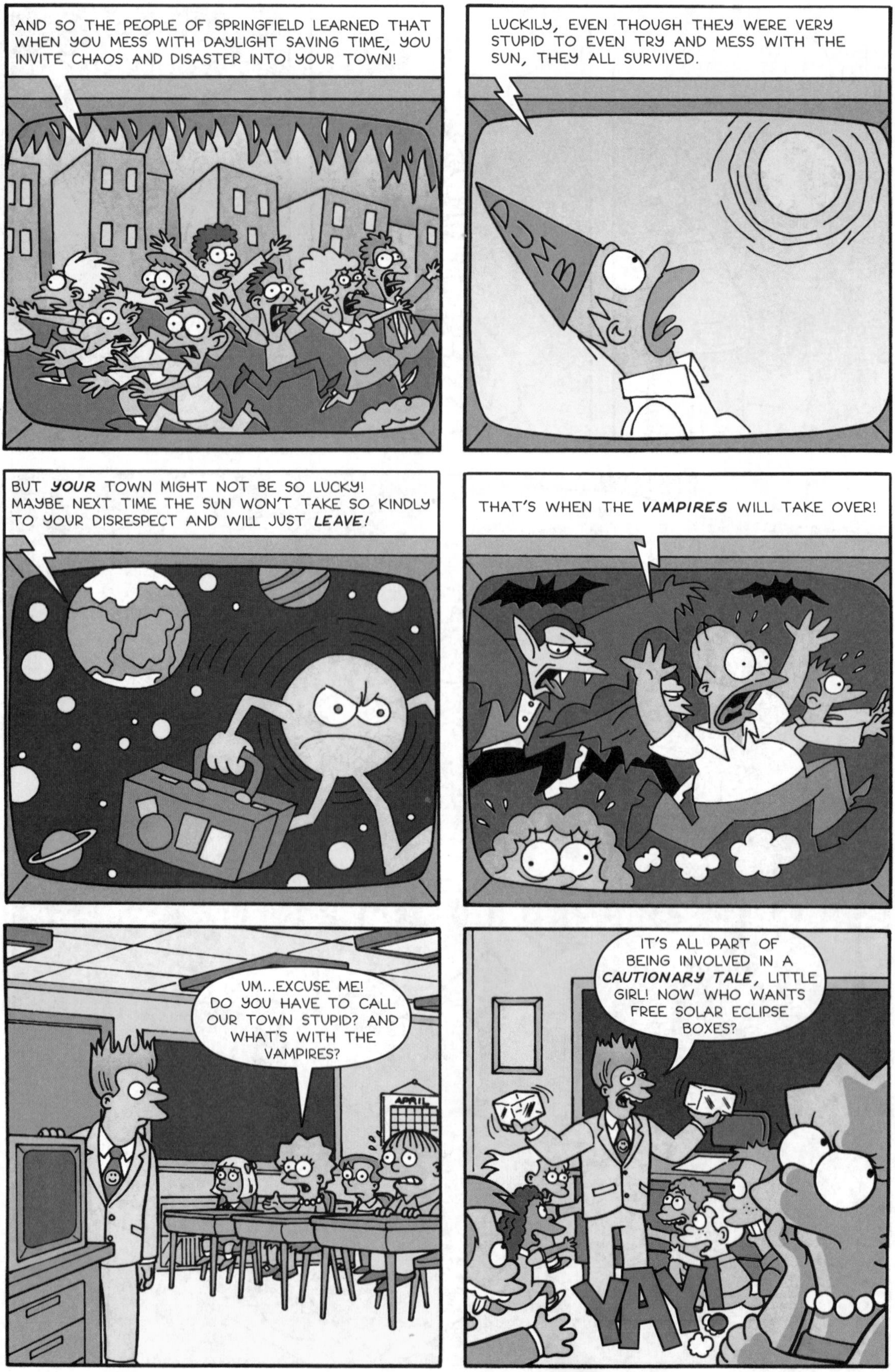

AND SO THE PEOPLE OF SPRINGFIELD LEARNED THAT WHEN YOU MESS WITH DAYLIGHT SAVING TIME, YOU INVITE CHAOS AND DISASTER INTO YOUR TOWN!
LUCKILY, EVEN THOUGH THEY WERE VERY STUPID TO EVEN TRY AND MESS WITH THE SUN, THEY ALL SURVIVED.
BUT YOUR TOWN MIGHT NOT BE SO LUCKY! MAYBE NEXT TIME THE SUN WON'T TAKE SO KINDLY TO YOUR DISRESPECT AND WILL JUST LEAVE!
THAT'S WHEN THE VAMPIRES WILL TAKE OVER!
UM...EXCUSE ME! DO YOU HAVE TO CALL OUR TOWN STUPID? AND WHAT'S WITH THE VAMPIRES?
APRIL
IT'S ALL PART OF BEING INVOLVED IN A CAUTIONARY TALE, LITTLE GIRL! NOW WHO WANTS FREE SOLAR ECLIPSE BOXES?
YAY!

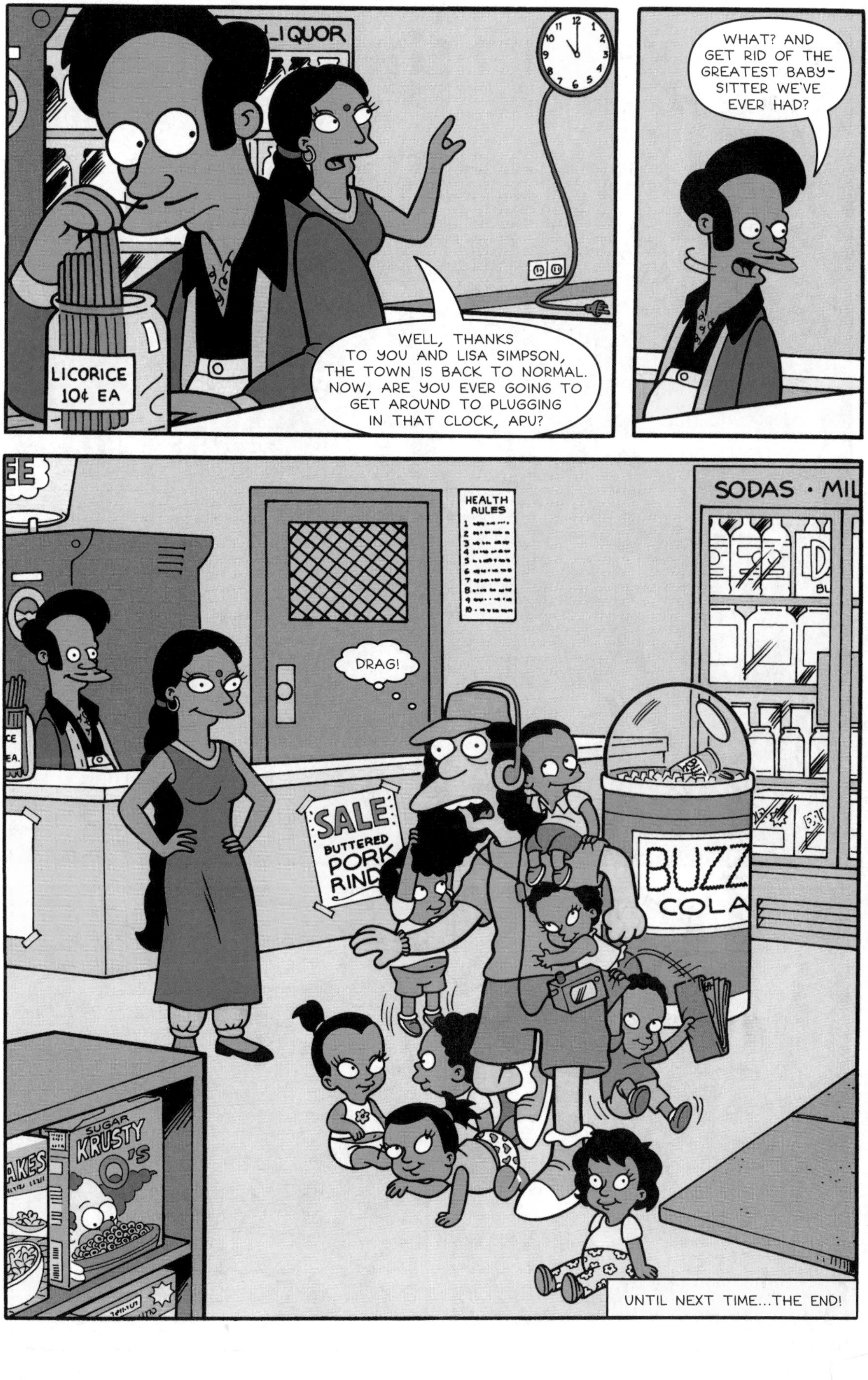

LIQUOR
LICORICE 10¢ EA
WELL, THANKS TO YOU AND LISA SIMPSON, THE TOWN IS BACK TO NORMAL. NOW, ARE YOU EVER GOING TO GET AROUND TO PLUGGING IN THAT CLOCK, APU?
WHAT? AND GET RID OF THE GREATEST BABY-SITTER WE'VE EVER HAD?
HEALTH RULES
SODAS · MIL
DRAG!
SALE BUTTERED PORK RIND
BUZZ COLA
SUGAR KRUSTY O's
UNTIL NEXT TIME...THE END!

MATT GROENING presents

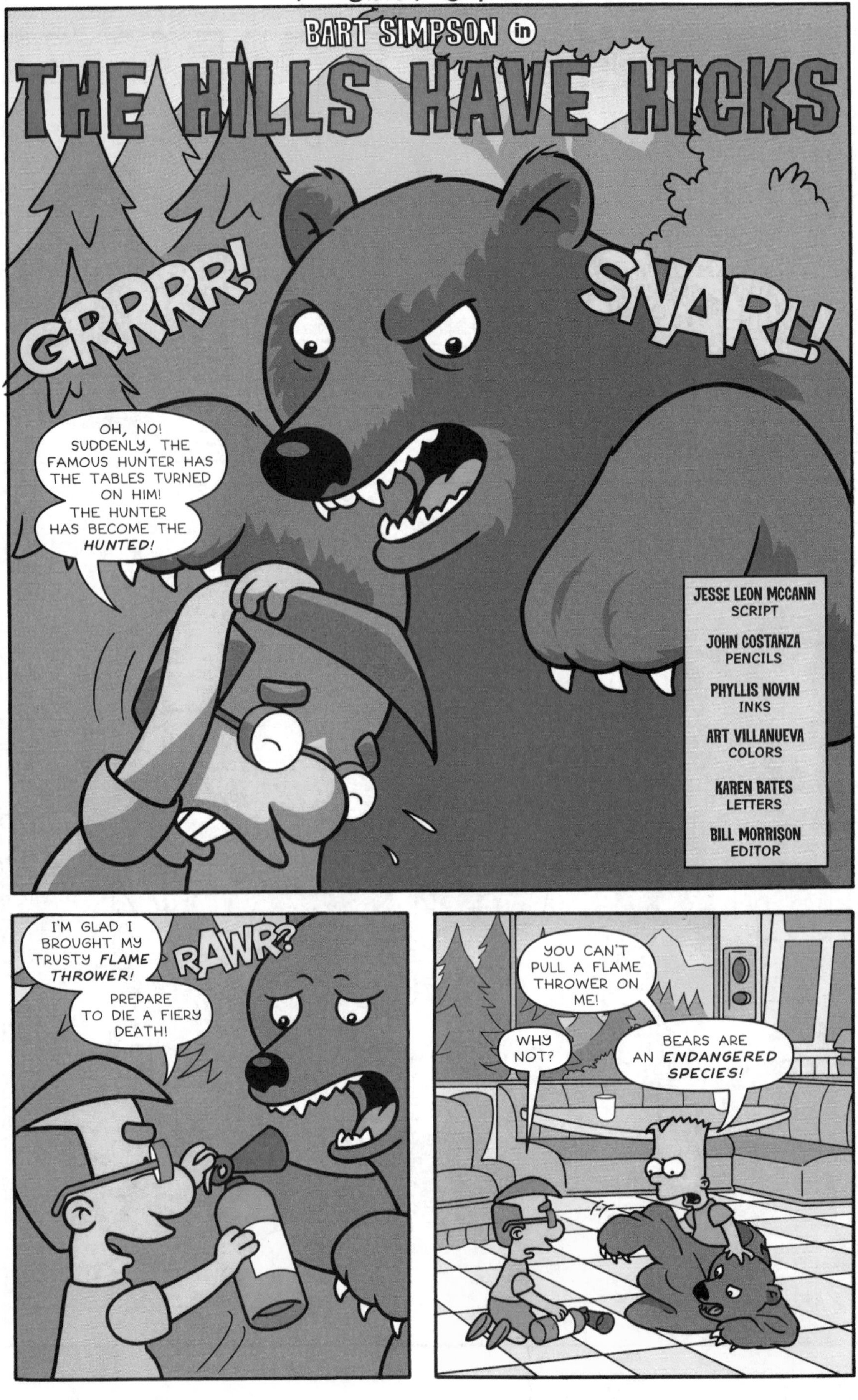
BART SIMPSON in
THE HILLS HAVE HICKS
GRRRR!
SNARL!
OH, NO! SUDDENLY, THE FAMOUS HUNTER HAS THE TABLES TURNED ON HIM! THE HUNTER HAS BECOME THE *HUNTED!*
JESSE LEON MCCANN SCRIPT
JOHN COSTANZA PENCILS
PHYLLIS NOVIN INKS
ART VILLANUEVA COLORS
KAREN BATES LETTERS
BILL MORRISON EDITOR
I'M GLAD I BROUGHT MY TRUSTY *FLAME THROWER!*
RAWR?
PREPARE TO DIE A FIERY DEATH!
YOU CAN'T PULL A FLAME THROWER ON ME!
WHY NOT?
BEARS ARE AN *ENDANGERED SPECIES!*

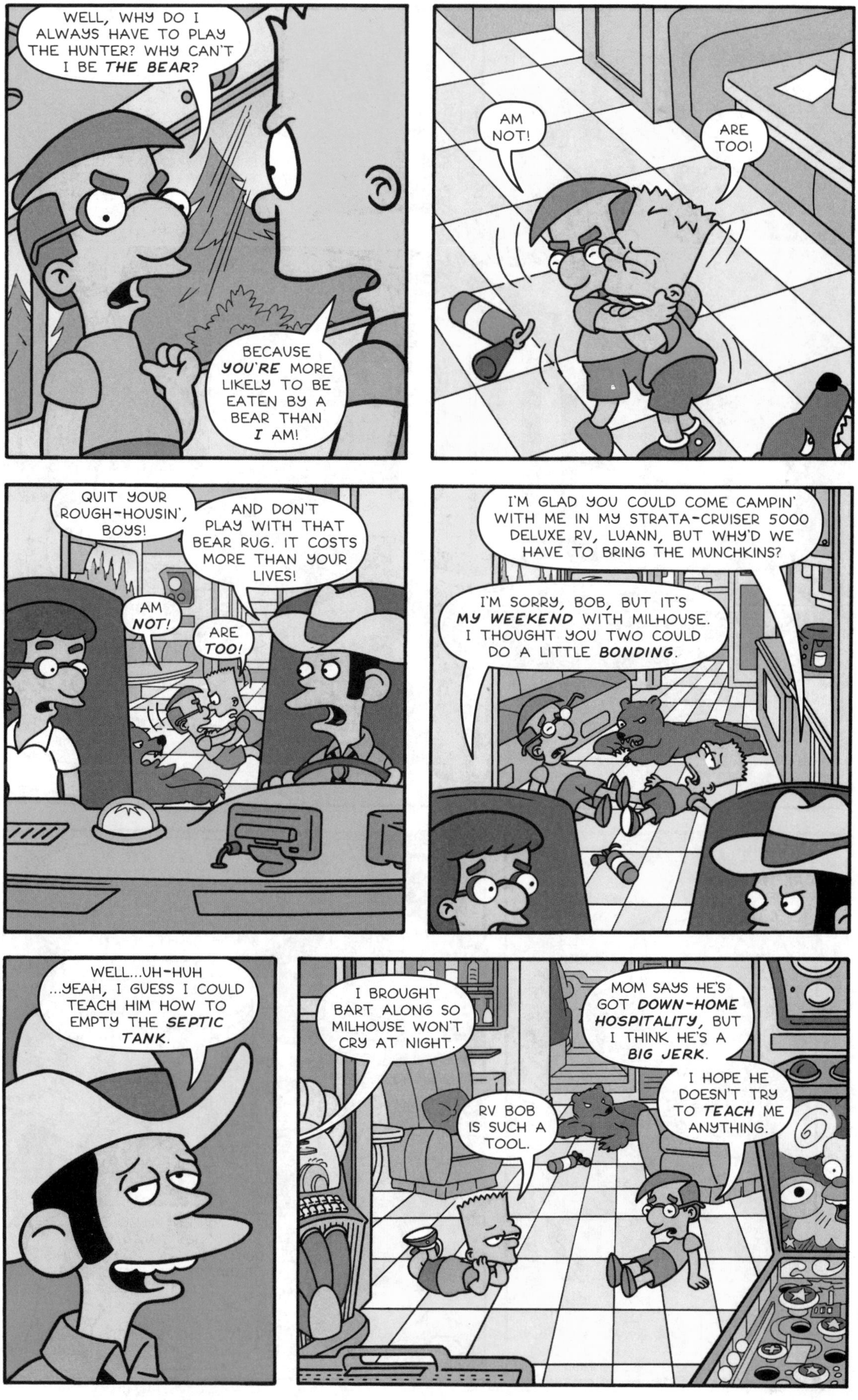
WELL, WHY DO I ALWAYS HAVE TO PLAY THE HUNTER? WHY CAN'T I BE THE BEAR?
BECAUSE YOU'RE MORE LIKELY TO BE EATEN BY A BEAR THAN I AM!
AM NOT!
ARE TOO!
QUIT YOUR ROUGH-HOUSIN', BOYS!
AND DON'T PLAY WITH THAT BEAR RUG. IT COSTS MORE THAN YOUR LIVES!
AM NOT!
ARE TOO!
I'M GLAD YOU COULD COME CAMPIN' WITH ME IN MY STRATA-CRUISER 5000 DELUXE RV, LUANN, BUT WHY'D WE HAVE TO BRING THE MUNCHKINS?
I'M SORRY, BOB, BUT IT'S MY WEEKEND WITH MILHOUSE. I THOUGHT YOU TWO COULD DO A LITTLE BONDING.
WELL...UH-HUH ...YEAH, I GUESS I COULD TEACH HIM HOW TO EMPTY THE SEPTIC TANK.
I BROUGHT BART ALONG SO MILHOUSE WON'T CRY AT NIGHT.
MOM SAYS HE'S GOT DOWN-HOME HOSPITALITY, BUT I THINK HE'S A BIG JERK.
RV BOB IS SUCH A TOOL.
I HOPE HE DOESN'T TRY TO TEACH ME ANYTHING.

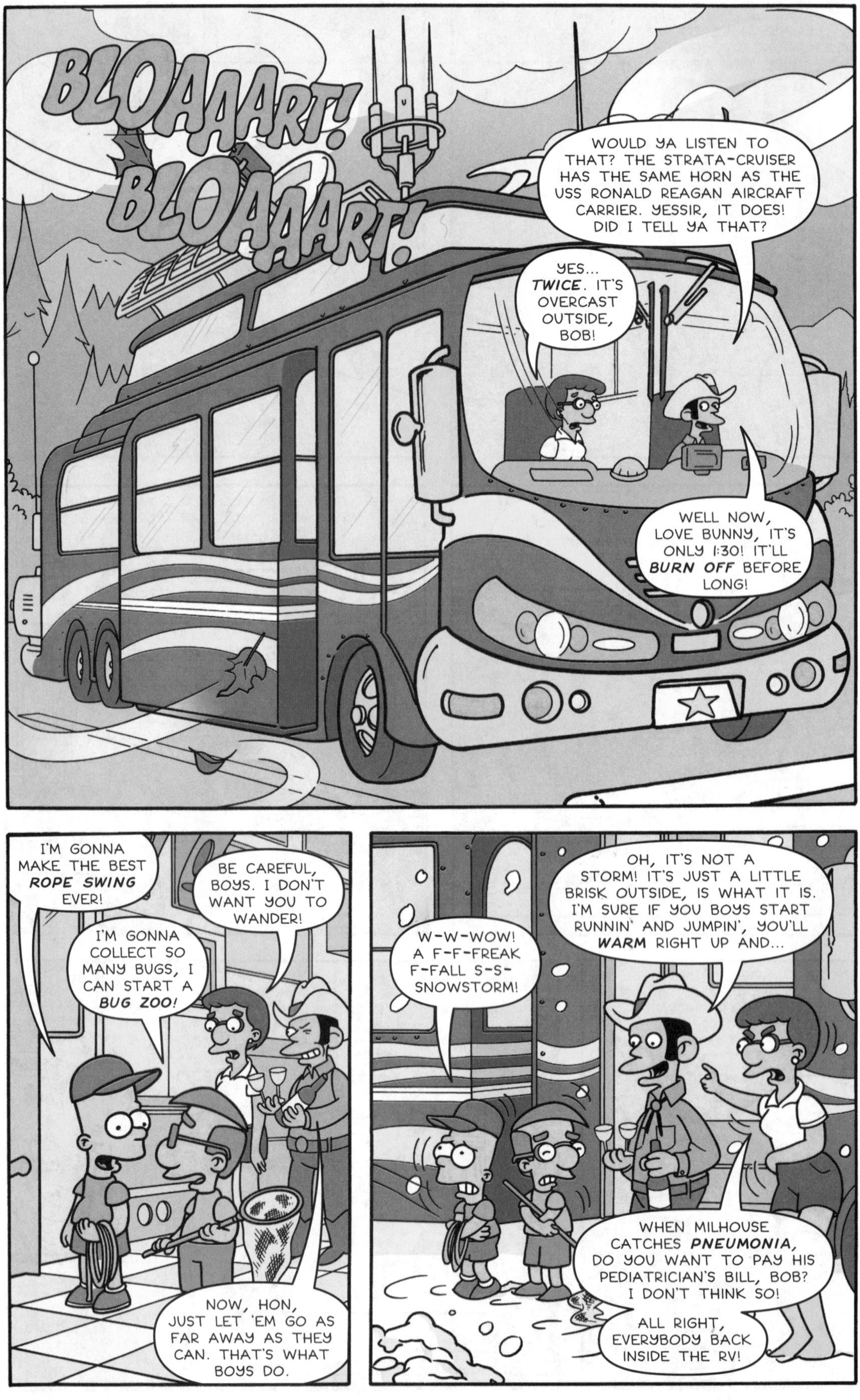
BLOAAAART! BLOAAAART!
WOULD YA LISTEN TO THAT? THE STRATA-CRUISER HAS THE SAME HORN AS THE USS RONALD REAGAN AIRCRAFT CARRIER. YESSIR, IT DOES! DID I TELL YA THAT?
YES... TWICE. IT'S OVERCAST OUTSIDE, BOB!
WELL NOW, LOVE BUNNY, IT'S ONLY 1:30! IT'LL BURN OFF BEFORE LONG!
I'M GONNA MAKE THE BEST ROPE SWING EVER!
I'M GONNA COLLECT SO MANY BUGS, I CAN START A BUG ZOO!
BE CAREFUL, BOYS. I DON'T WANT YOU TO WANDER!
NOW, HON, JUST LET 'EM GO AS FAR AWAY AS THEY CAN. THAT'S WHAT BOYS DO.
W-W-WOW! A F-F-FREAK F-FALL S-S-SNOWSTORM!
OH, IT'S NOT A STORM! IT'S JUST A LITTLE BRISK OUTSIDE, IS WHAT IT IS. I'M SURE IF YOU BOYS START RUNNIN' AND JUMPIN', YOU'LL WARM RIGHT UP AND...
WHEN MILHOUSE CATCHES PNEUMONIA, DO YOU WANT TO PAY HIS PEDIATRICIAN'S BILL, BOB? I DON'T THINK SO!
ALL RIGHT, EVERYBODY BACK INSIDE THE RV!

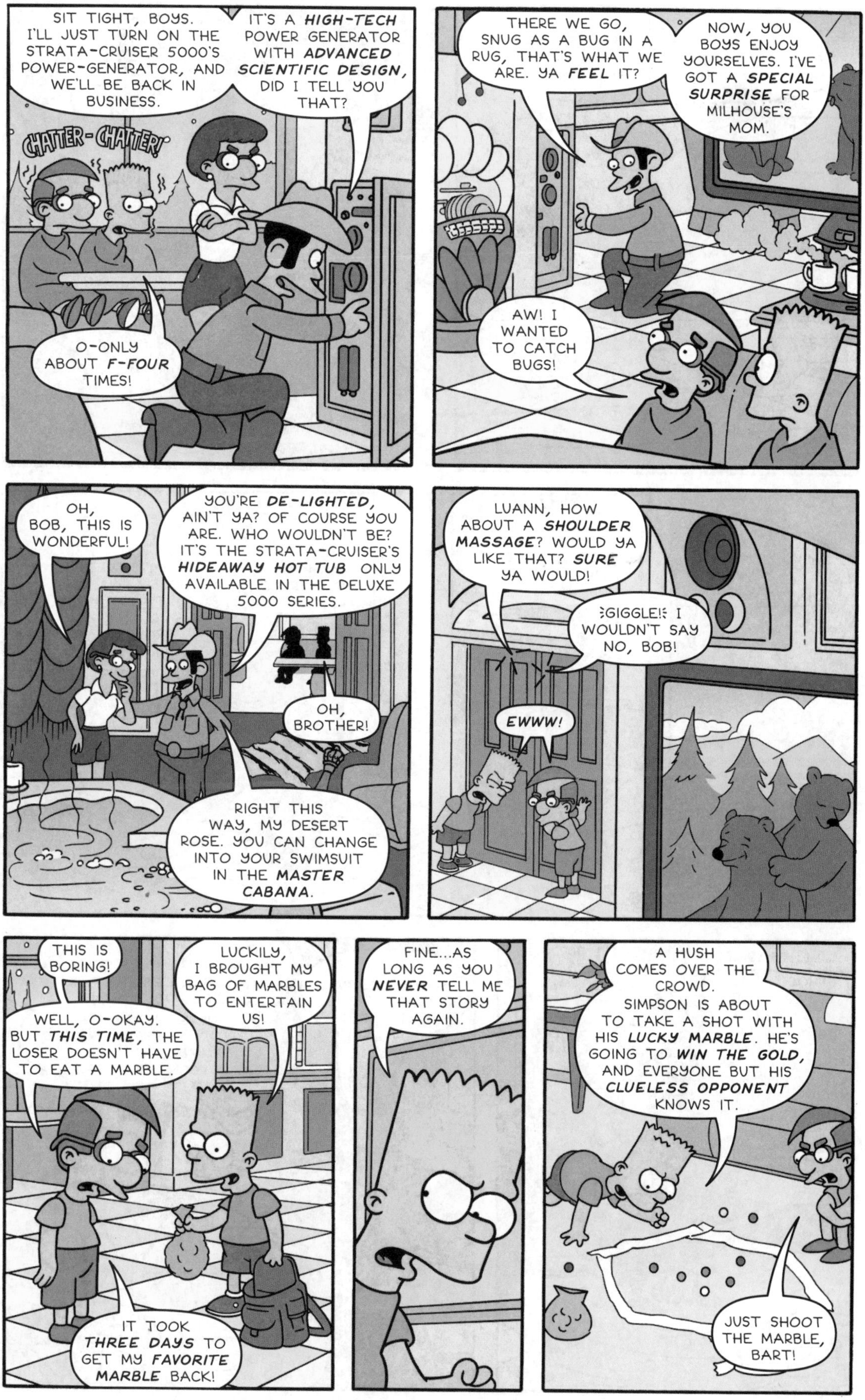

SIT TIGHT, BOYS. I'LL JUST TURN ON THE STRATA-CRUISER 5000'S POWER-GENERATOR, AND WE'LL BE BACK IN BUSINESS.
IT'S A **HIGH-TECH** POWER GENERATOR WITH **ADVANCED SCIENTIFIC DESIGN,** DID I TELL YOU THAT?
CHATTER-CHATTER!
O-ONLY ABOUT **F-FOUR** TIMES!
THERE WE GO, SNUG AS A BUG IN A RUG, THAT'S WHAT WE ARE. YA **FEEL** IT?
NOW, YOU BOYS ENJOY YOURSELVES. I'VE GOT A **SPECIAL SURPRISE** FOR MILHOUSE'S MOM.
AW! I WANTED TO CATCH BUGS!
OH, BOB, THIS IS WONDERFUL!
YOU'RE **DE-LIGHTED,** AIN'T YA? OF COURSE YOU ARE. WHO WOULDN'T BE? IT'S THE STRATA-CRUISER'S **HIDEAWAY HOT TUB** ONLY AVAILABLE IN THE DELUXE 5000 SERIES.
OH, BROTHER!
RIGHT THIS WAY, MY DESERT ROSE. YOU CAN CHANGE INTO YOUR SWIMSUIT IN THE **MASTER CABANA**.
LUANN, HOW ABOUT A **SHOULDER MASSAGE**? WOULD YA LIKE THAT? **SURE** YA WOULD!
GIGGLE! I WOULDN'T SAY NO, BOB!
EWWW!
THIS IS BORING!
LUCKILY, I BROUGHT MY BAG OF MARBLES TO ENTERTAIN US!
WELL, O-OKAY. BUT **THIS TIME,** THE LOSER DOESN'T HAVE TO EAT A MARBLE.
IT TOOK **THREE DAYS** TO GET MY **FAVORITE MARBLE** BACK!
FINE...AS LONG AS YOU **NEVER** TELL ME THAT STORY AGAIN.
A HUSH COMES OVER THE CROWD. SIMPSON IS ABOUT TO TAKE A SHOT WITH HIS **LUCKY MARBLE**. HE'S GOING TO **WIN THE GOLD,** AND EVERYONE BUT HIS **CLUELESS OPPONENT** KNOWS IT.
JUST SHOOT THE MARBLE, BART!

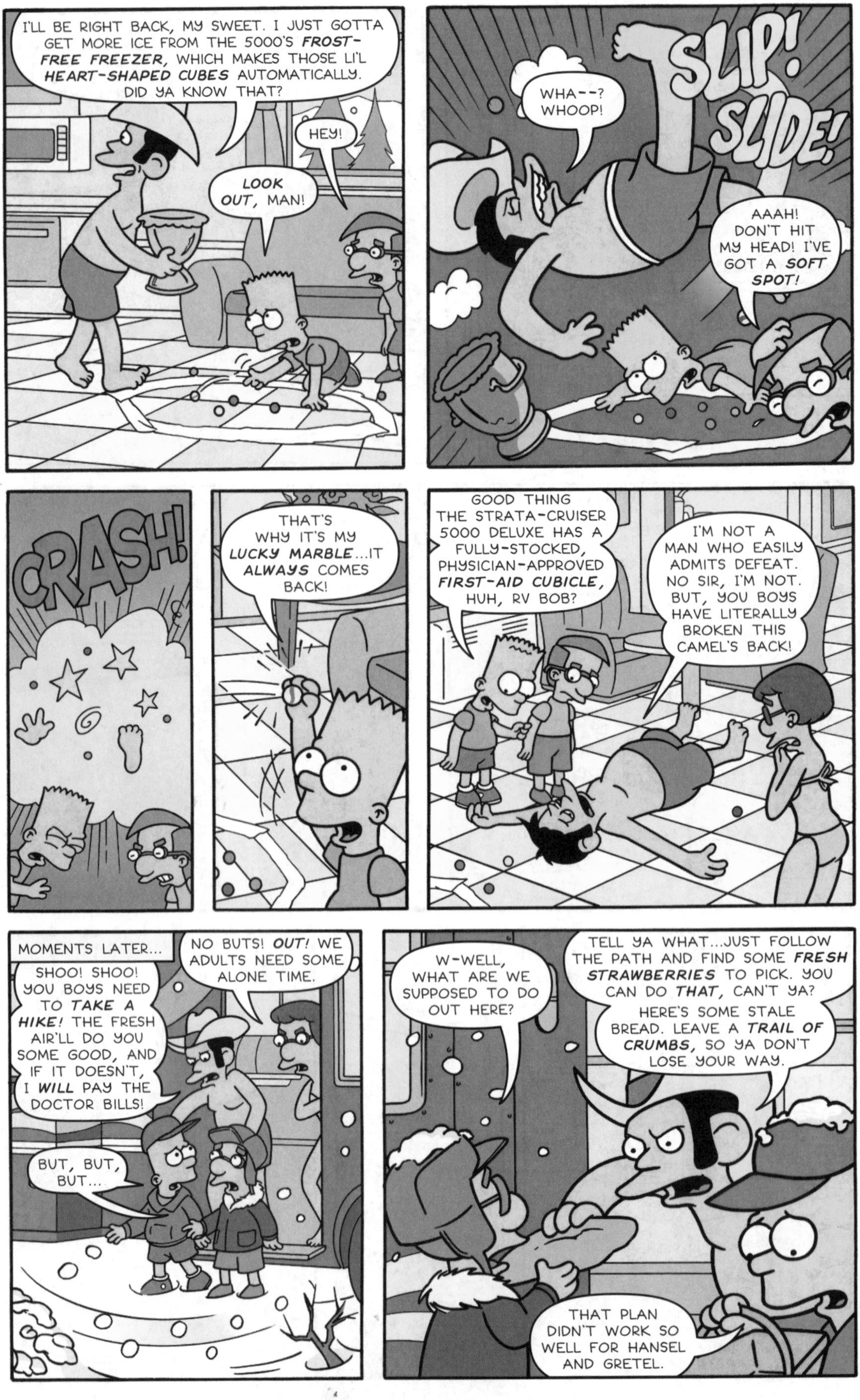
I'LL BE RIGHT BACK, MY SWEET. I JUST GOTTA GET MORE ICE FROM THE 5000'S ***FROST-FREE FREEZER,*** WHICH MAKES THOSE LI'L ***HEART-SHAPED CUBES*** AUTOMATICALLY. DID YA KNOW THAT?
HEY!
LOOK OUT, MAN!
WHA--? WHOOP!
SLIP! SLIDE!
AAAH! DON'T HIT MY HEAD! I'VE GOT A ***SOFT SPOT!***
CRASH!
THAT'S WHY IT'S MY ***LUCKY MARBLE***...IT ***ALWAYS*** COMES BACK!
GOOD THING THE STRATA-CRUISER 5000 DELUXE HAS A FULLY-STOCKED, PHYSICIAN-APPROVED ***FIRST-AID CUBICLE,*** HUH, RV BOB?
I'M NOT A MAN WHO EASILY ADMITS DEFEAT. NO SIR, I'M NOT. BUT, YOU BOYS HAVE LITERALLY BROKEN THIS CAMEL'S BACK!
MOMENTS LATER...
SHOO! SHOO! YOU BOYS NEED TO ***TAKE A HIKE!*** THE FRESH AIR'LL DO YOU SOME GOOD, AND IF IT DOESN'T, I ***WILL*** PAY THE DOCTOR BILLS!
NO BUTS! ***OUT!*** WE ADULTS NEED SOME ALONE TIME.
BUT, BUT, BUT...
W-WELL, WHAT ARE WE SUPPOSED TO DO OUT HERE?
TELL YA WHAT...JUST FOLLOW THE PATH AND FIND SOME ***FRESH STRAWBERRIES*** TO PICK. YOU CAN DO ***THAT,*** CAN'T YA?
HERE'S SOME STALE BREAD. LEAVE A ***TRAIL OF CRUMBS,*** SO YA DON'T LOSE YOUR WAY.
THAT PLAN DIDN'T WORK SO WELL FOR HANSEL AND GRETEL.

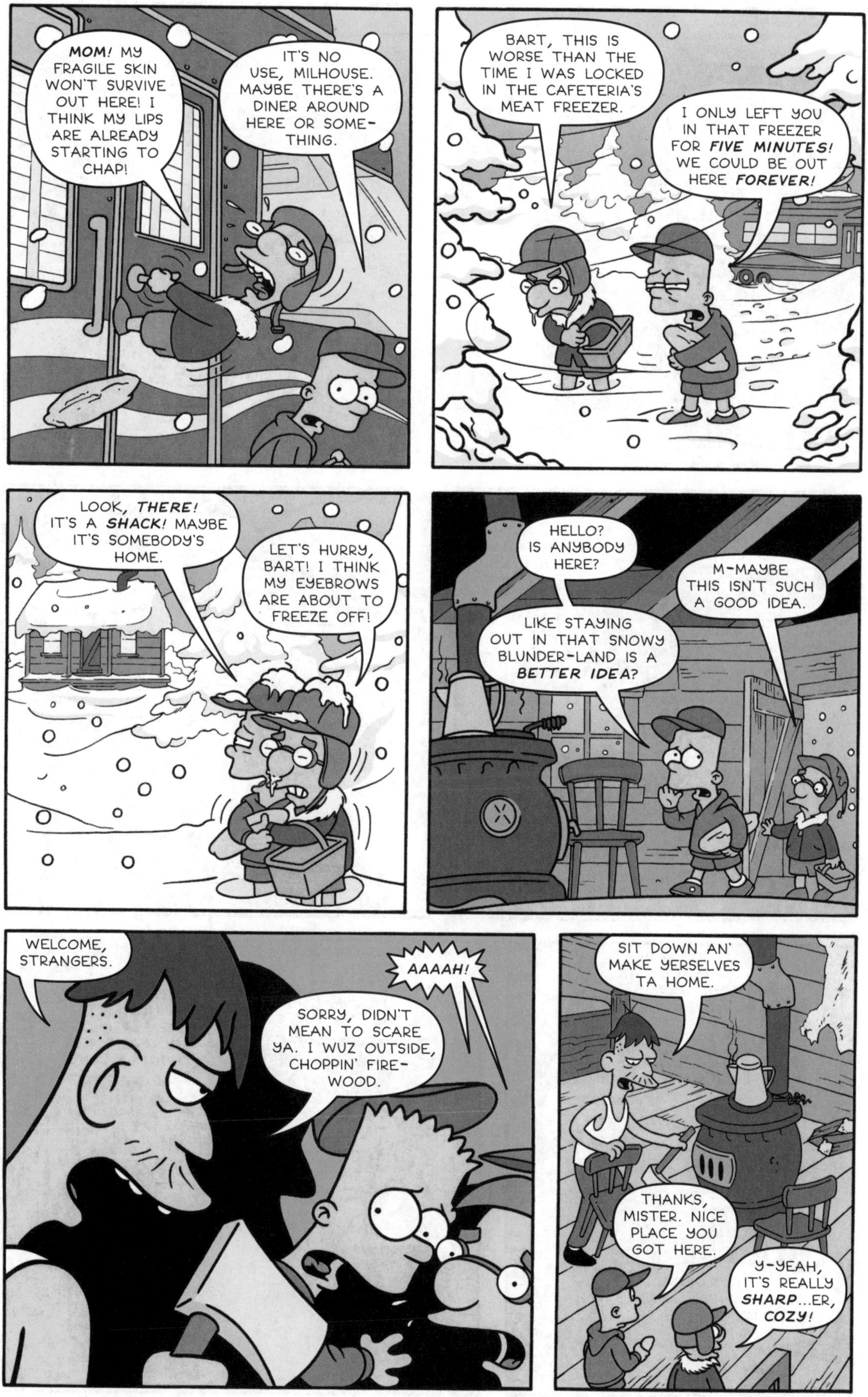

MOM! MY FRAGILE SKIN WON'T SURVIVE OUT HERE! I THINK MY LIPS ARE ALREADY STARTING TO CHAP!
IT'S NO USE, MILHOUSE. MAYBE THERE'S A DINER AROUND HERE OR SOMETHING.
BART, THIS IS WORSE THAN THE TIME I WAS LOCKED IN THE CAFETERIA'S MEAT FREEZER.
I ONLY LEFT YOU IN THAT FREEZER FOR FIVE MINUTES! WE COULD BE OUT HERE FOREVER!
LOOK, THERE! IT'S A SHACK! MAYBE IT'S SOMEBODY'S HOME.
LET'S HURRY, BART! I THINK MY EYEBROWS ARE ABOUT TO FREEZE OFF!
HELLO? IS ANYBODY HERE?
M-MAYBE THIS ISN'T SUCH A GOOD IDEA.
LIKE STAYING OUT IN THAT SNOWY BLUNDER-LAND IS A BETTER IDEA?
WELCOME, STRANGERS.
AAAAH!
SORRY, DIDN'T MEAN TO SCARE YA. I WUZ OUTSIDE, CHOPPIN' FIREWOOD.
SIT DOWN AN' MAKE YERSELVES TA HOME.
THANKS, MISTER. NICE PLACE YOU GOT HERE.
Y-YEAH, IT'S REALLY SHARP...ER, COZY!

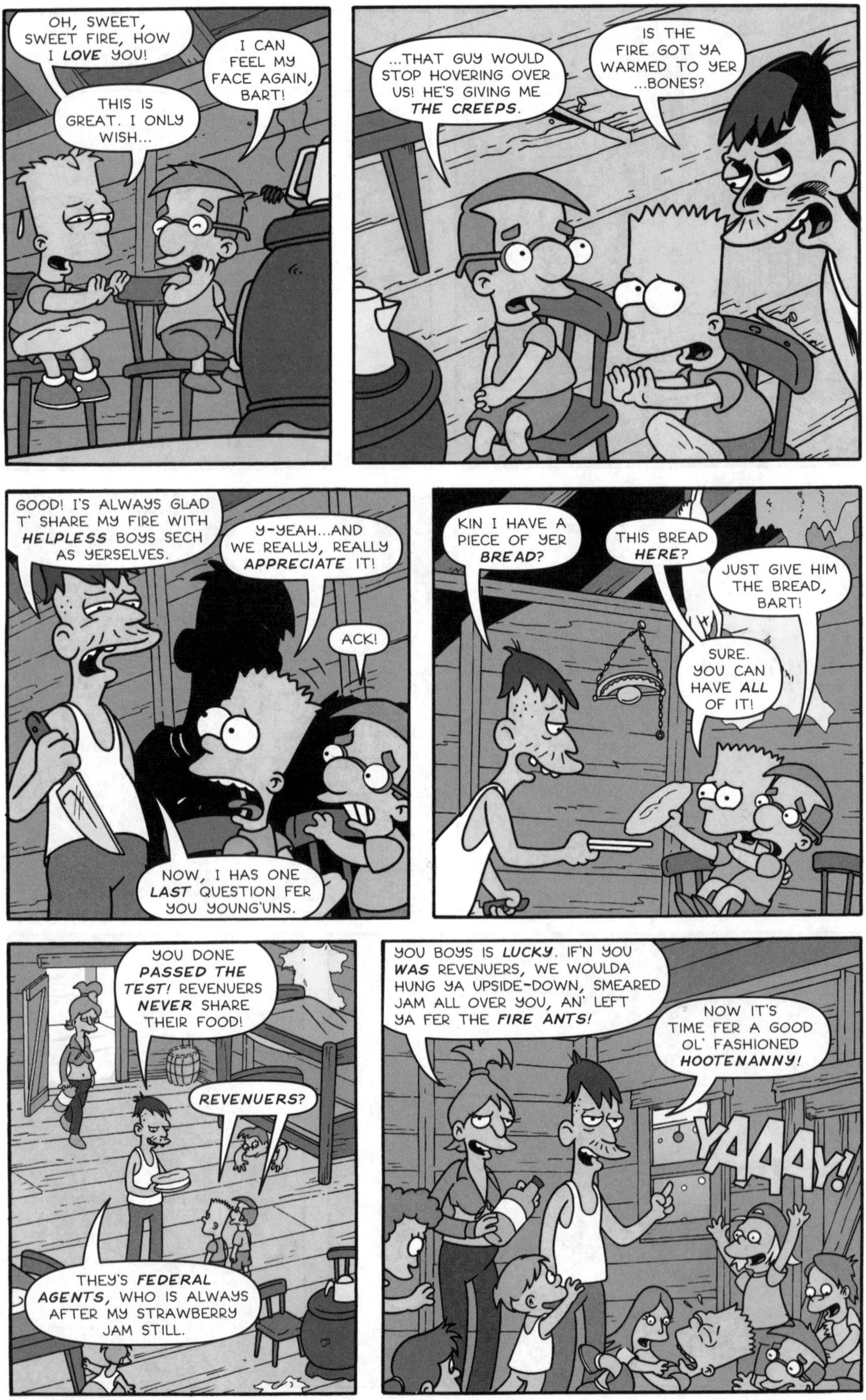
OH, SWEET, SWEET FIRE, HOW I LOVE YOU!
THIS IS GREAT. I ONLY WISH...
I CAN FEEL MY FACE AGAIN, BART!
...THAT GUY WOULD STOP HOVERING OVER US! HE'S GIVING ME THE CREEPS.
IS THE FIRE GOT YA WARMED TO YER ...BONES?
GOOD! I'S ALWAYS GLAD T' SHARE MY FIRE WITH HELPLESS BOYS SECH AS YERSELVES.
Y-YEAH...AND WE REALLY, REALLY APPRECIATE IT!
ACK!
NOW, I HAS ONE LAST QUESTION FER YOU YOUNG'UNS.
KIN I HAVE A PIECE OF YER BREAD?
THIS BREAD HERE?
JUST GIVE HIM THE BREAD, BART!
SURE. YOU CAN HAVE ALL OF IT!
YOU DONE PASSED THE TEST! REVENUERS NEVER SHARE THEIR FOOD!
REVENUERS?
THEY'S FEDERAL AGENTS, WHO IS ALWAYS AFTER MY STRAWBERRY JAM STILL.
YOU BOYS IS LUCKY. IF'N YOU WAS REVENUERS, WE WOULDA HUNG YA UPSIDE-DOWN, SMEARED JAM ALL OVER YOU, AN' LEFT YA FER THE FIRE ANTS!
NOW IT'S TIME FER A GOOD OL' FASHIONED HOOTENANNY!
YAAAY!

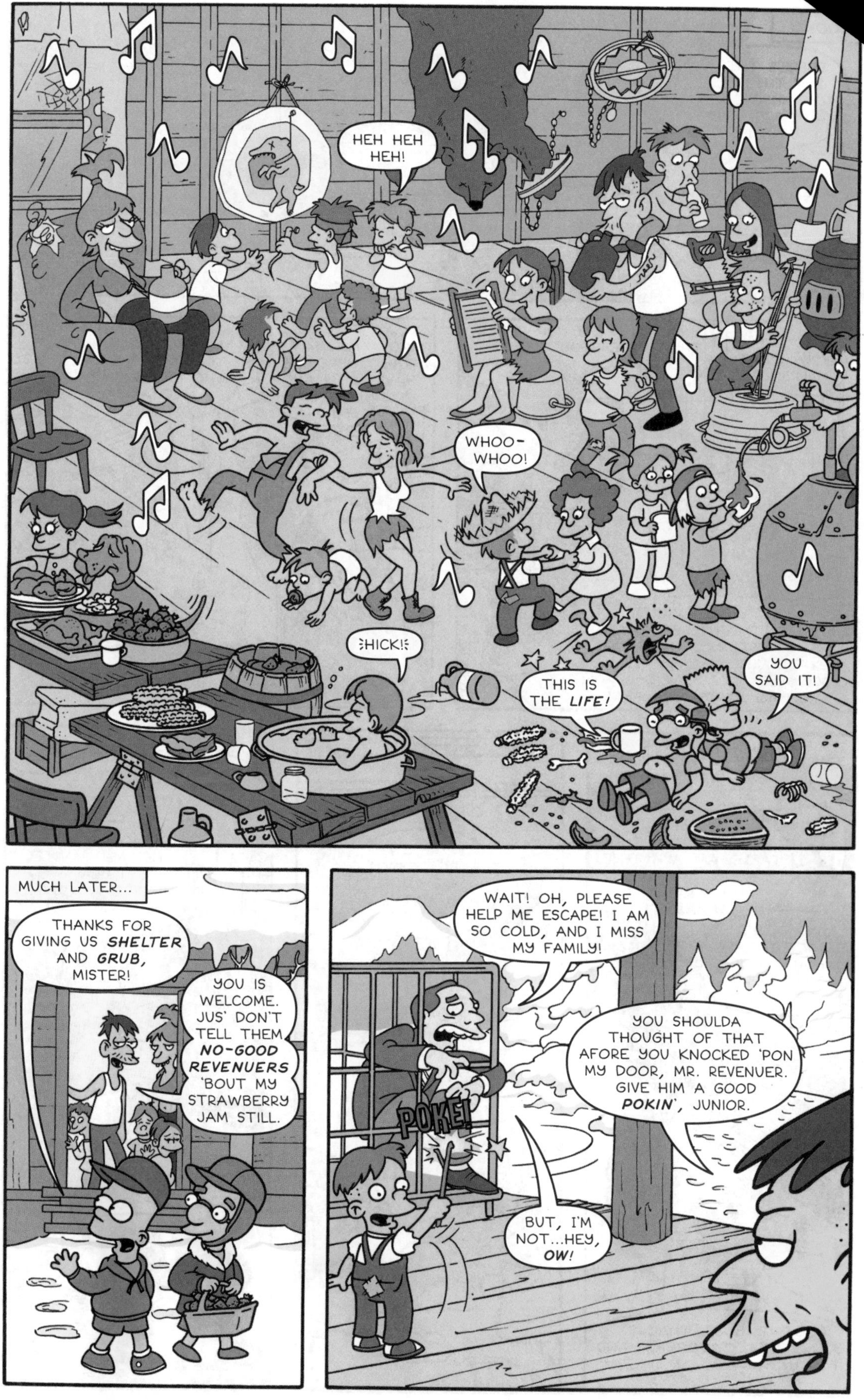
HEH HEH HEH!
WHOO-WHOO!
HICK!
THIS IS THE *LIFE!*
YOU SAID IT!
MUCH LATER...
THANKS FOR GIVING US ***SHELTER*** AND ***GRUB,*** MISTER!
YOU IS WELCOME. JUS' DON'T TELL THEM ***NO-GOOD REVENUERS*** 'BOUT MY STRAWBERRY JAM STILL.
WAIT! OH, PLEASE HELP ME ESCAPE! I AM SO COLD, AND I MISS MY FAMILY!
YOU SHOULDA THOUGHT OF THAT AFORE YOU KNOCKED 'PON MY DOOR, MR. REVENUER. GIVE HIM A GOOD ***POKIN'***, JUNIOR.
POKE!
BUT, I'M NOT...HEY, ***OW!***

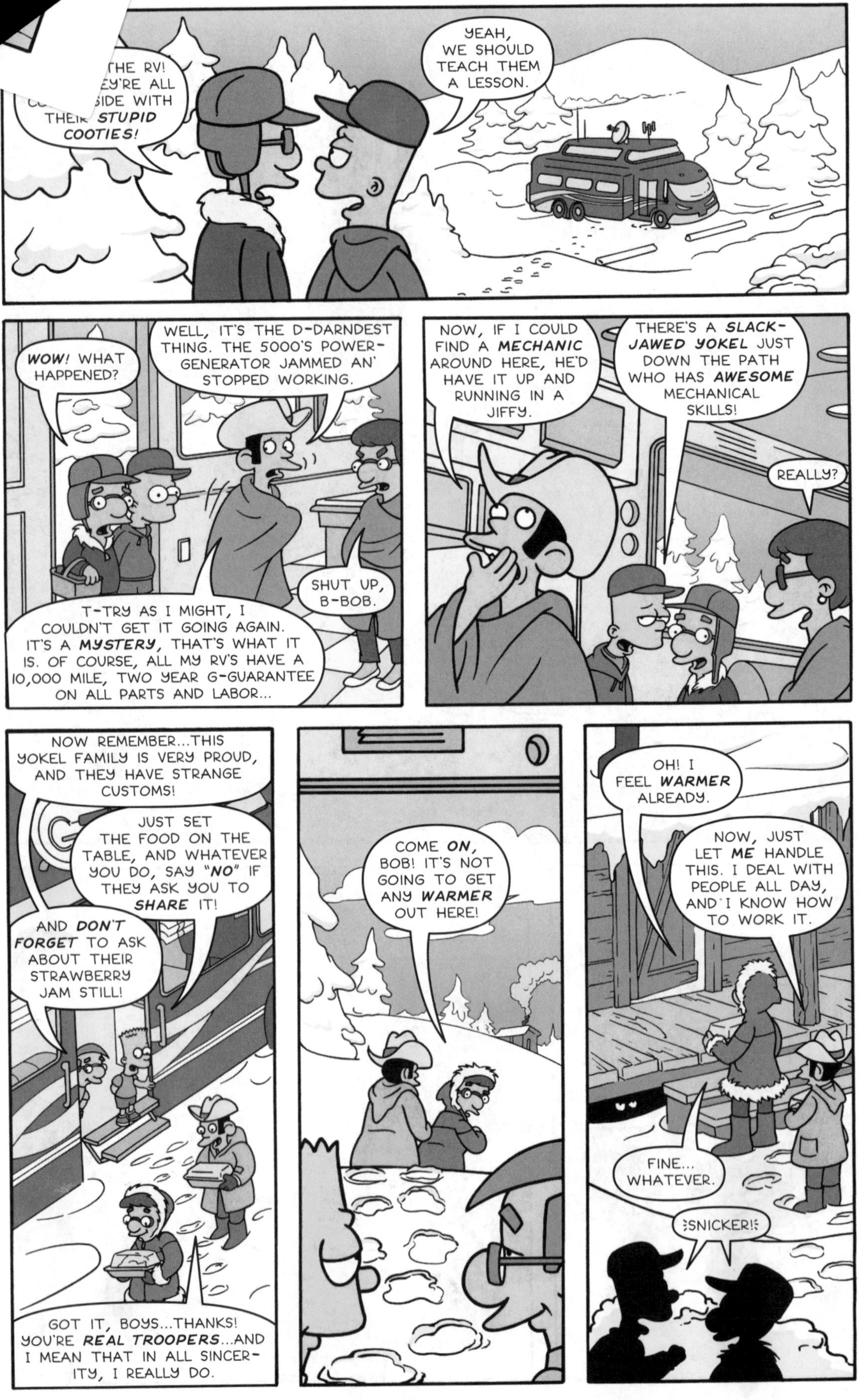
THE RV! EY'RE ALL SIDE WITH THEI STUPID COOTIES!
YEAH, WE SHOULD TEACH THEM A LESSON.
WOW! WHAT HAPPENED?
WELL, IT'S THE D-DARNDEST THING. THE 5000'S POWER-GENERATOR JAMMED AN' STOPPED WORKING.
SHUT UP, B-BOB.
T-TRY AS I MIGHT, I COULDN'T GET IT GOING AGAIN. IT'S A MYSTERY, THAT'S WHAT IT IS. OF COURSE, ALL MY RV'S HAVE A 10,000 MILE, TWO YEAR G-GUARANTEE ON ALL PARTS AND LABOR...
NOW, IF I COULD FIND A MECHANIC AROUND HERE, HE'D HAVE IT UP AND RUNNING IN A JIFFY.
THERE'S A SLACK-JAWED YOKEL JUST DOWN THE PATH WHO HAS AWESOME MECHANICAL SKILLS!
REALLY?
NOW REMEMBER...THIS YOKEL FAMILY IS VERY PROUD, AND THEY HAVE STRANGE CUSTOMS!
JUST SET THE FOOD ON THE TABLE, AND WHATEVER YOU DO, SAY "NO" IF THEY ASK YOU TO SHARE IT!
AND DON'T FORGET TO ASK ABOUT THEIR STRAWBERRY JAM STILL!
GOT IT, BOYS...THANKS! YOU'RE REAL TROOPERS...AND I MEAN THAT IN ALL SINCERITY, I REALLY DO.
COME ON, BOB! IT'S NOT GOING TO GET ANY WARMER OUT HERE!
OH! I FEEL WARMER ALREADY.
NOW, JUST LET ME HANDLE THIS. I DEAL WITH PEOPLE ALL DAY, AND I KNOW HOW TO WORK IT.
FINE... WHATEVER.
SNICKER!

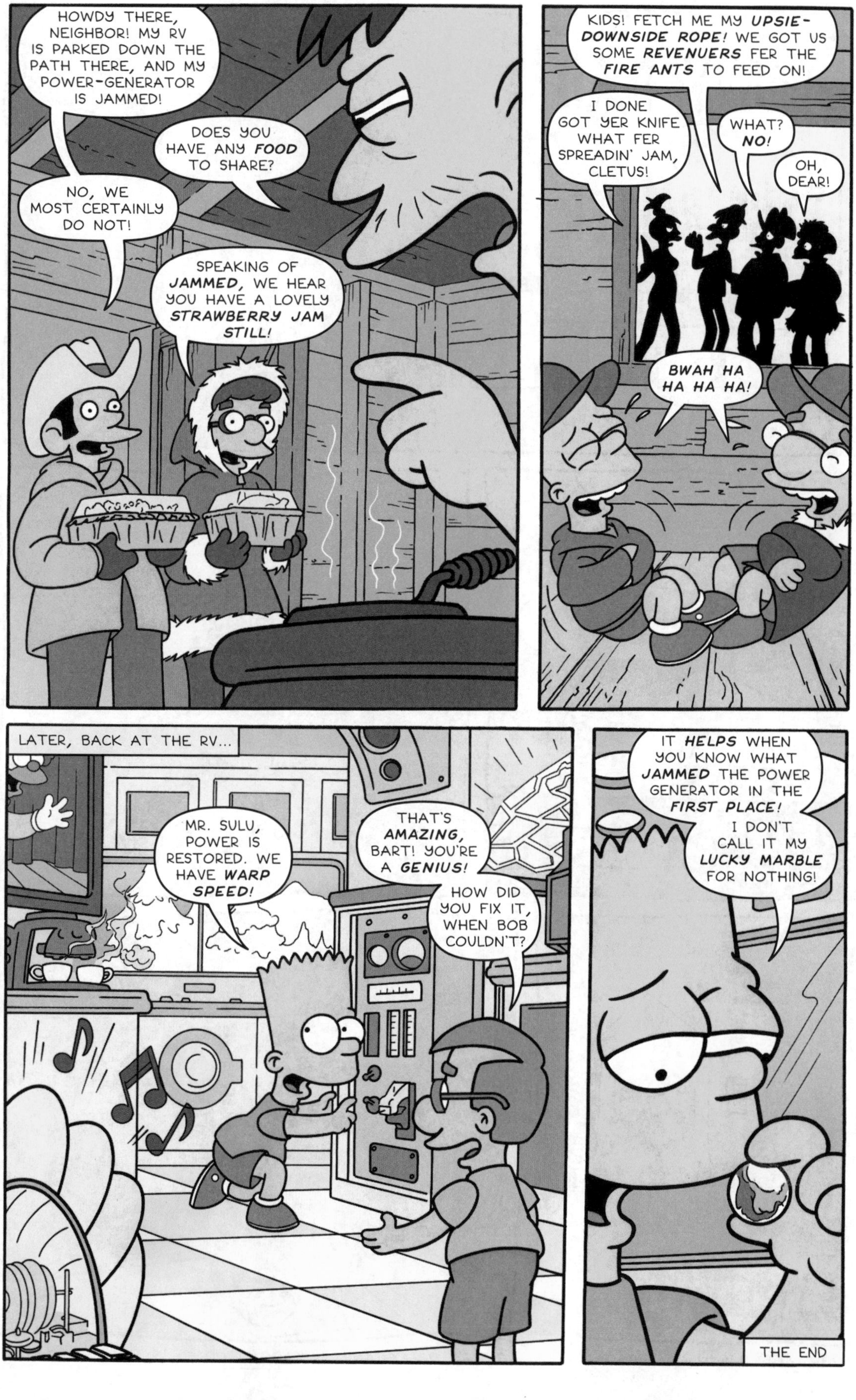
HOWDY THERE, NEIGHBOR! MY RV IS PARKED DOWN THE PATH THERE, AND MY POWER-GENERATOR IS JAMMED!
DOES YOU HAVE ANY **FOOD** TO SHARE?
NO, WE MOST CERTAINLY DO NOT!
SPEAKING OF **JAMMED**, WE HEAR YOU HAVE A LOVELY **STRAWBERRY JAM STILL!**
KIDS! FETCH ME MY **UPSIE-DOWNSIDE ROPE!** WE GOT US SOME **REVENUERS** FER THE **FIRE ANTS** TO FEED ON!
I DONE GOT YER KNIFE WHAT FER SPREADIN' JAM, CLETUS!
WHAT? **NO!**
OH, DEAR!
BWAH HA HA HA HA!
LATER, BACK AT THE RV...
MR. SULU, POWER IS RESTORED. WE HAVE **WARP SPEED!**
THAT'S **AMAZING**, BART! YOU'RE A **GENIUS!**
HOW DID YOU FIX IT, WHEN BOB COULDN'T?
IT **HELPS** WHEN YOU KNOW WHAT **JAMMED** THE POWER GENERATOR IN THE **FIRST PLACE!**
I DON'T CALL IT MY **LUCKY MARBLE** FOR NOTHING!
THE END

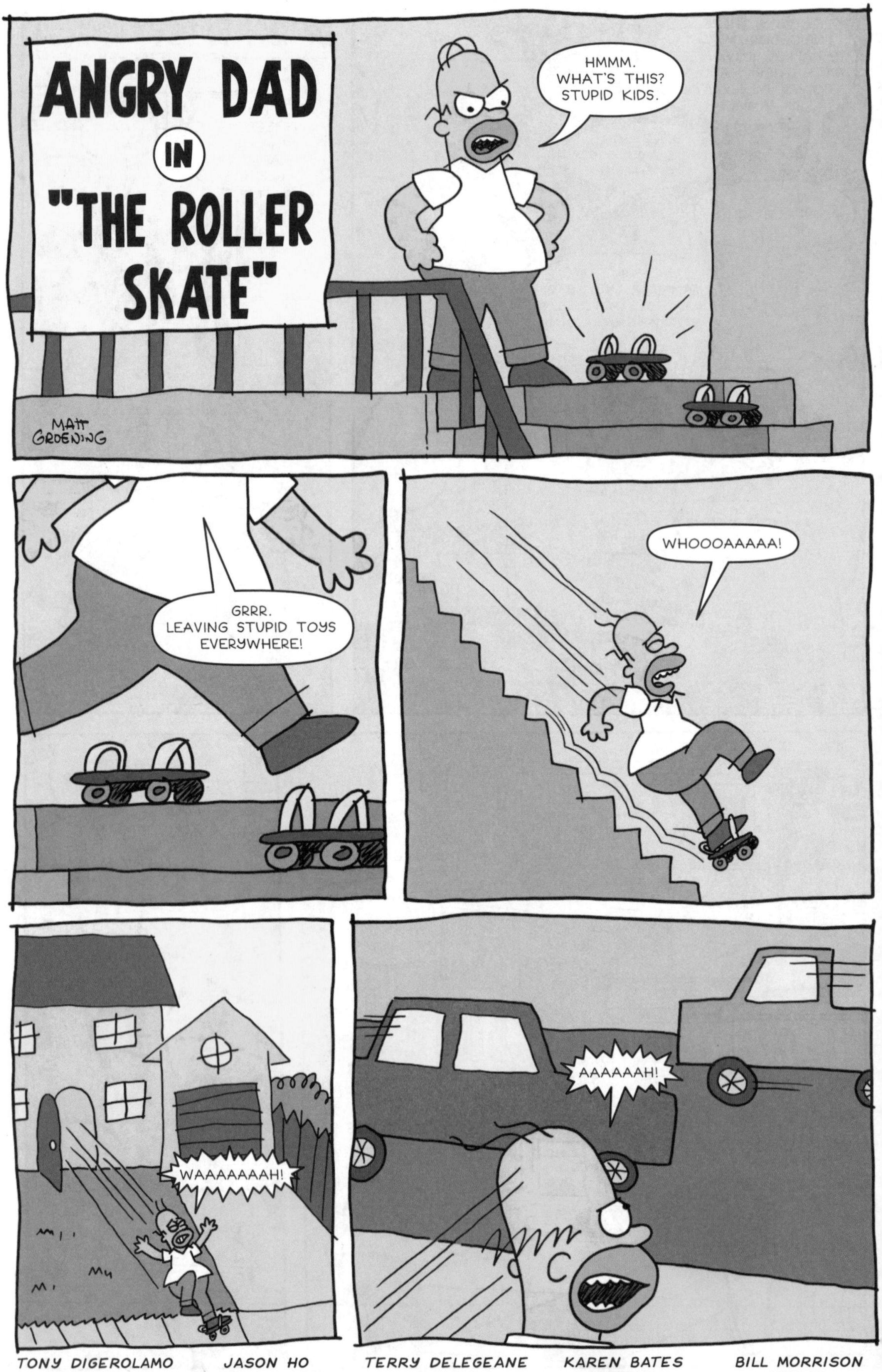
ANGRY DAD
IN
"THE ROLLER SKATE"
HMMM. WHAT'S THIS? STUPID KIDS.
MATT GROENING
GRRR. LEAVING STUPID TOYS EVERYWHERE!
WHOOOAAAAA!
WAAAAAAAAH!
AAAAAAH!

TONY DIGEROLAMO SCRIPT — *JASON HO* PENCILS & INKS — *TERRY DELEGEANE* COLORS — *KAREN BATES* LETTERS — *BILL MORRISON* EDITOR

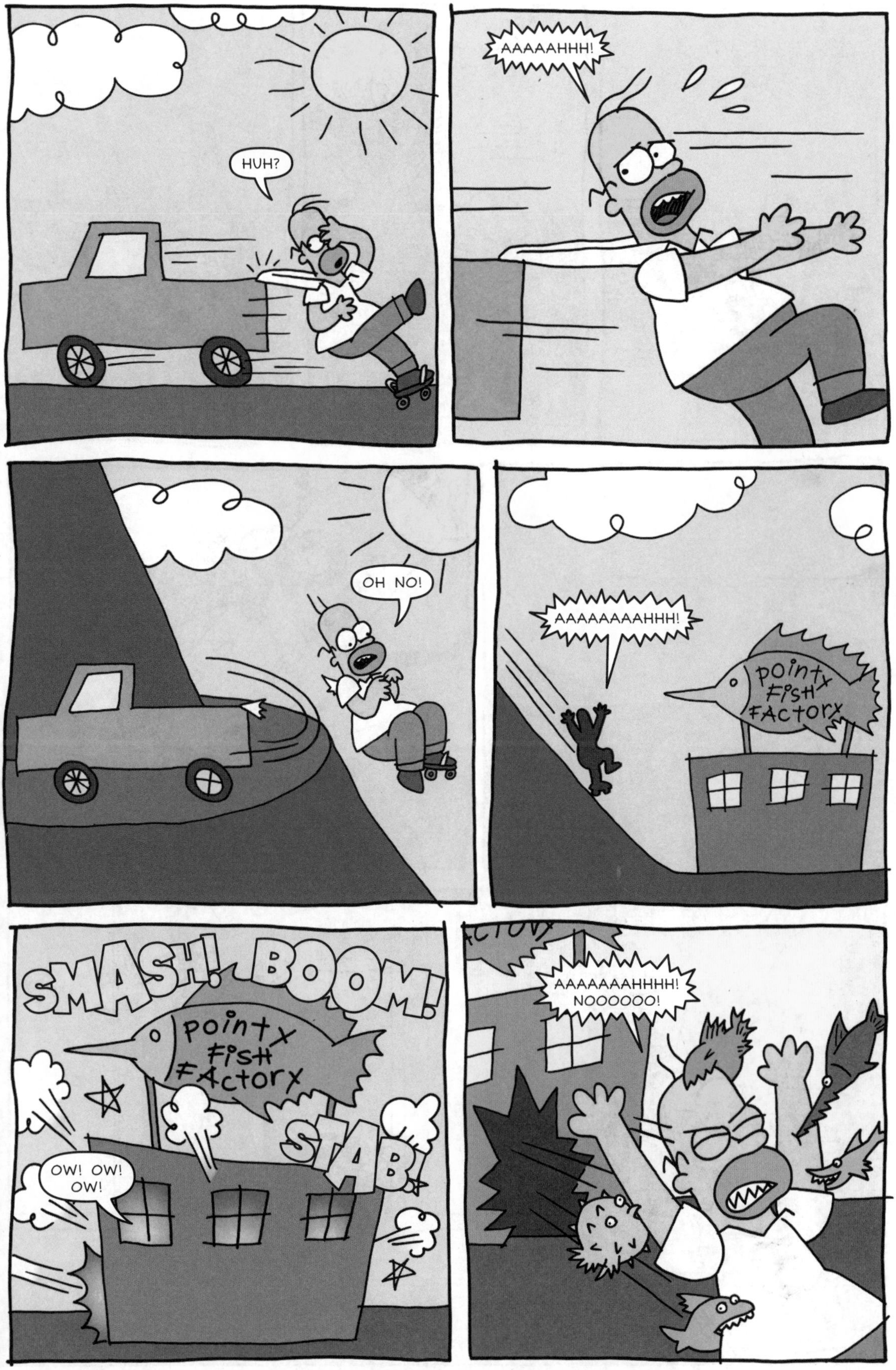
HUH?
AAAAAHHH!
OH NO!
AAAAAAAAHHH!
pointy fish factory
SMASH!
BOOM!
pointy fish factory
STAB!
OW! OW! OW!
AAAAAAAHHHH! NOOOOOO!

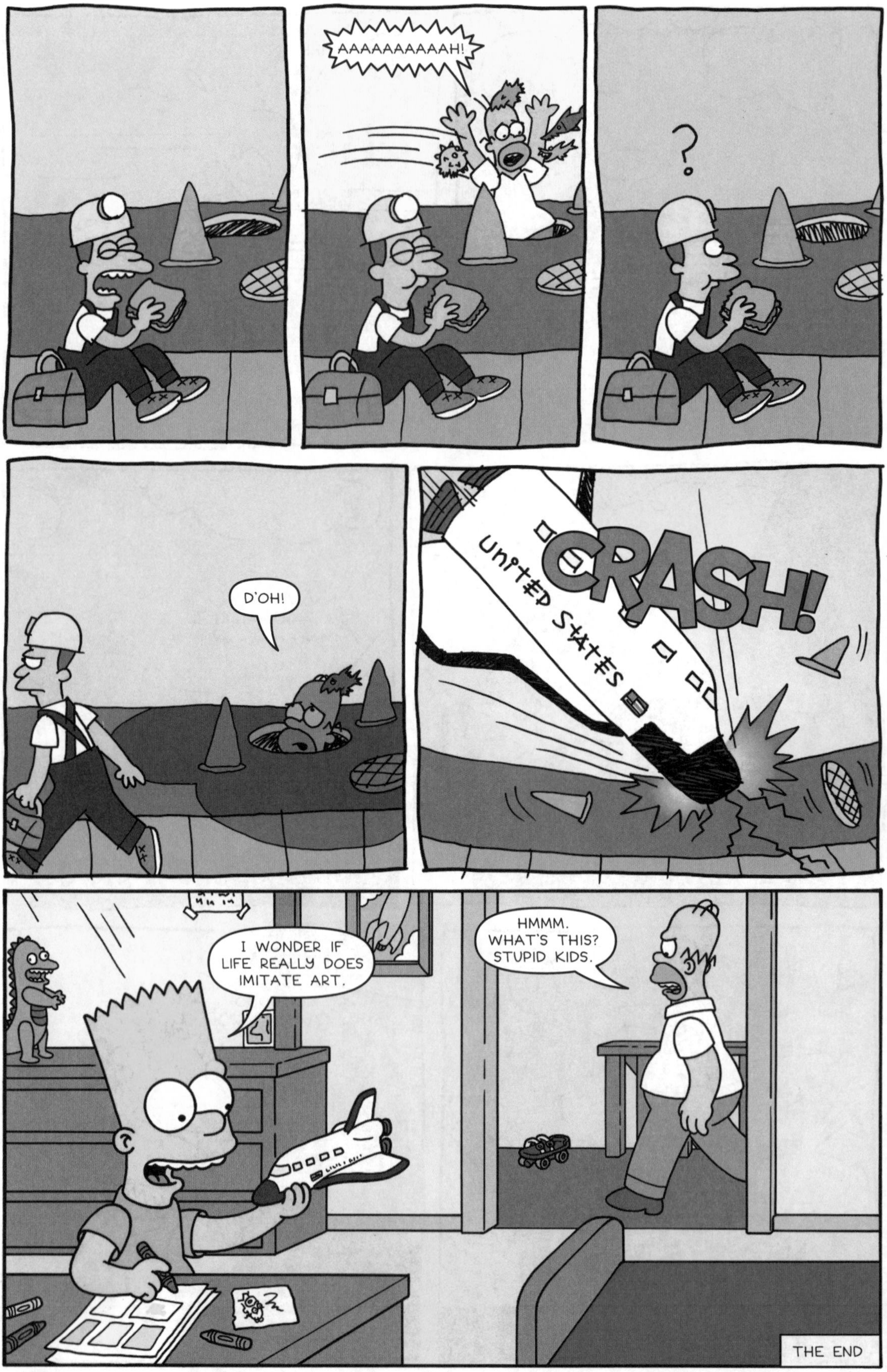
AAAAAAAAAAAH!
?
D'OH!
CRASH!
UNITED STATES
I WONDER IF LIFE REALLY DOES IMITATE ART.
HMMM. WHAT'S THIS? STUPID KIDS.
THE END

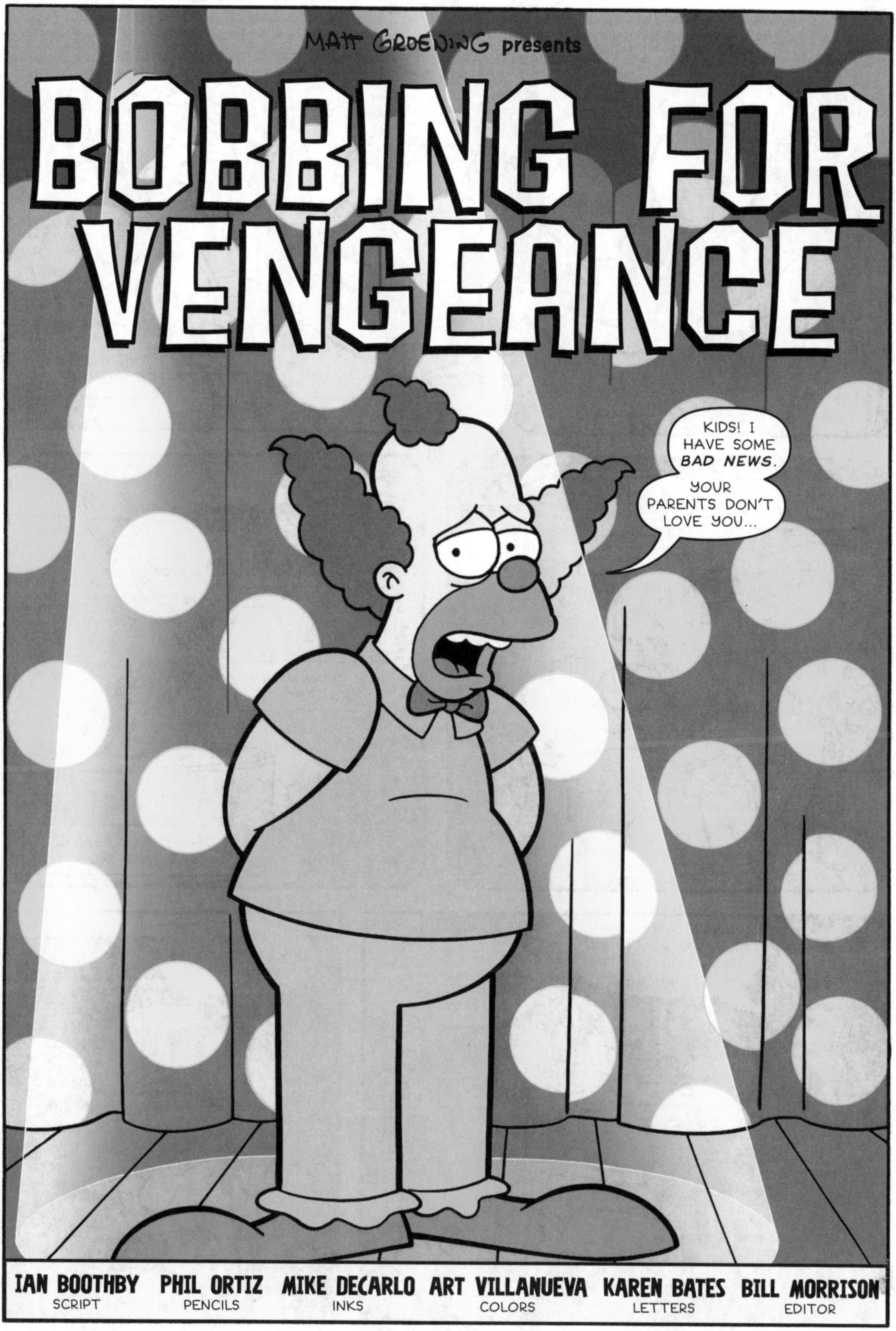
MATT GROENING presents
BOBBING FOR VENGEANCE
KIDS! I HAVE SOME BAD NEWS.
YOUR PARENTS DON'T LOVE YOU...
IAN BOOTHBY SCRIPT
PHIL ORTIZ PENCILS
MIKE DECARLO INKS
ART VILLANUEVA COLORS
KAREN BATES LETTERS
BILL MORRISON EDITOR

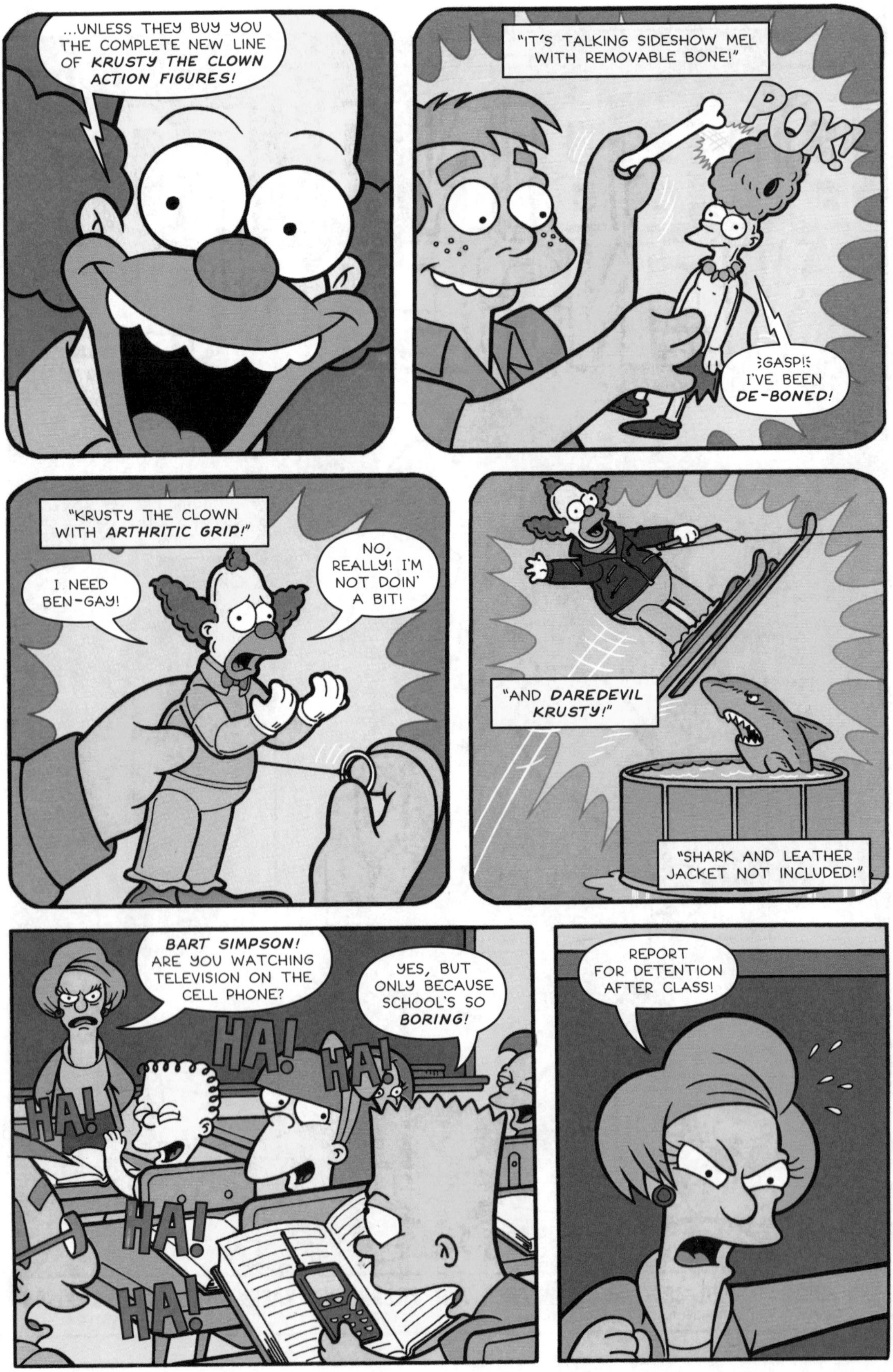
...UNLESS THEY BUY YOU THE COMPLETE NEW LINE OF KRUSTY THE CLOWN ACTION FIGURES!
"IT'S TALKING SIDESHOW MEL WITH REMOVABLE BONE!"
POK!
GASP! I'VE BEEN DE-BONED!
"KRUSTY THE CLOWN WITH ARTHRITIC GRIP!"
I NEED BEN-GAY!
NO, REALLY! I'M NOT DOIN' A BIT!
"AND DAREDEVIL KRUSTY!"
"SHARK AND LEATHER JACKET NOT INCLUDED!"
BART SIMPSON! ARE YOU WATCHING TELEVISION ON THE CELL PHONE?
YES, BUT ONLY BECAUSE SCHOOL'S SO BORING!
HA! HA! HA! HA! HA!
REPORT FOR DETENTION AFTER CLASS!

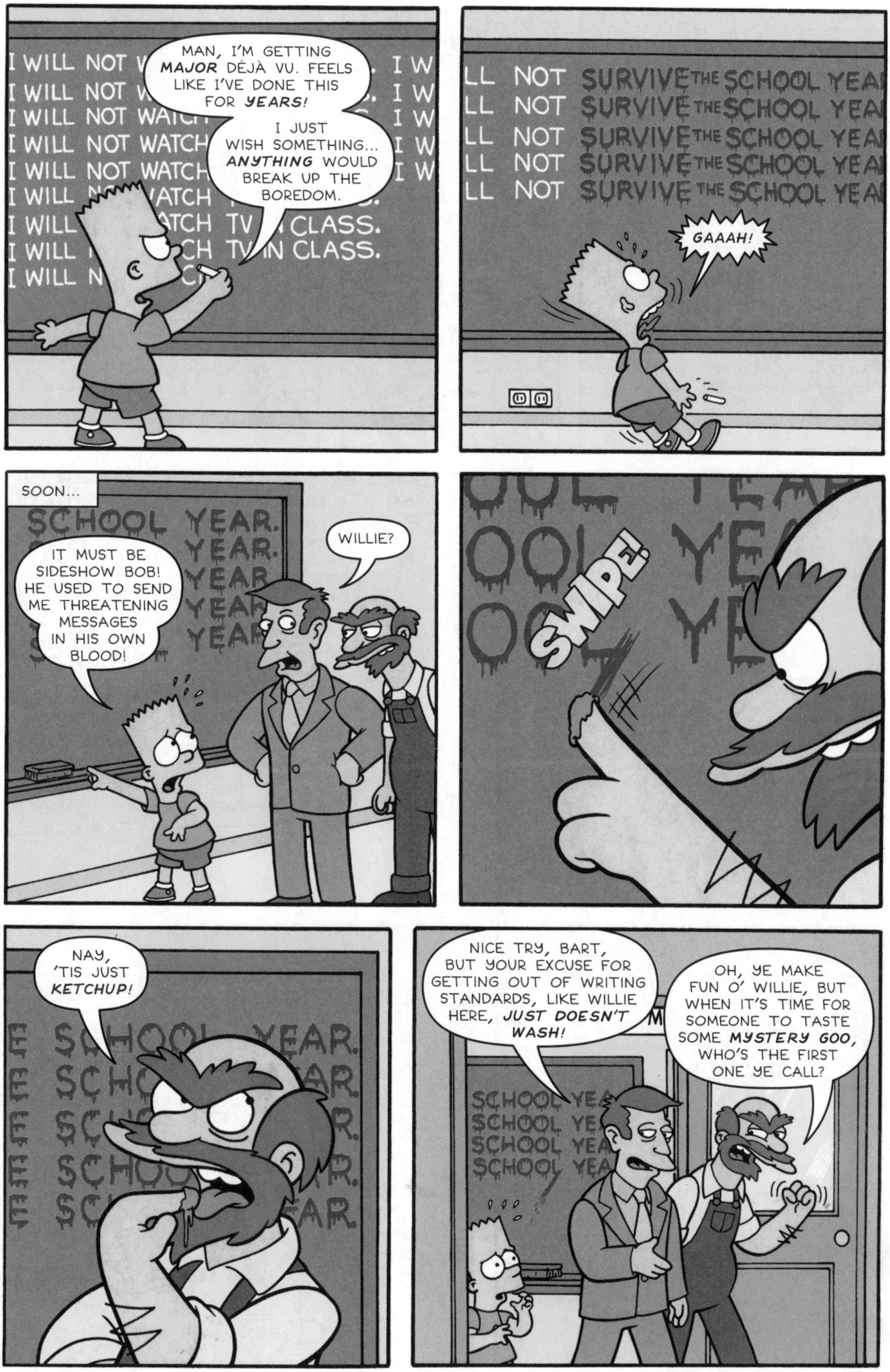

I WILL NOT WATCH TV IN CLASS.
MAN, I'M GETTING **MAJOR** DÉJÀ VU. FEELS LIKE I'VE DONE THIS FOR **YEARS!**
I JUST WISH SOMETHING... **ANYTHING** WOULD BREAK UP THE BOREDOM.
LL NOT SURVIVE THE SCHOOL YEA
GAAAH!
SOON...
SCHOOL YEAR.
IT MUST BE SIDESHOW BOB! HE USED TO SEND ME THREATENING MESSAGES IN HIS OWN BLOOD!
WILLIE?
SWIPE!
NAY, 'TIS JUST **KETCHUP!**
NICE TRY, BART, BUT YOUR EXCUSE FOR GETTING OUT OF WRITING STANDARDS, LIKE WILLIE HERE, **JUST DOESN'T WASH!**
OH, YE MAKE FUN O' WILLIE, BUT WHEN IT'S TIME FOR SOMEONE TO TASTE SOME **MYSTERY GOO,** WHO'S THE FIRST ONE YE CALL?

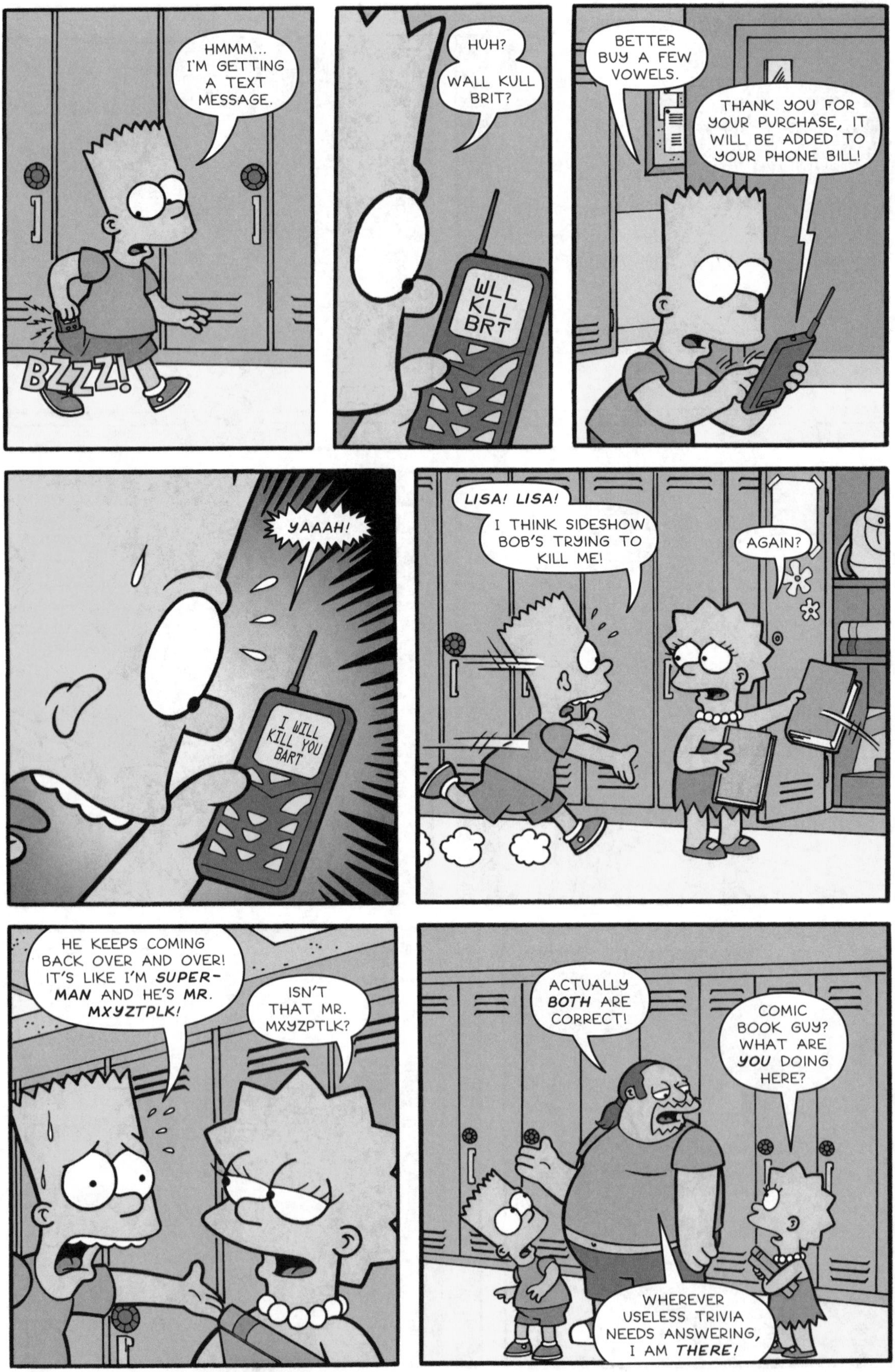

HMMM... I'M GETTING A TEXT MESSAGE.
BZZZ!
HUH?
WALL KULL BRIT?
WLL KLL BRT
BETTER BUY A FEW VOWELS.
THANK YOU FOR YOUR PURCHASE, IT WILL BE ADDED TO YOUR PHONE BILL!
YAAAH!
I WILL KILL YOU BART
LISA! LISA!
I THINK SIDESHOW BOB'S TRYING TO KILL ME!
AGAIN?
HE KEEPS COMING BACK OVER AND OVER! IT'S LIKE I'M SUPERMAN AND HE'S MR. MXYZTPLK!
ISN'T THAT MR. MXYZPTLK?
ACTUALLY BOTH ARE CORRECT!
COMIC BOOK GUY? WHAT ARE YOU DOING HERE?
WHEREVER USELESS TRIVIA NEEDS ANSWERING, I AM THERE!

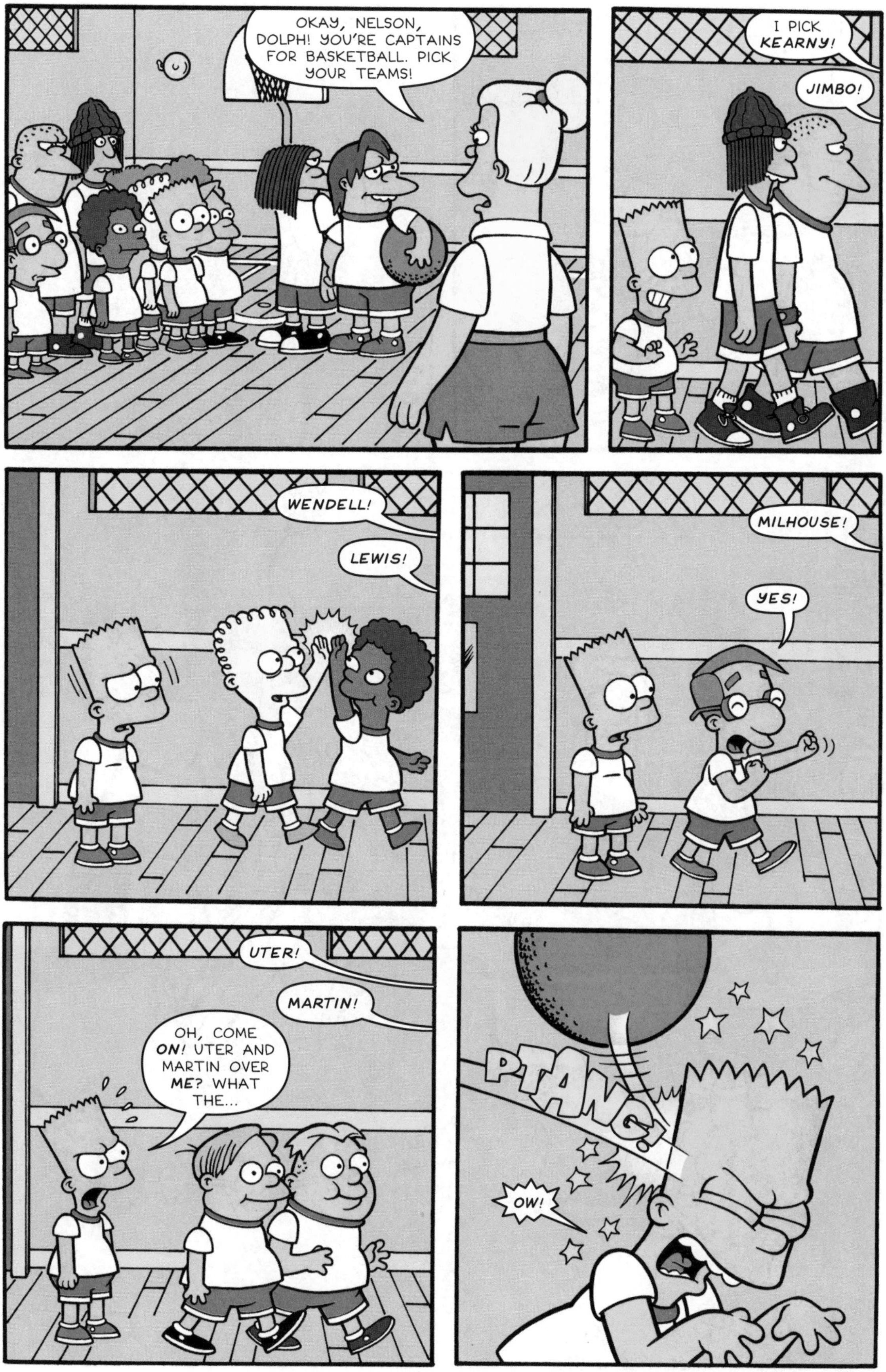
OKAY, NELSON, DOLPH! YOU'RE CAPTAINS FOR BASKETBALL. PICK YOUR TEAMS!
I PICK KEARNY!
JIMBO!
WENDELL!
LEWIS!
MILHOUSE!
YES!
UTER!
MARTIN!
OH, COME ON! UTER AND MARTIN OVER ME? WHAT THE...
PTANG!
OW!

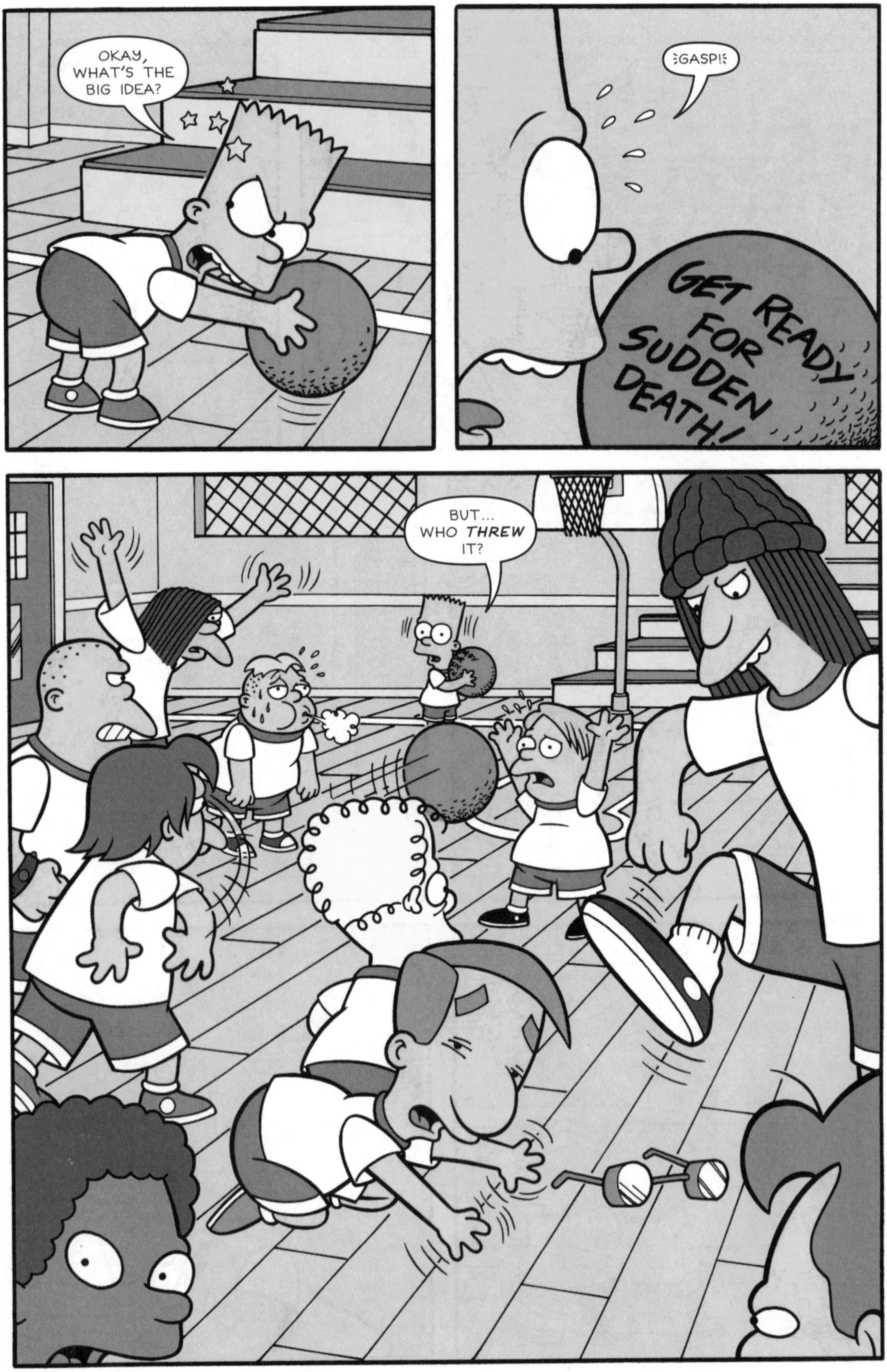
OKAY, WHAT'S THE BIG IDEA?
GASP!
GET READY FOR SUDDEN DEATH!
BUT... WHO *THREW* IT?

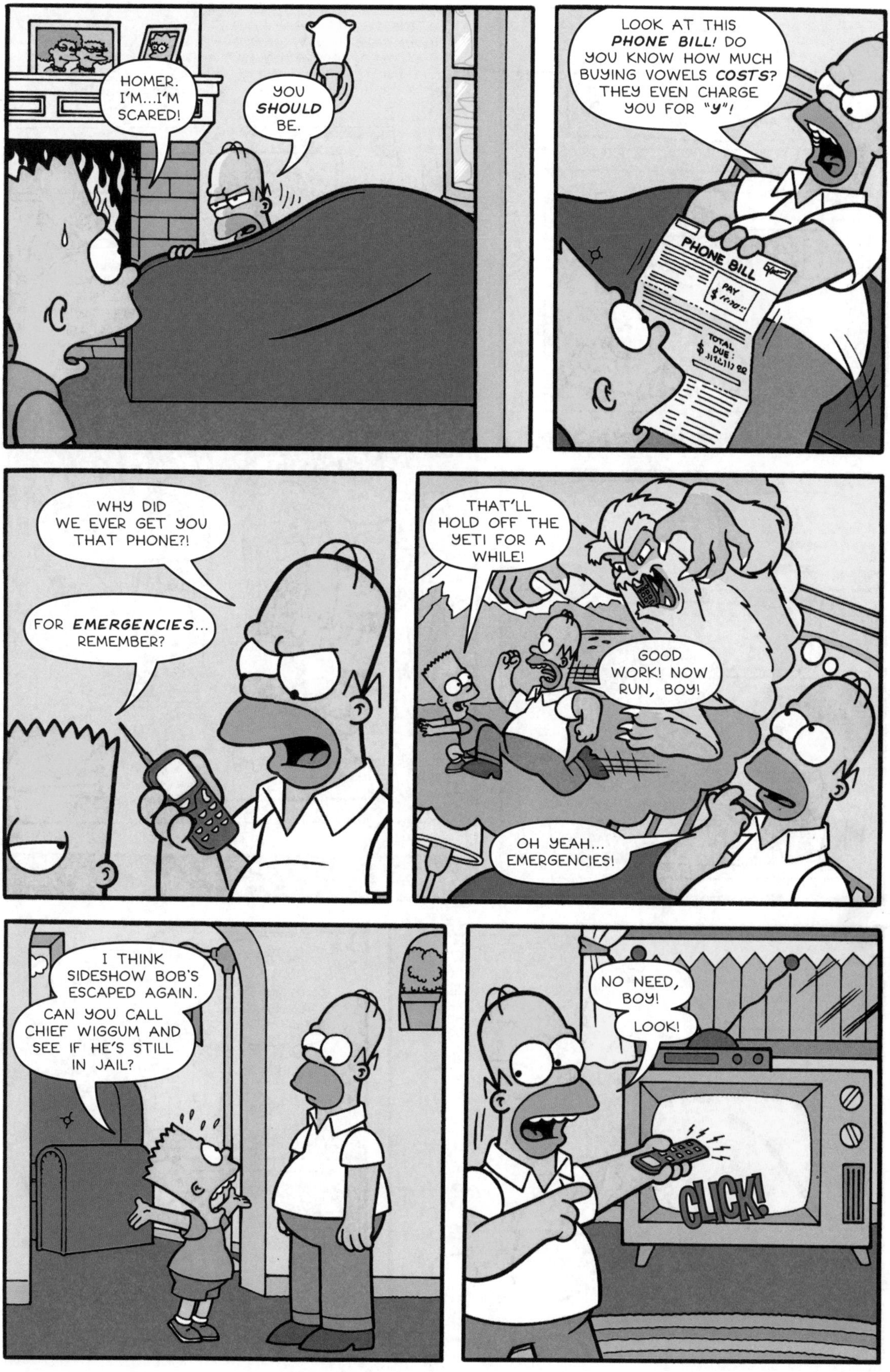
HOMER. I'M...I'M SCARED!
YOU *SHOULD* BE.
LOOK AT THIS *PHONE BILL*! DO YOU KNOW HOW MUCH BUYING VOWELS *COSTS*? THEY EVEN CHARGE YOU FOR "*Y*"!
PHONE BILL
PAY
TOTAL DUE:
WHY DID WE EVER GET YOU THAT PHONE?!
FOR *EMERGENCIES*... REMEMBER?
THAT'LL HOLD OFF THE YETI FOR A WHILE!
GOOD WORK! NOW RUN, BOY!
OH YEAH... EMERGENCIES!
I THINK SIDESHOW BOB'S ESCAPED AGAIN.
CAN YOU CALL CHIEF WIGGUM AND SEE IF HE'S STILL IN JAIL?
NO NEED, BOY!
LOOK!
CLICK!

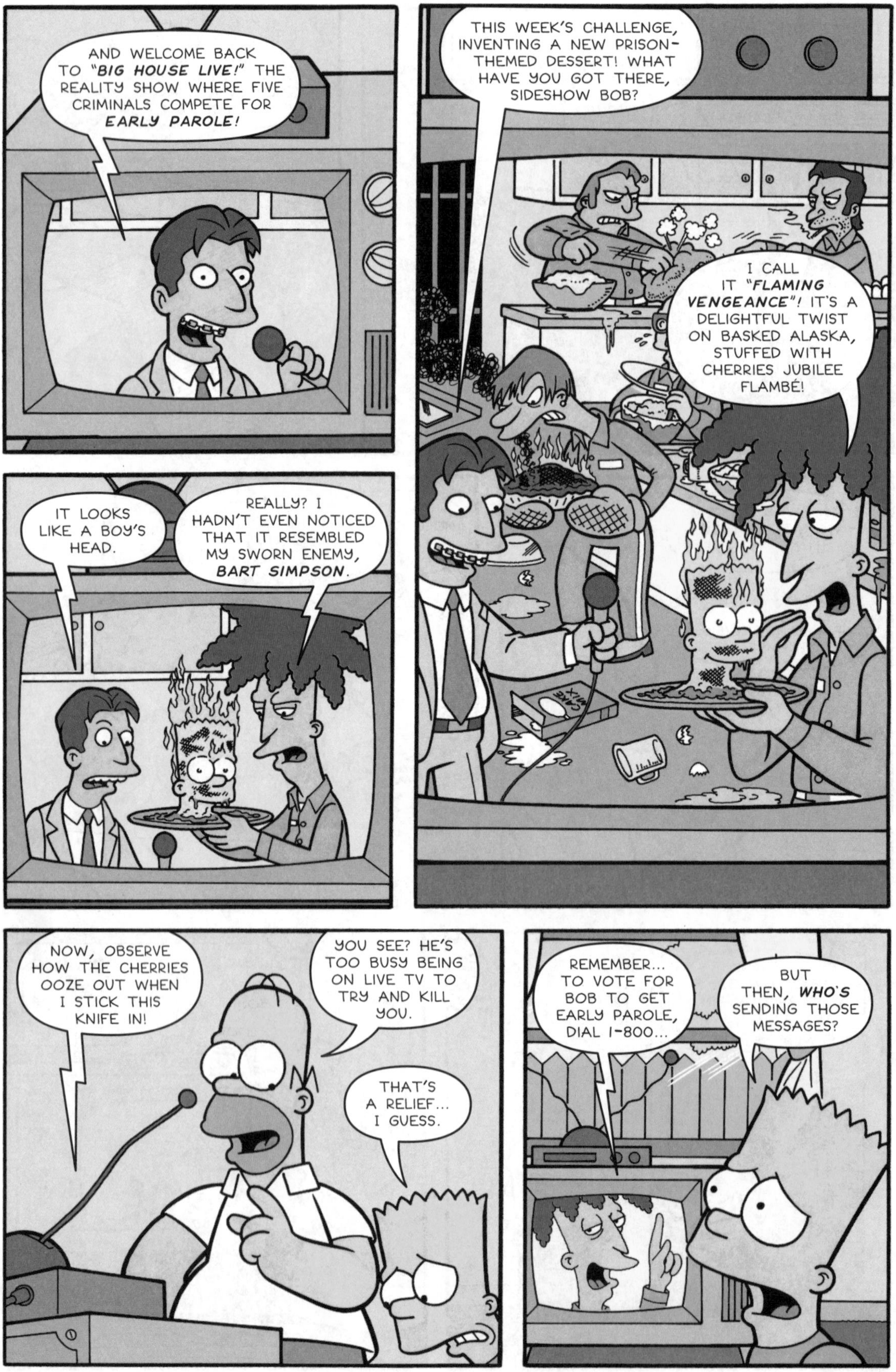
AND WELCOME BACK TO "BIG HOUSE LIVE!" THE REALITY SHOW WHERE FIVE CRIMINALS COMPETE FOR EARLY PAROLE!
THIS WEEK'S CHALLENGE, INVENTING A NEW PRISON-THEMED DESSERT! WHAT HAVE YOU GOT THERE, SIDESHOW BOB?
I CALL IT "FLAMING VENGEANCE"! IT'S A DELIGHTFUL TWIST ON BASKED ALASKA, STUFFED WITH CHERRIES JUBILEE FLAMBÉ!
CAKE MIX
IT LOOKS LIKE A BOY'S HEAD.
REALLY? I HADN'T EVEN NOTICED THAT IT RESEMBLED MY SWORN ENEMY, BART SIMPSON.
NOW, OBSERVE HOW THE CHERRIES OOZE OUT WHEN I STICK THIS KNIFE IN!
YOU SEE? HE'S TOO BUSY BEING ON LIVE TV TO TRY AND KILL YOU.
THAT'S A RELIEF... I GUESS.
REMEMBER... TO VOTE FOR BOB TO GET EARLY PAROLE, DIAL 1-800...
BUT THEN, WHO'S SENDING THOSE MESSAGES?

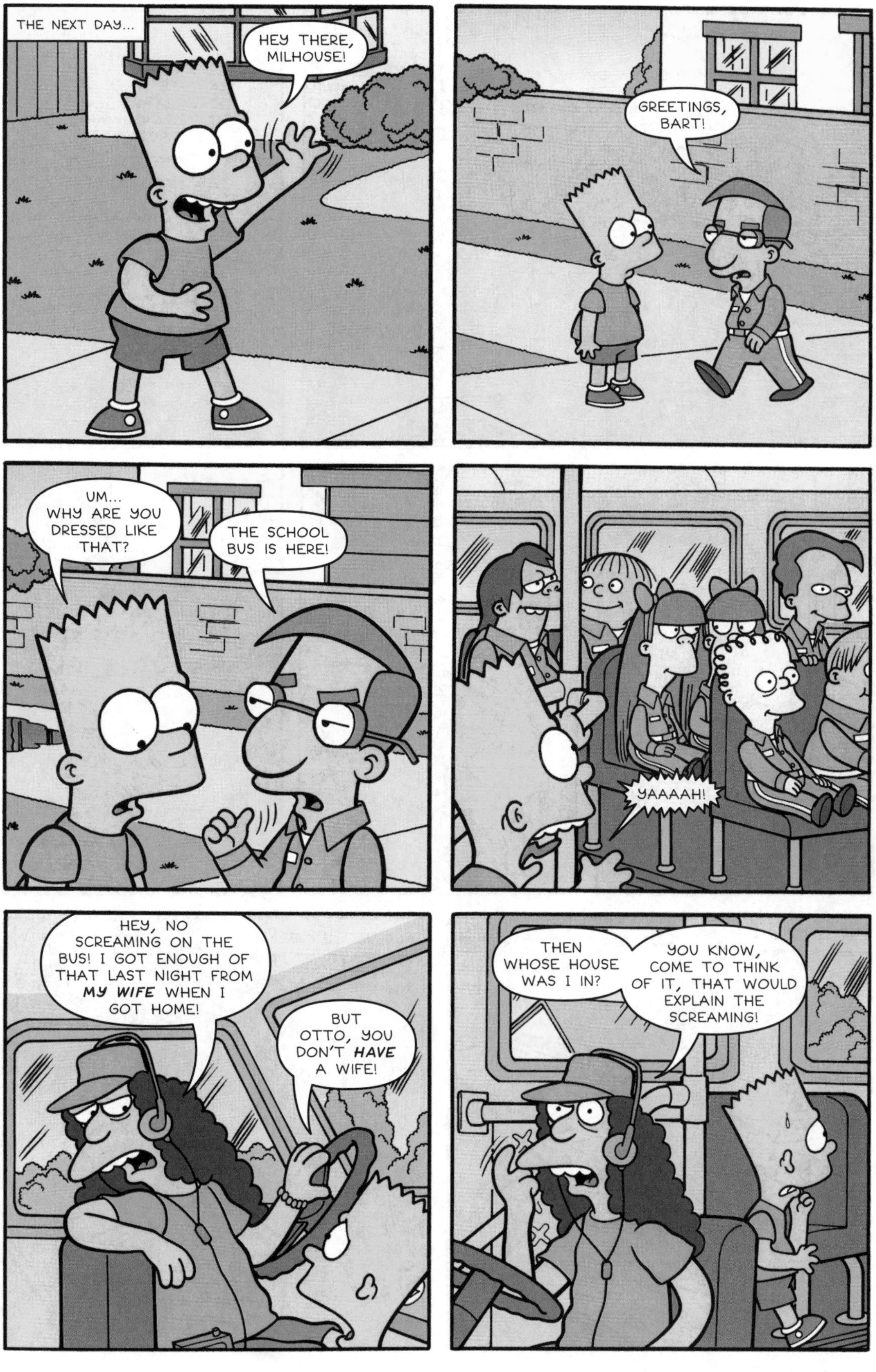
THE NEXT DAY...
HEY THERE, MILHOUSE!
GREETINGS, BART!
UM... WHY ARE YOU DRESSED LIKE THAT?
THE SCHOOL BUS IS HERE!
YAAAAH!
HEY, NO SCREAMING ON THE BUS! I GOT ENOUGH OF THAT LAST NIGHT FROM MY WIFE WHEN I GOT HOME!
BUT OTTO, YOU DON'T HAVE A WIFE!
THEN WHOSE HOUSE WAS I IN?
YOU KNOW, COME TO THINK OF IT, THAT WOULD EXPLAIN THE SCREAMING!

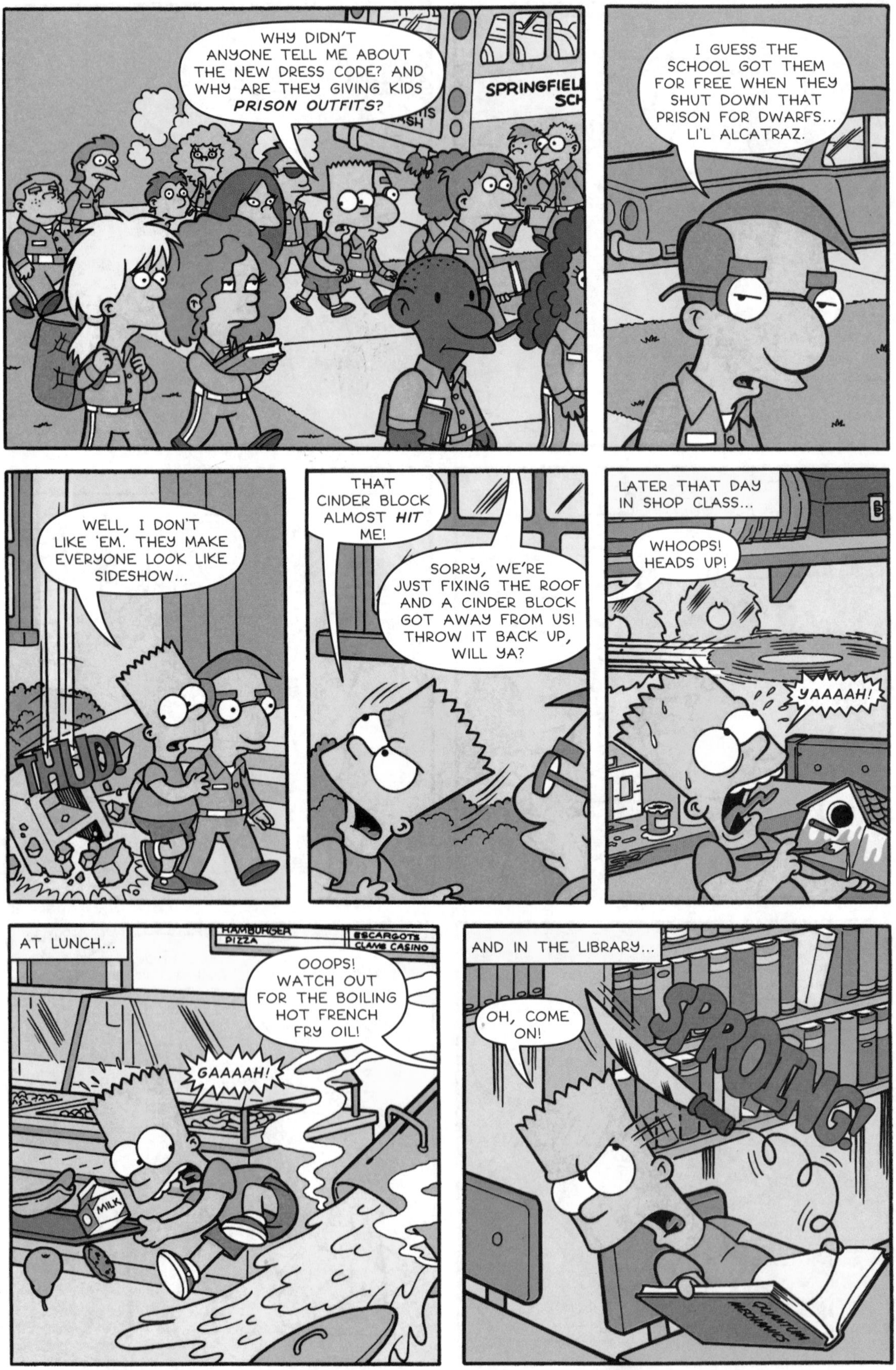

WHY DIDN'T ANYONE TELL ME ABOUT THE NEW DRESS CODE? AND WHY ARE THEY GIVING KIDS *PRISON OUTFITS*?
I GUESS THE SCHOOL GOT THEM FOR FREE WHEN THEY SHUT DOWN THAT PRISON FOR DWARFS... LI'L ALCATRAZ.
WELL, I DON'T LIKE 'EM. THEY MAKE EVERYONE LOOK LIKE SIDESHOW...
THUD!
THAT CINDER BLOCK ALMOST *HIT* ME!
SORRY, WE'RE JUST FIXING THE ROOF AND A CINDER BLOCK GOT AWAY FROM US! THROW IT BACK UP, WILL YA?
LATER THAT DAY IN SHOP CLASS...
WHOOPS! HEADS UP!
YAAAAH!
AT LUNCH...
OOOPS! WATCH OUT FOR THE BOILING HOT FRENCH FRY OIL!
GAAAAH!
MILK
AND IN THE LIBRARY...
OH, COME ON!
SPROING!

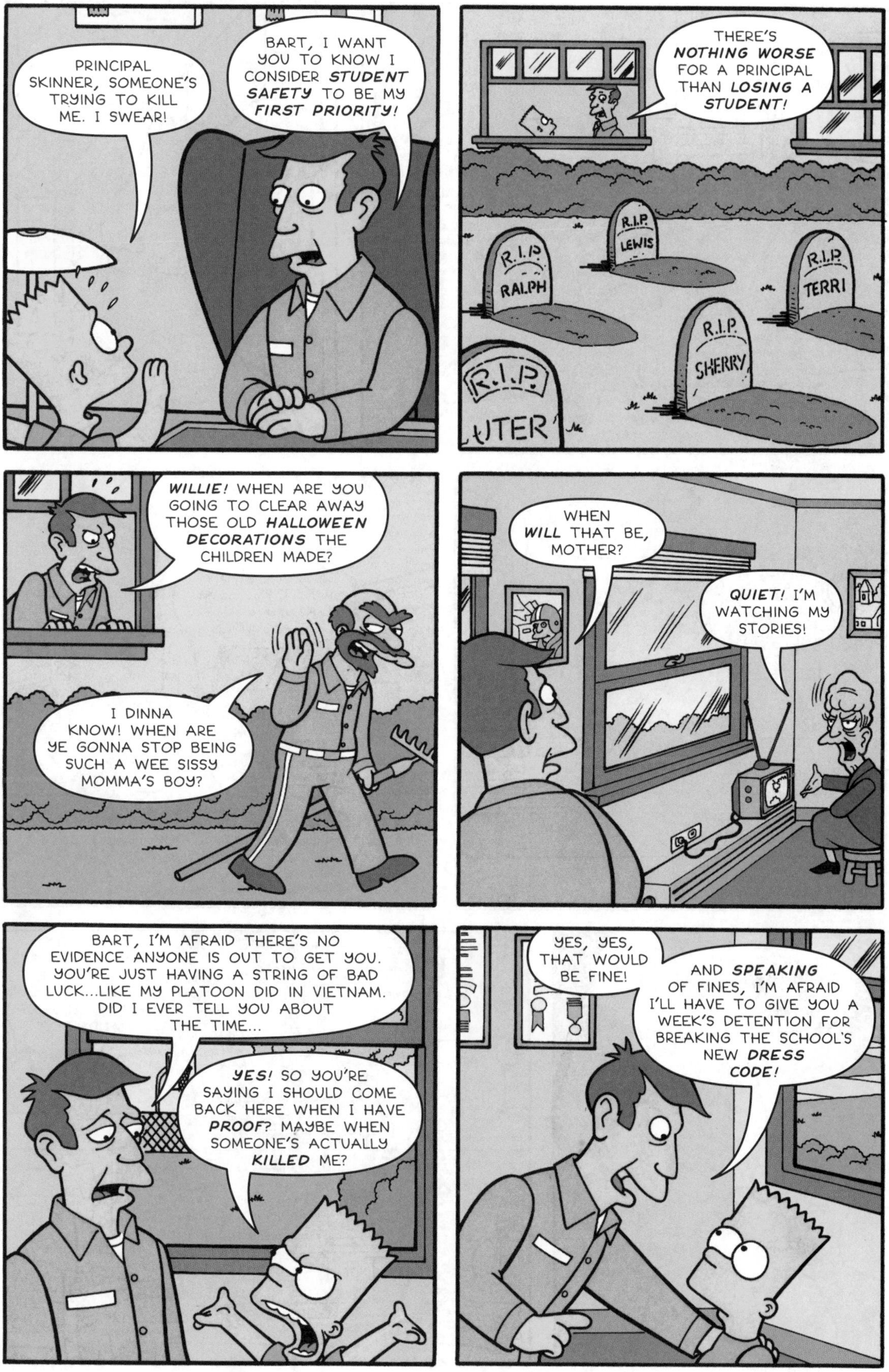
PRINCIPAL SKINNER, SOMEONE'S TRYING TO KILL ME. I SWEAR!
BART, I WANT YOU TO KNOW I CONSIDER STUDENT SAFETY TO BE MY FIRST PRIORITY!
THERE'S NOTHING WORSE FOR A PRINCIPAL THAN LOSING A STUDENT!
R.I.P. LEWIS
R.I.P. RALPH
R.I.P. TERRI
R.I.P. SHERRY
R.I.P. UTER
WILLIE! WHEN ARE YOU GOING TO CLEAR AWAY THOSE OLD HALLOWEEN DECORATIONS THE CHILDREN MADE?
I DINNA KNOW! WHEN ARE YE GONNA STOP BEING SUCH A WEE SISSY MOMMA'S BOY?
WHEN WILL THAT BE, MOTHER?
QUIET! I'M WATCHING MY STORIES!
BART, I'M AFRAID THERE'S NO EVIDENCE ANYONE IS OUT TO GET YOU. YOU'RE JUST HAVING A STRING OF BAD LUCK...LIKE MY PLATOON DID IN VIETNAM. DID I EVER TELL YOU ABOUT THE TIME...
YES! SO YOU'RE SAYING I SHOULD COME BACK HERE WHEN I HAVE PROOF? MAYBE WHEN SOMEONE'S ACTUALLY KILLED ME?
YES, YES, THAT WOULD BE FINE!
AND SPEAKING OF FINES, I'M AFRAID I'LL HAVE TO GIVE YOU A WEEK'S DETENTION FOR BREAKING THE SCHOOL'S NEW DRESS CODE!

YOU BELIEVE ME...RIGHT, LIS?

SURE, BART. I KNOW YOU WOULDN'T MAKE SOMETHING LIKE THIS UP...UNLESS YOU THOUGHT IT WAS FUNNY.

OR YOU WERE BORED.

OR JUST BEING A JERK.

THE PERSON DOING IT MUST BE SOMEONE CLOSE.

WHAM!

OW!

WHY'D YOU THROW THAT ROCK AT ME?

I DON'T KNOW. I JUST FELT LIKE *HURTING* YOU ALL OF A SUDDEN.

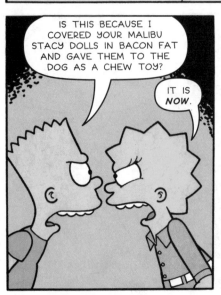

IS THIS BECAUSE I COVERED YOUR MALIBU STACY DOLLS IN BACON FAT AND GAVE THEM TO THE DOG AS A CHEW TOY?

IT IS *NOW*.

AAAAAH! MOM! LISA'S TRYING TO KILL ME!

LISA! STOP TRYING TO KILL YOUR BROTHER, AND BOTH OF YOU WASH YOUR HANDS FOR DINNER!

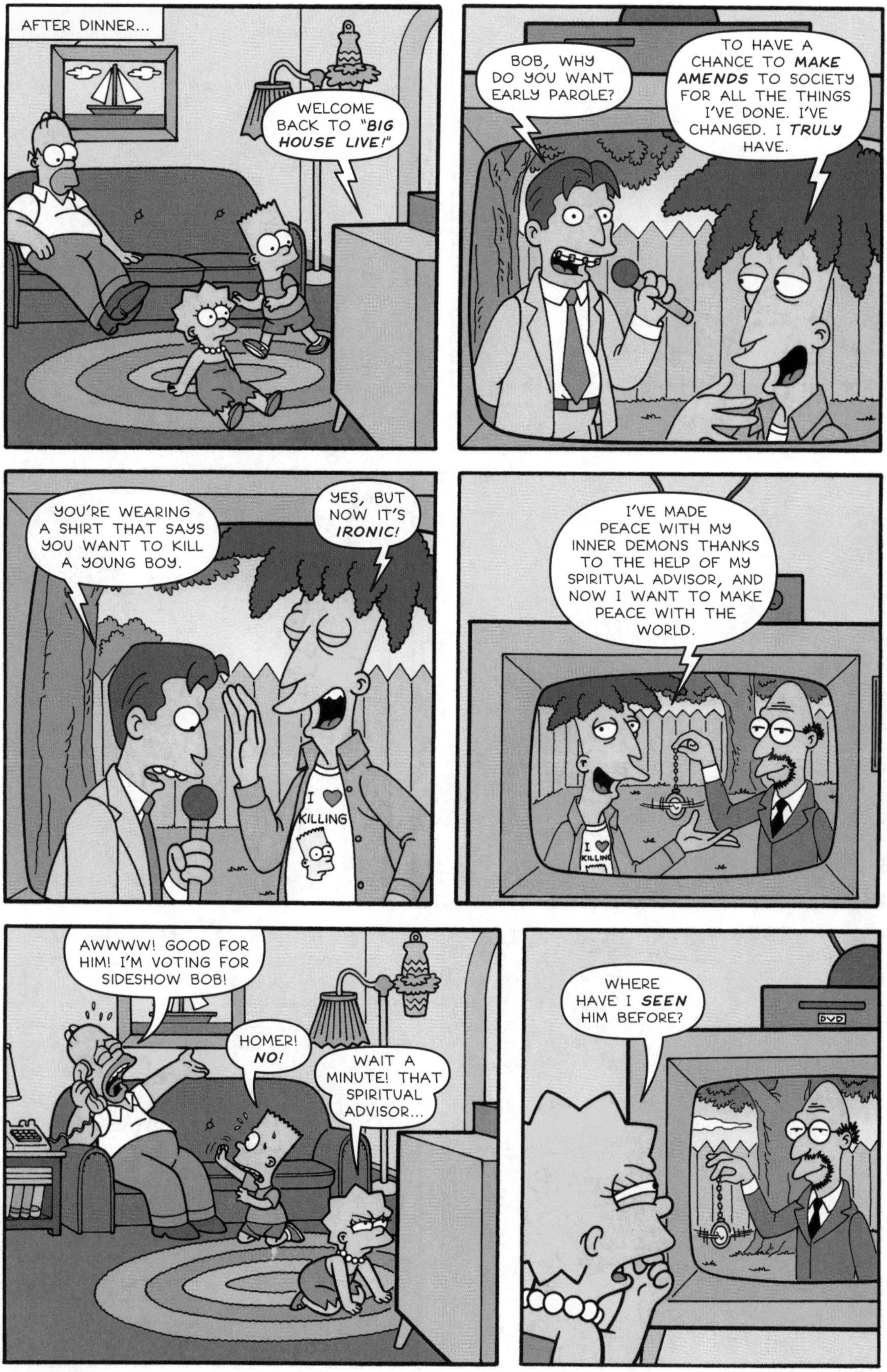
AFTER DINNER...
WELCOME BACK TO "BIG HOUSE LIVE!"
BOB, WHY DO YOU WANT EARLY PAROLE?
TO HAVE A CHANCE TO MAKE AMENDS TO SOCIETY FOR ALL THE THINGS I'VE DONE. I'VE CHANGED. I TRULY HAVE.
YOU'RE WEARING A SHIRT THAT SAYS YOU WANT TO KILL A YOUNG BOY.
YES, BUT NOW IT'S IRONIC!
I ♥ KILLING
I'VE MADE PEACE WITH MY INNER DEMONS THANKS TO THE HELP OF MY SPIRITUAL ADVISOR, AND NOW I WANT TO MAKE PEACE WITH THE WORLD.
AWWWW! GOOD FOR HIM! I'M VOTING FOR SIDESHOW BOB!
HOMER! NO!
WAIT A MINUTE! THAT SPIRITUAL ADVISOR...
WHERE HAVE I SEEN HIM BEFORE?
DVD

COMIC BOOK GUY, DO YOU KNOW WHERE I COULD FIND COPIES OF THE TV SERIES "BIG HOUSE LIVE!"?

THEY HAVE NOT YET RELEASED THE SHOW ON DVD, AND AS A LEGITIMATE BUSINESS-MAN I CANNOT HELP YOU IN OBTAINING *PIRATED COPIES* OF THE SHOW.

Richie Rich
THE INSIDER TRADING YEARS

BUT PERHAPS MY FRIEND *BOBBY BOOTLEG* MIGHT BE ABLE TO HELP YOU.

HEY THERE, KID! WHAT CAN I *DOWNLOAD AND BURN* FOR YOU TODAY?

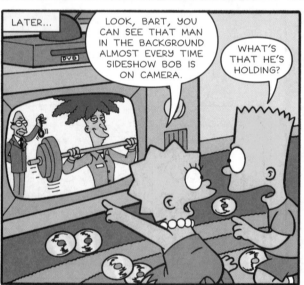

LATER...

LOOK, BART, YOU CAN SEE THAT MAN IN THE BACKGROUND ALMOST EVERY TIME SIDESHOW BOB IS ON CAMERA.

WHAT'S THAT HE'S HOLDING?

TV! MAGNIFY IMAGE!

IT CAN'T *DO* THAT, BART!

BUT *THIS* CAN!

IT'S A *POCKET WATCH!*

I THINK I KNOW WHAT'S HAPPENING! THAT'S A *HYPNOTIST!*

LET ME JUST PAUSE THE DVD!

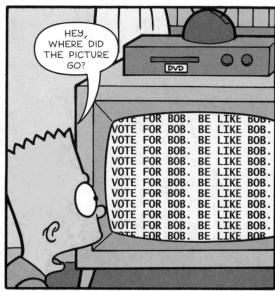

HEY, WHERE DID THE PICTURE GO?

VOTE FOR BOB. BE LIKE BOB.
VOTE FOR BOB. BE LIKE BOB.
VOTE FOR BOB. BE LIKE BOB.
VOTE FOR BOB. BE LIKE BOB.
VOTE FOR BOB. BE LIKE BOB.
VOTE FOR BOB. BE LIKE BOB.
VOTE FOR BOB. BE LIKE BOB.
VOTE FOR BOB. BE LIKE BOB.
VOTE FOR BOB. BE LIKE BOB.
VOTE FOR BOB. BE LIKE BOB.
VOTE FOR BOB. BE LIKE BOB.

THIS IS A HIDDEN IMAGE. IT MUST HAVE FLASHED ON THE SCREEN FOR LESS THAN A SECOND!

BOB'S USING HYPNOSIS AND SUBLIMINAL MESSAGES TO TRY AND WIN THE REALITY SHOW!

THAT DOESN'T EXPLAIN HOW HE'S GETTING OUT AND TRYING TO KILL ME.

HE'S NOT TRYING TO KILL YOU, BART!

THEN WHO IS?

EVERYONE ELSE.

HUH?

ANYONE WHO SEES THE SHOW GETS THE MESSAGE TO *LIKE* SIDESHOW BOB AND TO *BE LIKE* SIDESHOW BOB. SINCE HE CLEARLY *HATES* YOU, SO DO *THEY*.

I FELT LIKE HURTING YOU MYSELF, AND I HAVE ONLY SEEN THE SHOW *ONCE*! I FEEL LIKE SLUGGING YOU *NOW*!

BART! BART! BART! BART! BART! BART!

UH-OH!

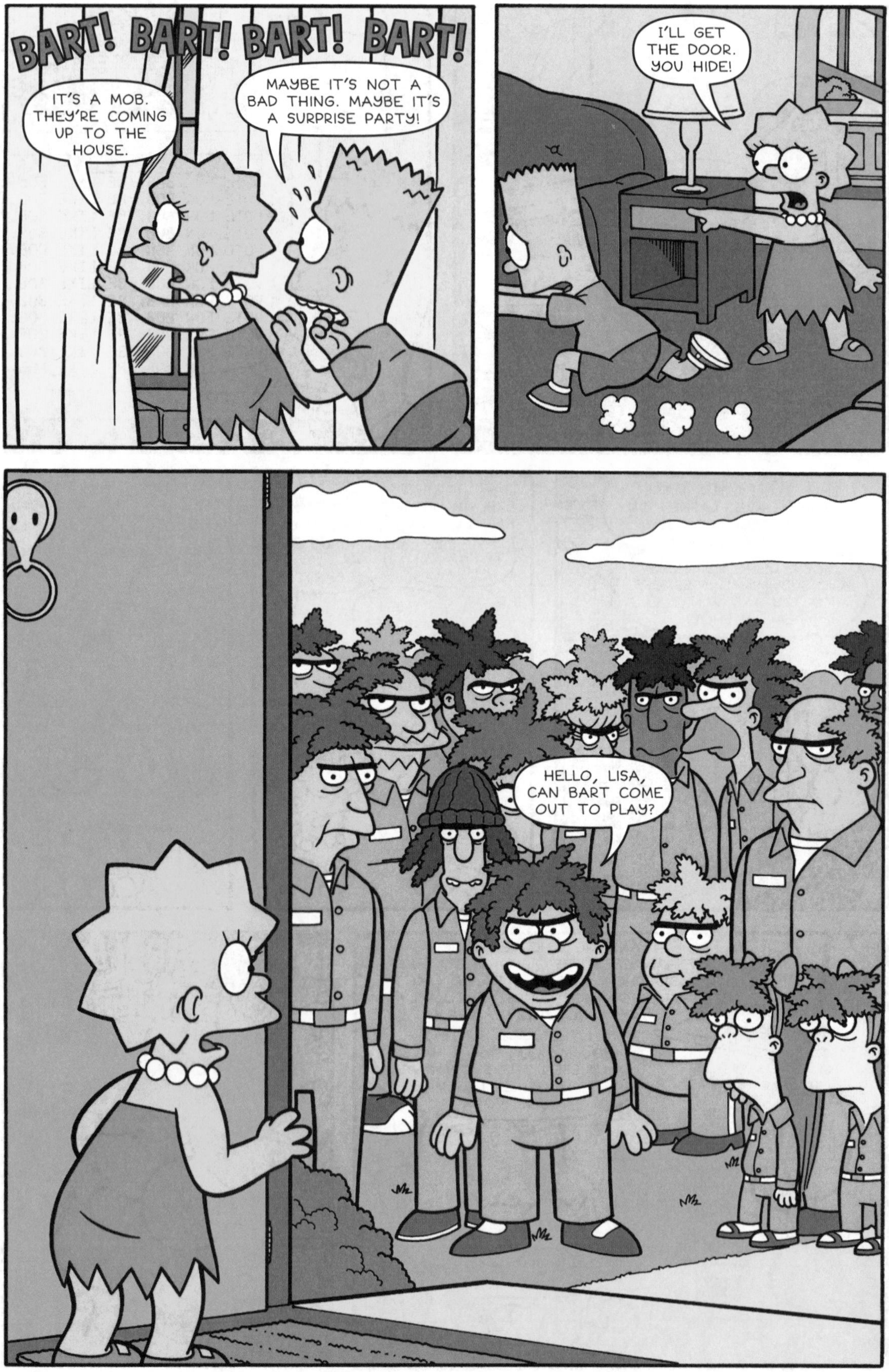
BART! BART! BART! BART!
IT'S A MOB. THEY'RE COMING UP TO THE HOUSE.
MAYBE IT'S NOT A BAD THING. MAYBE IT'S A SURPRISE PARTY!
I'LL GET THE DOOR. YOU HIDE!
HELLO, LISA, CAN BART COME OUT TO PLAY?

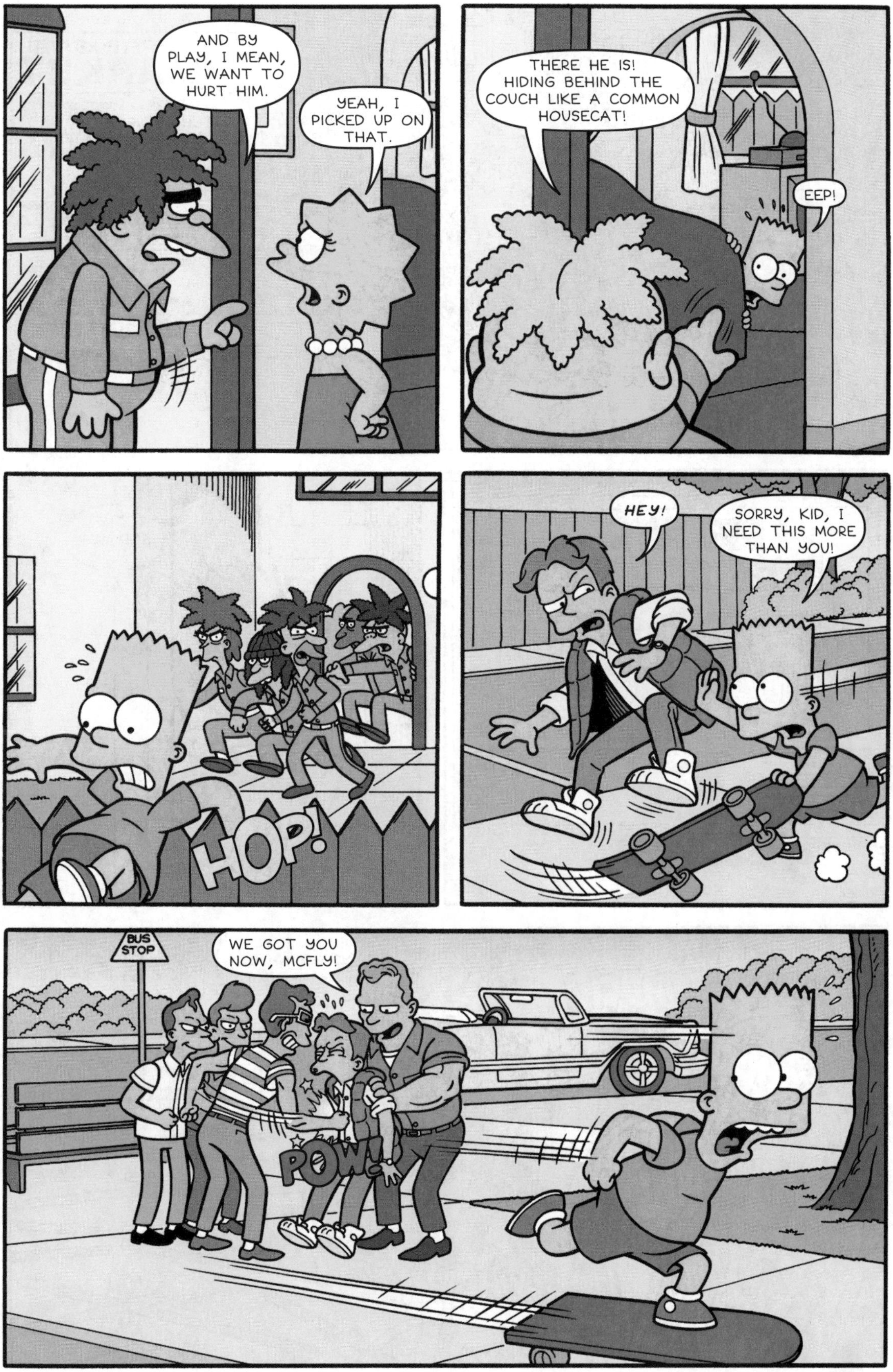

AND BY PLAY, I MEAN, WE WANT TO HURT HIM.
YEAH, I PICKED UP ON THAT.
THERE HE IS! HIDING BEHIND THE COUCH LIKE A COMMON HOUSECAT!
EEP!
HOP!
HEY!
SORRY, KID, I NEED THIS MORE THAN YOU!
BUS STOP
WE GOT YOU NOW, MCFLY!
POW!

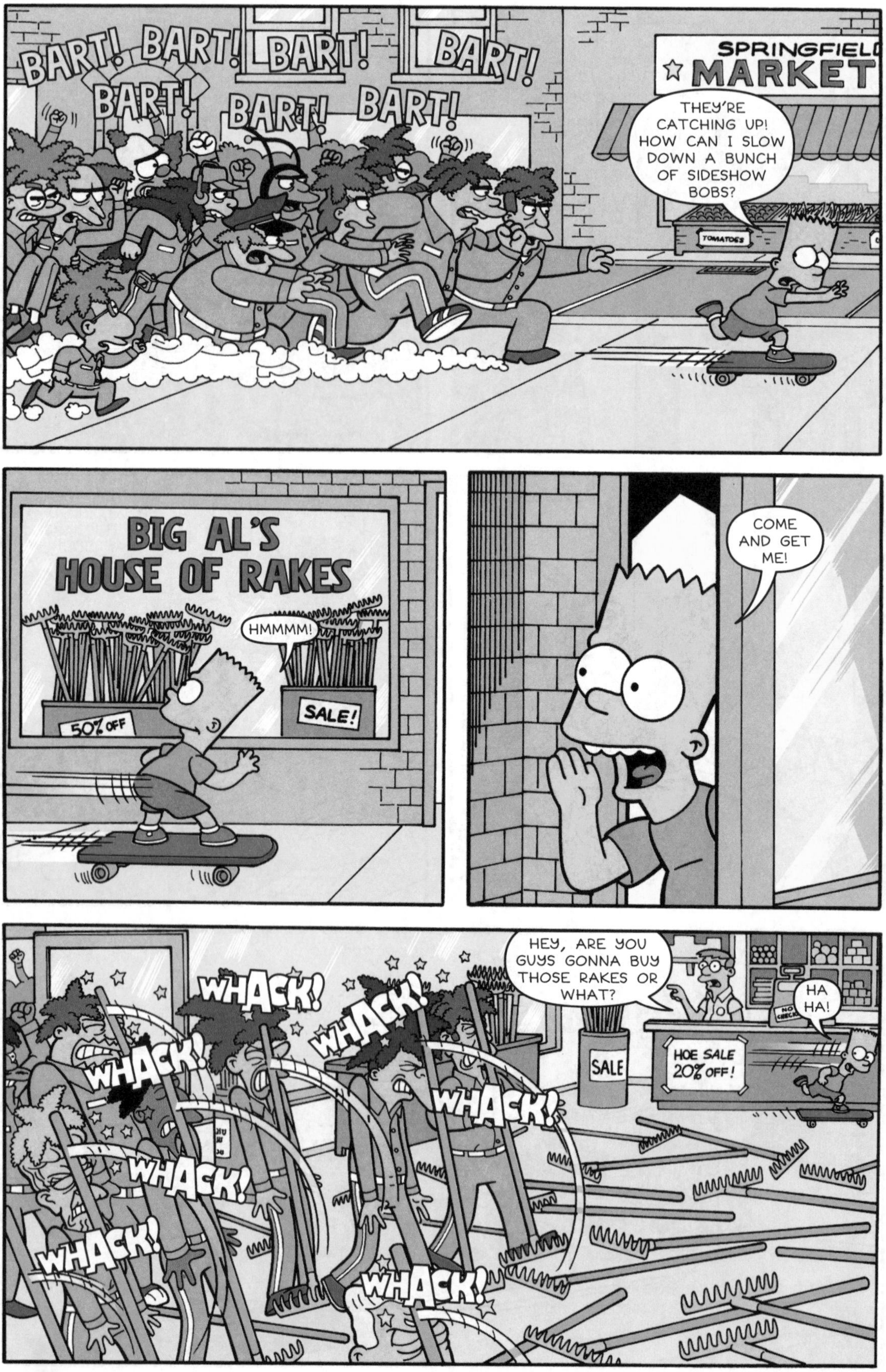
BART! BART! BART! BART!
BART! BART! BART!
SPRINGFIELD MARKET
THEY'RE CATCHING UP! HOW CAN I SLOW DOWN A BUNCH OF SIDESHOW BOBS?
TOMATOES
BIG AL'S HOUSE OF RAKES
HMMMM!
50% OFF
SALE!
COME AND GET ME!
WHACK!
WHACK!
WHACK!
WHACK!
WHACK!
WHACK!
WHACK!
HEY, ARE YOU GUYS GONNA BUY THOSE RAKES OR WHAT?
HA HA!
SALE
HOE SALE 20% OFF!

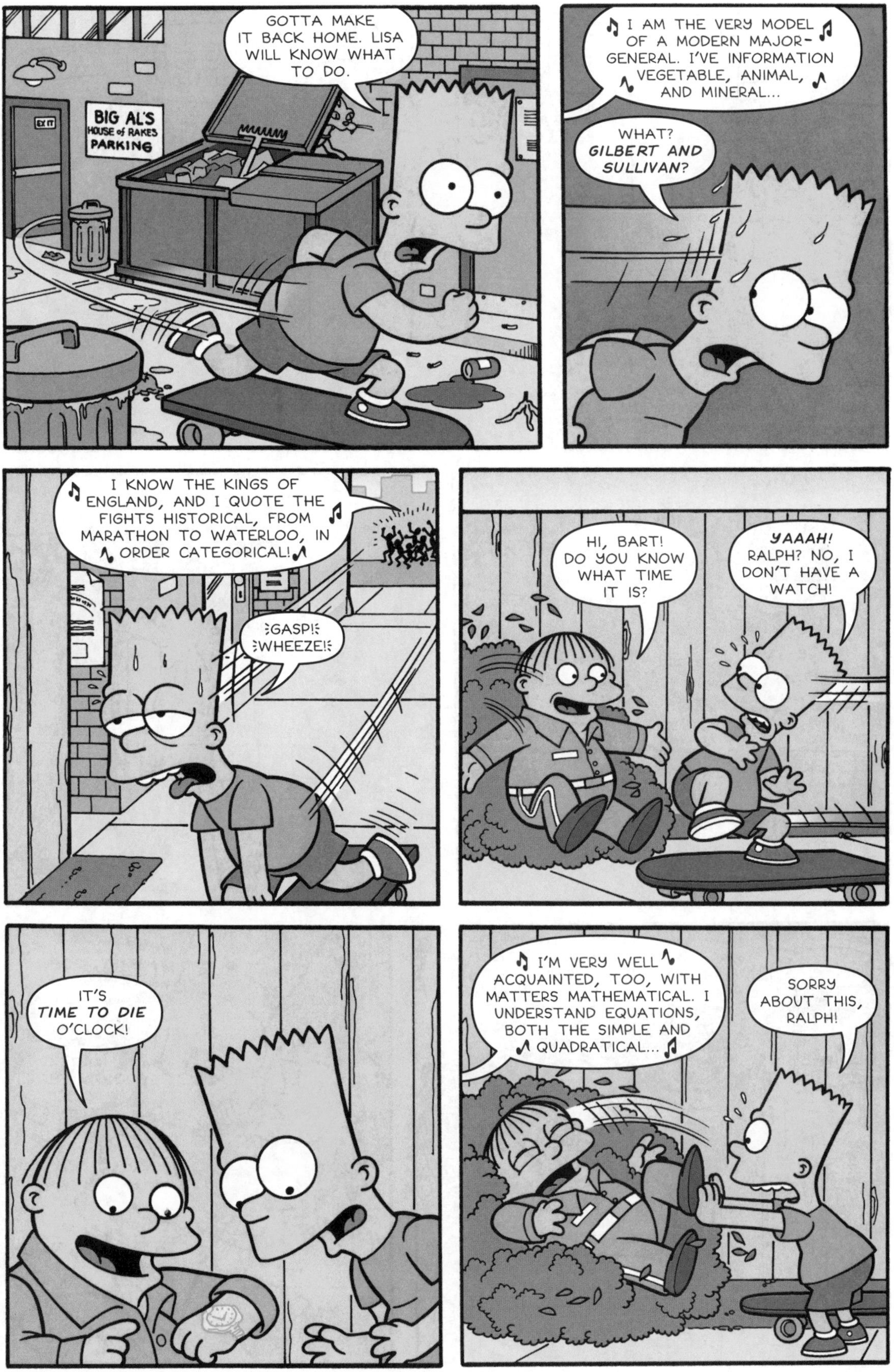
GOTTA MAKE IT BACK HOME. LISA WILL KNOW WHAT TO DO.
EXIT
BIG AL'S HOUSE of RAKES PARKING
I AM THE VERY MODEL OF A MODERN MAJOR-GENERAL. I'VE INFORMATION VEGETABLE, ANIMAL, AND MINERAL...
WHAT? *GILBERT AND SULLIVAN?*
I KNOW THE KINGS OF ENGLAND, AND I QUOTE THE FIGHTS HISTORICAL, FROM MARATHON TO WATERLOO, IN ORDER CATEGORICAL!
GASP! WHEEZE!
HI, BART! DO YOU KNOW WHAT TIME IT IS?
YAAAH! RALPH? NO, I DON'T HAVE A WATCH!
IT'S *TIME TO DIE* O'CLOCK!
I'M VERY WELL ACQUAINTED, TOO, WITH MATTERS MATHEMATICAL. I UNDERSTAND EQUATIONS, BOTH THE SIMPLE AND QUADRATICAL...
SORRY ABOUT THIS, RALPH!

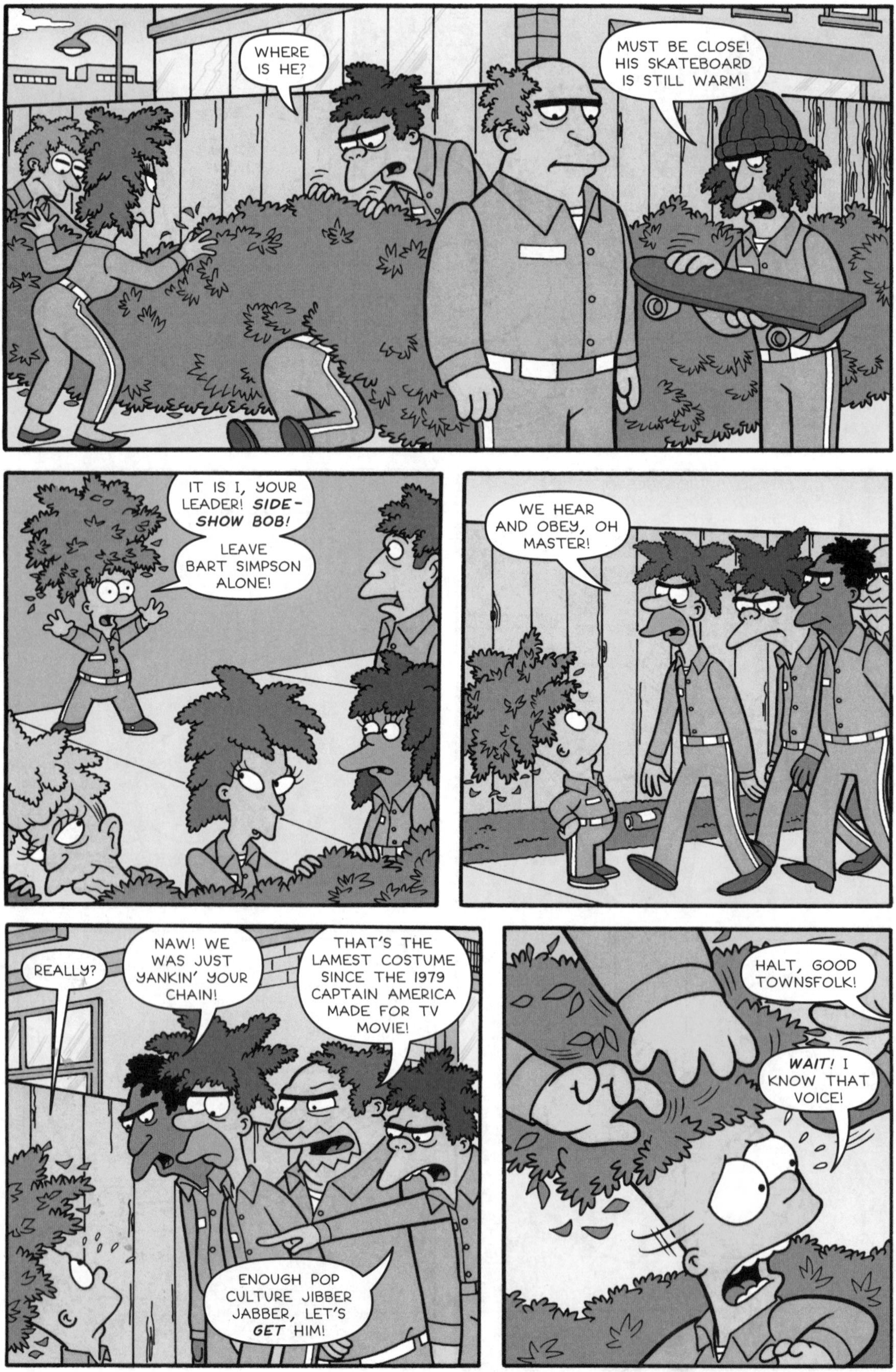
WHERE IS HE?
MUST BE CLOSE! HIS SKATEBOARD IS STILL WARM!
IT IS I, YOUR LEADER! SIDE-SHOW BOB!
LEAVE BART SIMPSON ALONE!
WE HEAR AND OBEY, OH MASTER!
REALLY?
NAW! WE WAS JUST YANKIN' YOUR CHAIN!
THAT'S THE LAMEST COSTUME SINCE THE 1979 CAPTAIN AMERICA MADE FOR TV MOVIE!
ENOUGH POP CULTURE JIBBER JABBER, LET'S GET HIM!
HALT, GOOD TOWNSFOLK!
WAIT! I KNOW THAT VOICE!

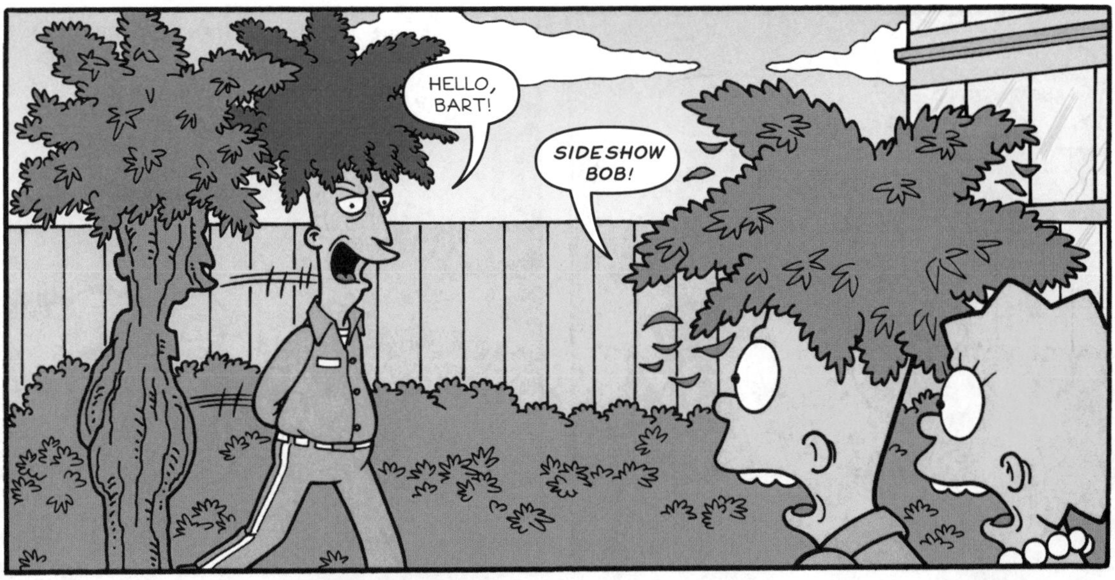
HELLO, BART!
SIDESHOW BOB!

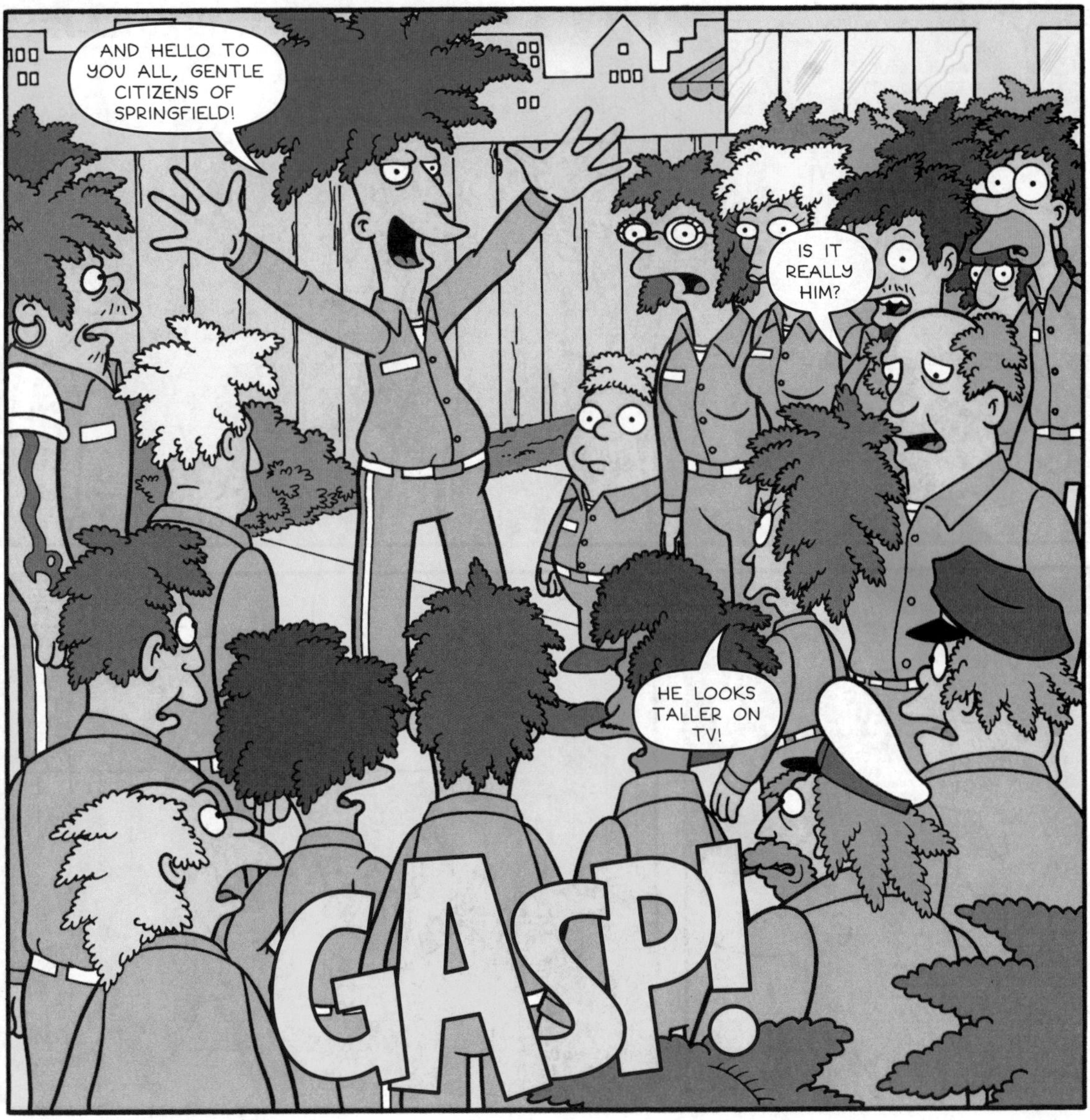
AND HELLO TO YOU ALL, GENTLE CITIZENS OF SPRINGFIELD!
IS IT REALLY HIM?
HE LOOKS TALLER ON TV!
GASP!

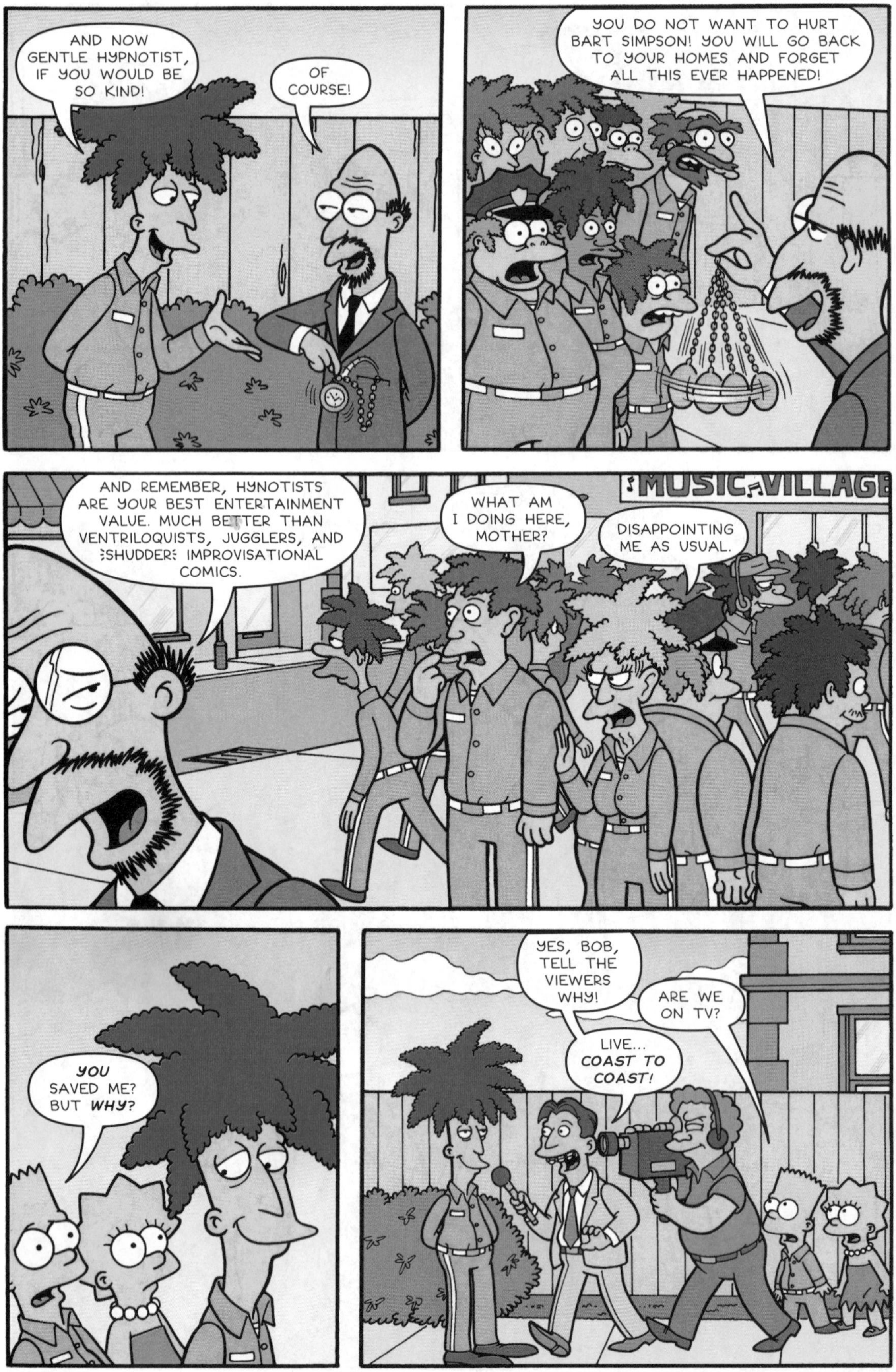
AND NOW GENTLE HYPNOTIST, IF YOU WOULD BE SO KIND!
OF COURSE!
YOU DO NOT WANT TO HURT BART SIMPSON! YOU WILL GO BACK TO YOUR HOMES AND FORGET ALL THIS EVER HAPPENED!
AND REMEMBER, HYNOTISTS ARE YOUR BEST ENTERTAINMENT VALUE. MUCH BETTER THAN VENTRILOQUISTS, JUGGLERS, AND ⁝SHUDDER⁝ IMPROVISATIONAL COMICS.
MUSIC VILLAGE
WHAT AM I DOING HERE, MOTHER?
DISAPPOINTING ME AS USUAL.
YOU SAVED ME? BUT *WHY*?
YES, BOB, TELL THE VIEWERS WHY!
ARE WE ON TV?
LIVE... *COAST TO COAST!*

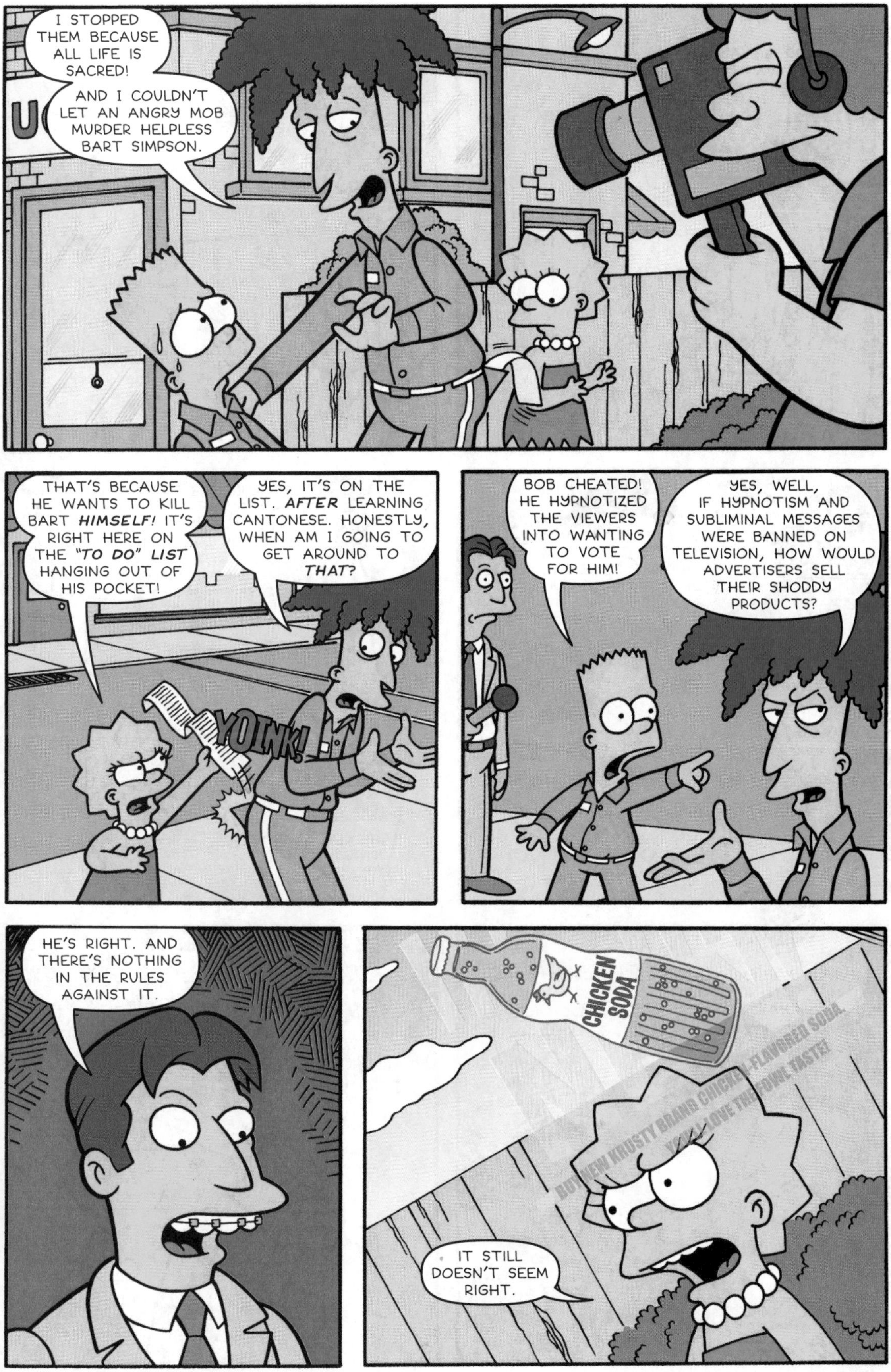
I STOPPED THEM BECAUSE ALL LIFE IS SACRED!
AND I COULDN'T LET AN ANGRY MOB MURDER HELPLESS BART SIMPSON.
THAT'S BECAUSE HE WANTS TO KILL BART **HIMSELF**! IT'S RIGHT HERE ON THE "*TO DO*" *LIST* HANGING OUT OF HIS POCKET!
YOINK!
YES, IT'S ON THE LIST. **AFTER** LEARNING CANTONESE. HONESTLY, WHEN AM I GOING TO GET AROUND TO *THAT*?
BOB CHEATED! HE HYPNOTIZED THE VIEWERS INTO WANTING TO VOTE FOR HIM!
YES, WELL, IF HYPNOTISM AND SUBLIMINAL MESSAGES WERE BANNED ON TELEVISION, HOW WOULD ADVERTISERS SELL THEIR SHODDY PRODUCTS?
HE'S RIGHT. AND THERE'S NOTHING IN THE RULES AGAINST IT.
CHICKEN SODA
BUY NEW KRUSTY BRAND CHICKEN-FLAVORED SODA. YOU'LL LOVE THE FOWL TASTE!
IT STILL DOESN'T SEEM RIGHT.

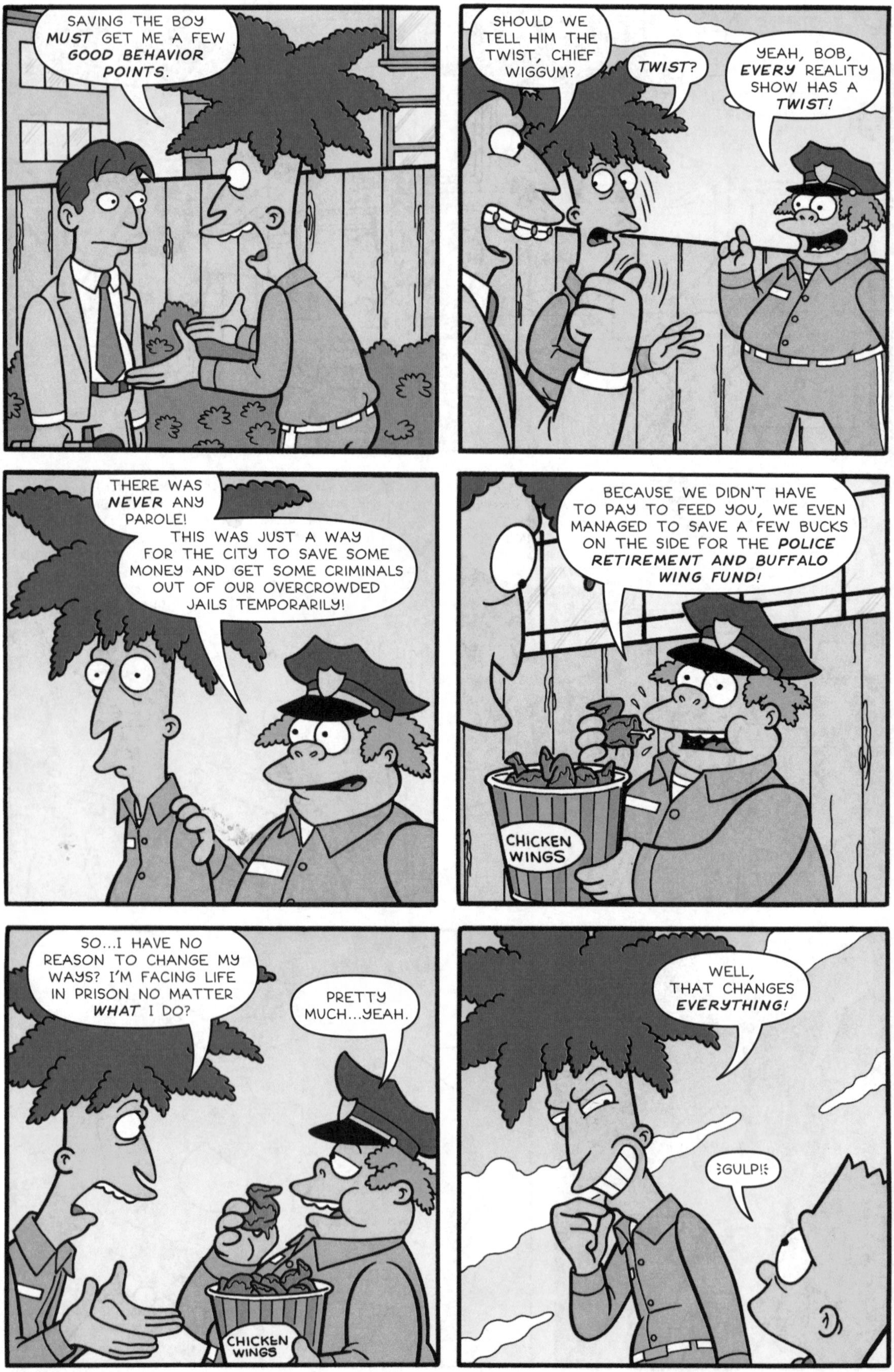
SAVING THE BOY MUST GET ME A FEW GOOD BEHAVIOR POINTS.
SHOULD WE TELL HIM THE TWIST, CHIEF WIGGUM?
TWIST?
YEAH, BOB, EVERY REALITY SHOW HAS A TWIST!
THERE WAS NEVER ANY PAROLE!
THIS WAS JUST A WAY FOR THE CITY TO SAVE SOME MONEY AND GET SOME CRIMINALS OUT OF OUR OVERCROWDED JAILS TEMPORARILY!
BECAUSE WE DIDN'T HAVE TO PAY TO FEED YOU, WE EVEN MANAGED TO SAVE A FEW BUCKS ON THE SIDE FOR THE POLICE RETIREMENT AND BUFFALO WING FUND!
CHICKEN WINGS
SO...I HAVE NO REASON TO CHANGE MY WAYS? I'M FACING LIFE IN PRISON NO MATTER WHAT I DO?
PRETTY MUCH...YEAH.
CHICKEN WINGS
WELL, THAT CHANGES EVERYTHING!
GULP!

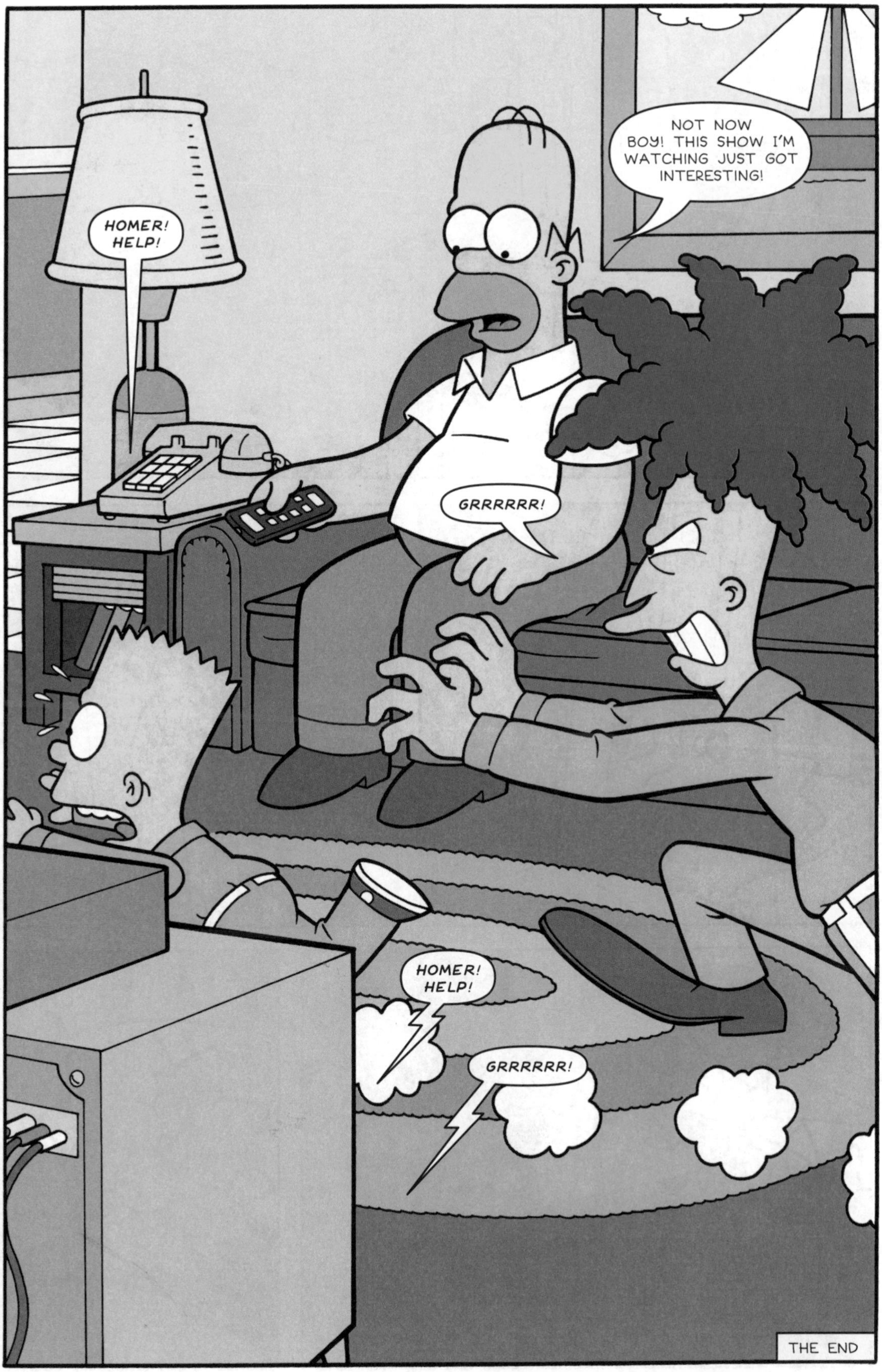
HOMER! HELP!
NOT NOW BOY! THIS SHOW I'M WATCHING JUST GOT INTERESTING!
GRRRRRR!
HOMER! HELP!
GRRRRRR!
THE END

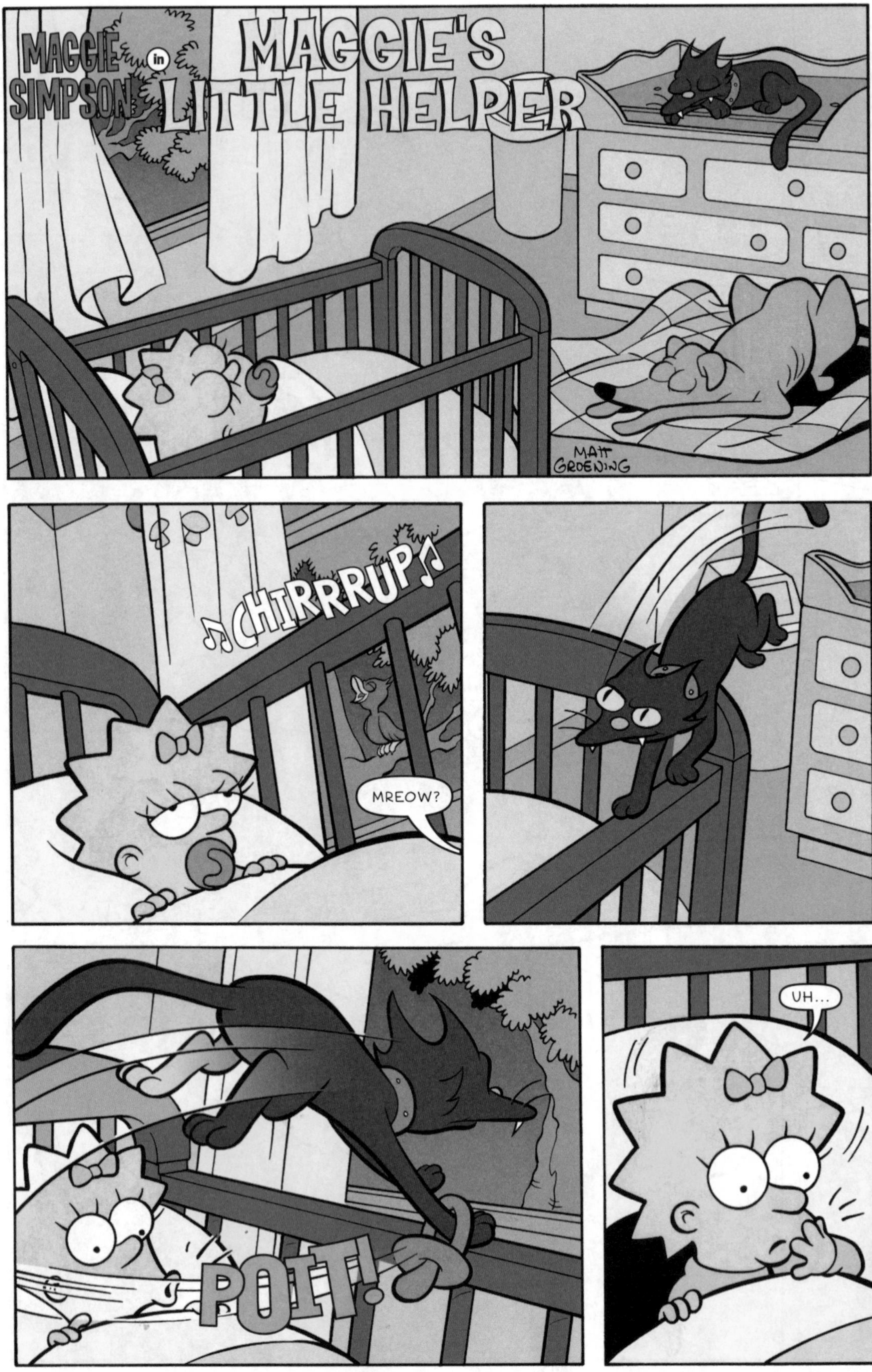
MAGGIE SIMPSON in
MAGGIE'S LITTLE HELPER
MATT GROENING
♫CHIRRRUP♫
MREOW?
POIT!
UH...

TOM PEYER
SCRIPT

CARLOS VALENTI
PENCILS

ANDREW PEPOY
INKS

ART VILLANUEVA
COLORS

KAREN BATES
LETTERS

BILL MORRISON
EDITOR

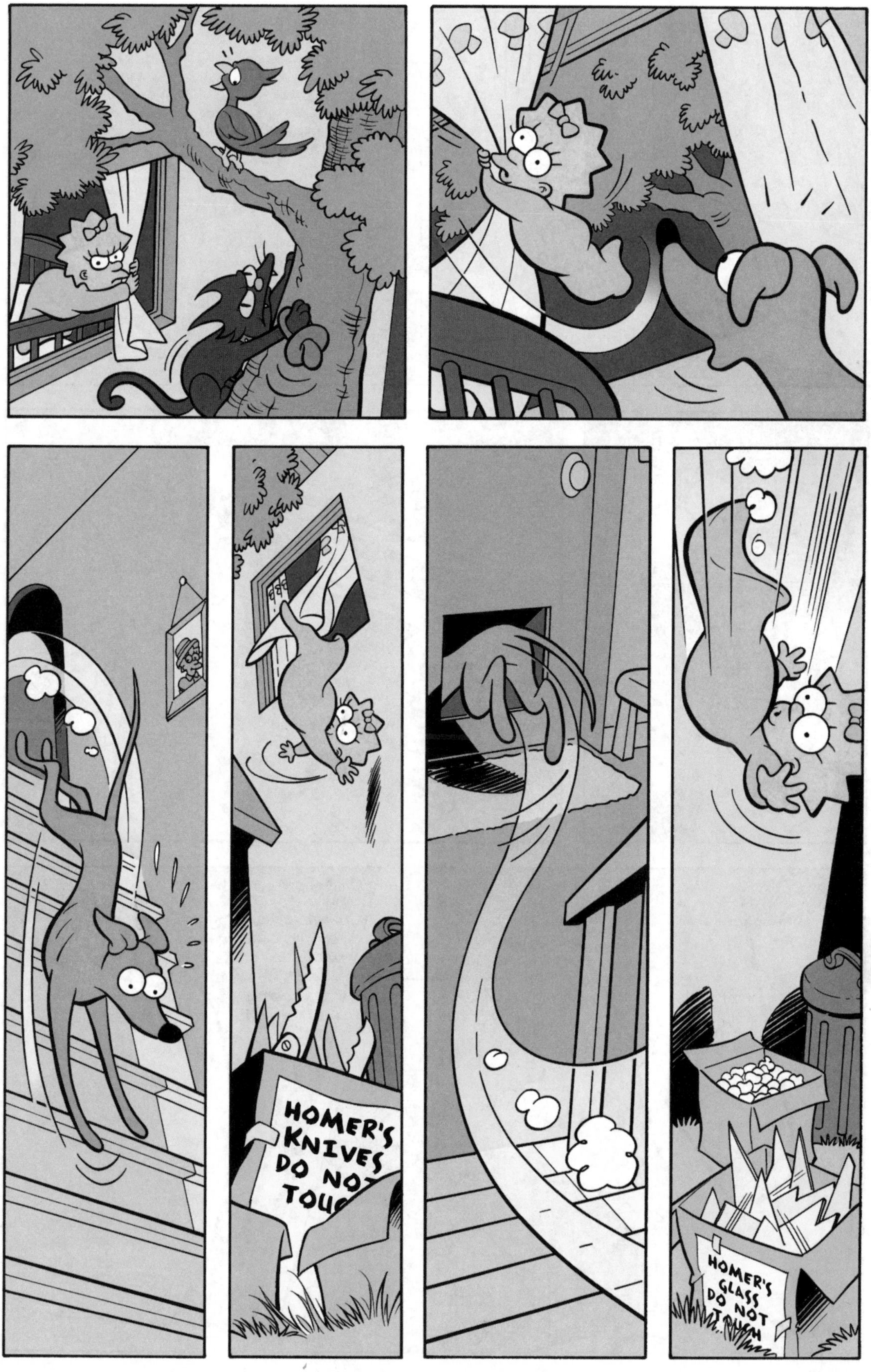

HOMER'S
KNIVES
DO NOT
TOUC
HOMER'S
GLASS
DO NOT
TOUCH

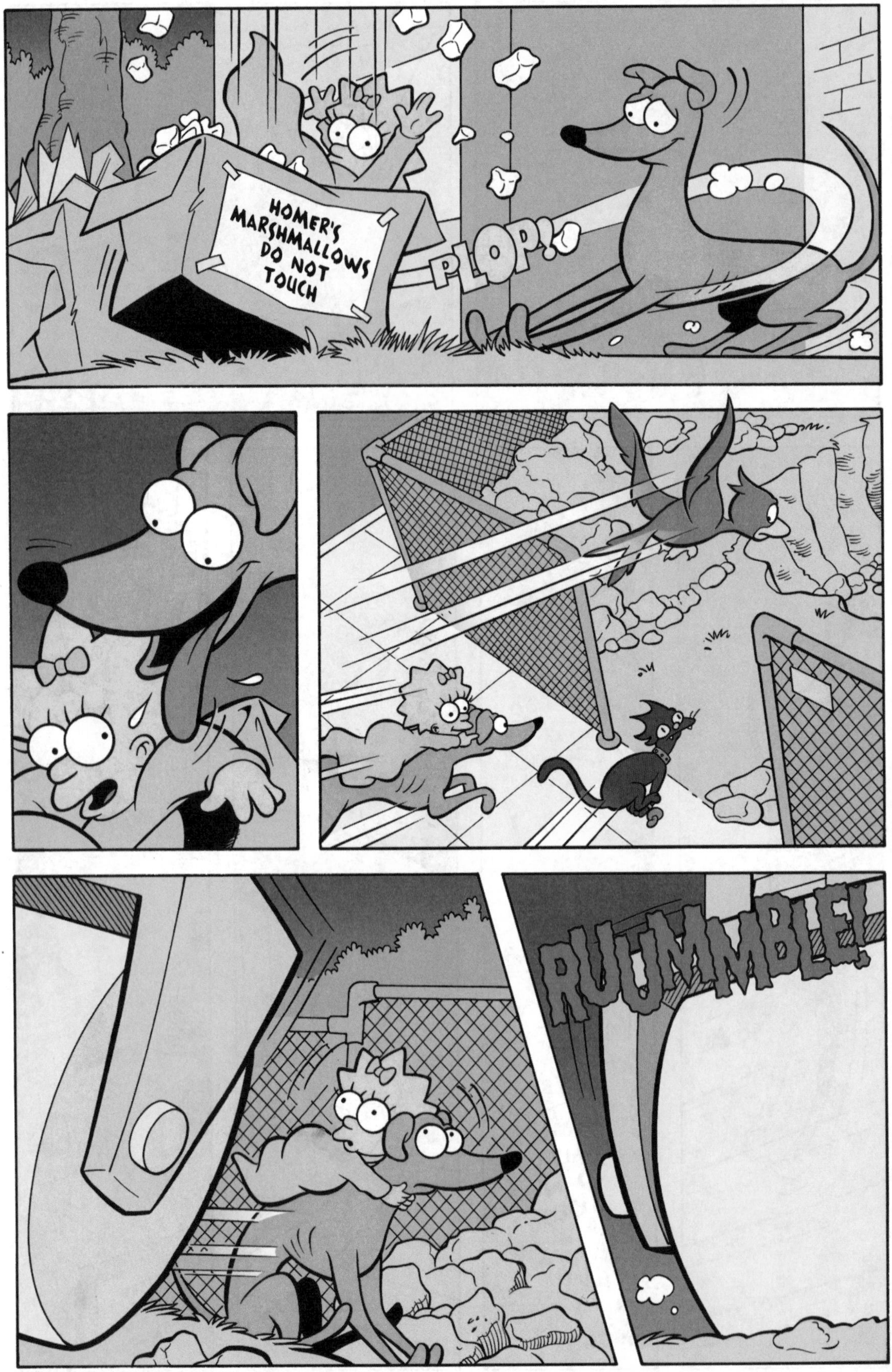
HOMER'S MARSHMALLOWS DO NOT TOUCH
PLOP!
RUUMMBLE!

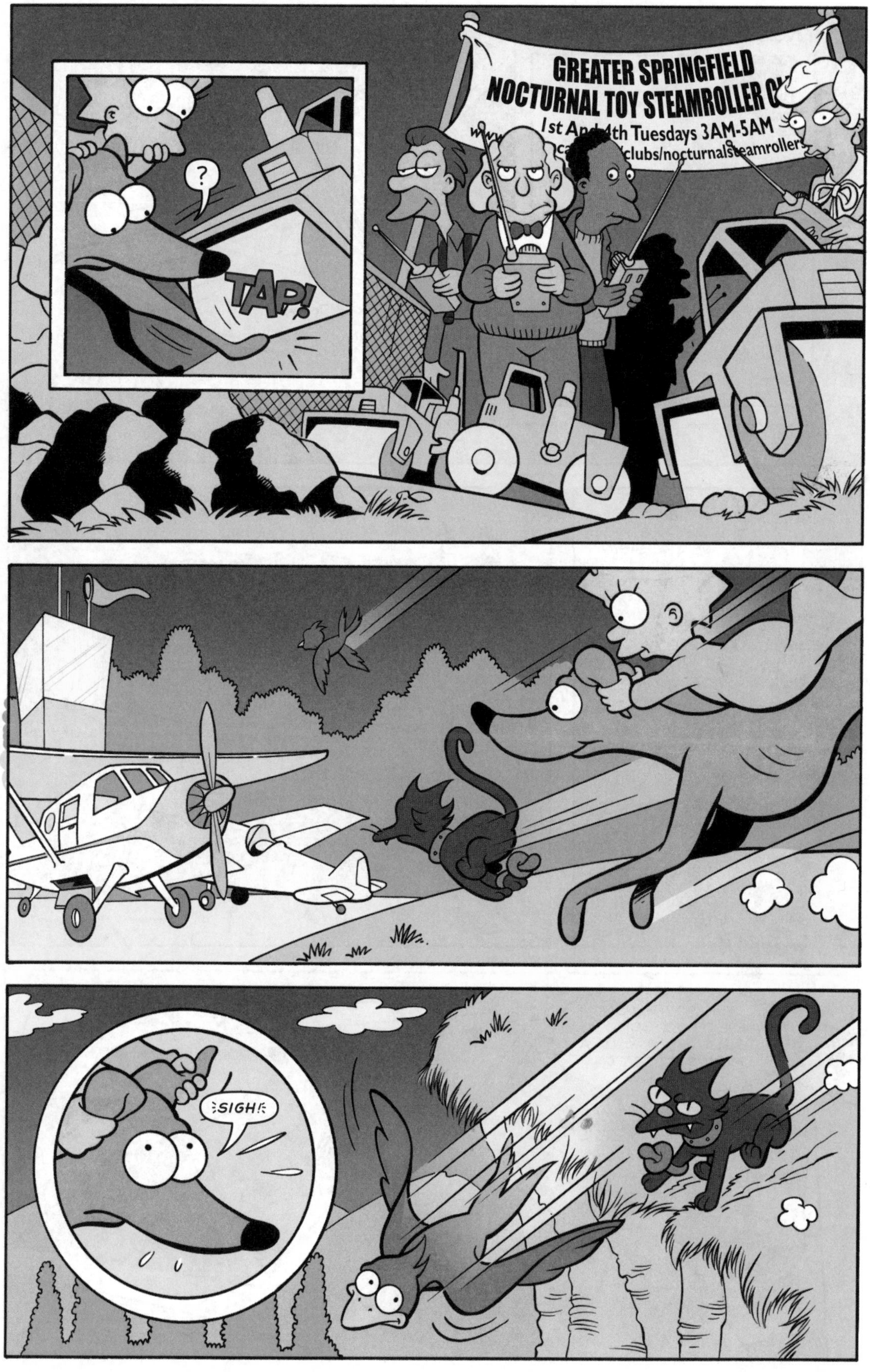
GREATER SPRINGFIELD
NOCTURNAL TOY STEAMROLLER
1st And 4th Tuesdays 3AM-5AM
/clubs/nocturnalsteamrollers
?
TAP!
SIGH!

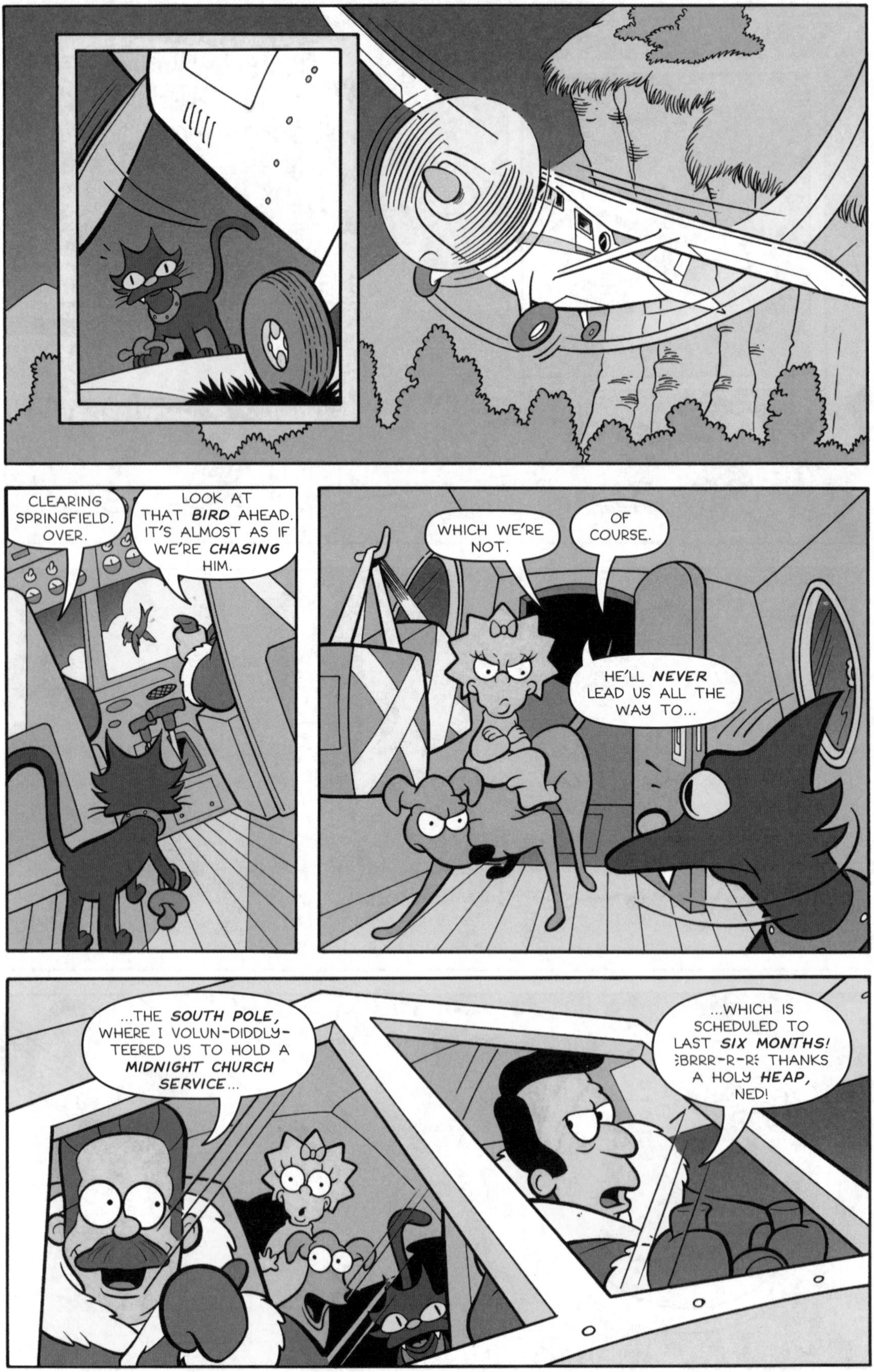

CLEARING SPRINGFIELD. OVER.
LOOK AT THAT BIRD AHEAD. IT'S ALMOST AS IF WE'RE CHASING HIM.
WHICH WE'RE NOT.
OF COURSE.
HE'LL NEVER LEAD US ALL THE WAY TO...
...THE SOUTH POLE, WHERE I VOLUN-DIDDLY-TEERED US TO HOLD A MIDNIGHT CHURCH SERVICE...
...WHICH IS SCHEDULED TO LAST SIX MONTHS! BRRR-R-R! THANKS A HOLY HEAP, NED!

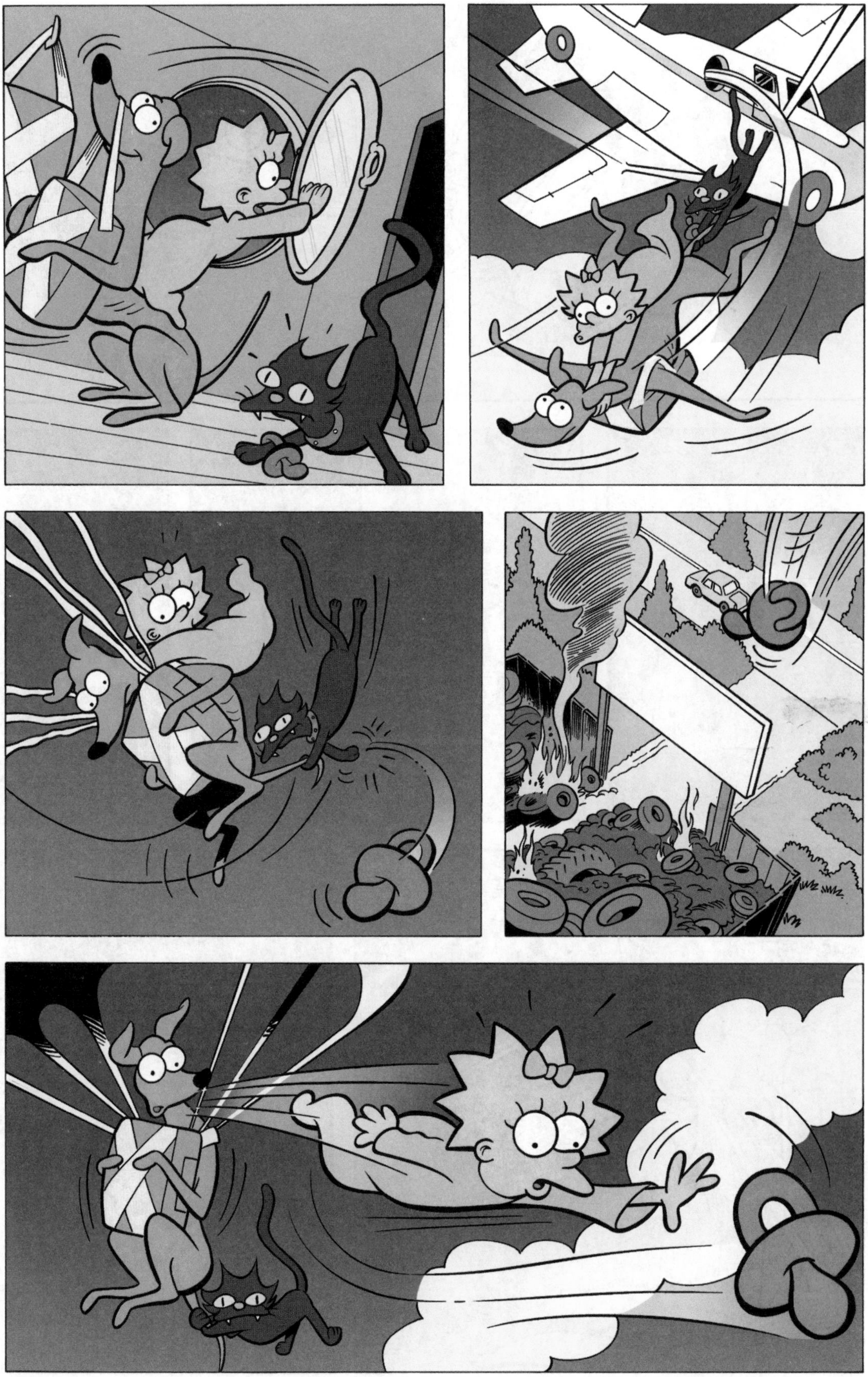

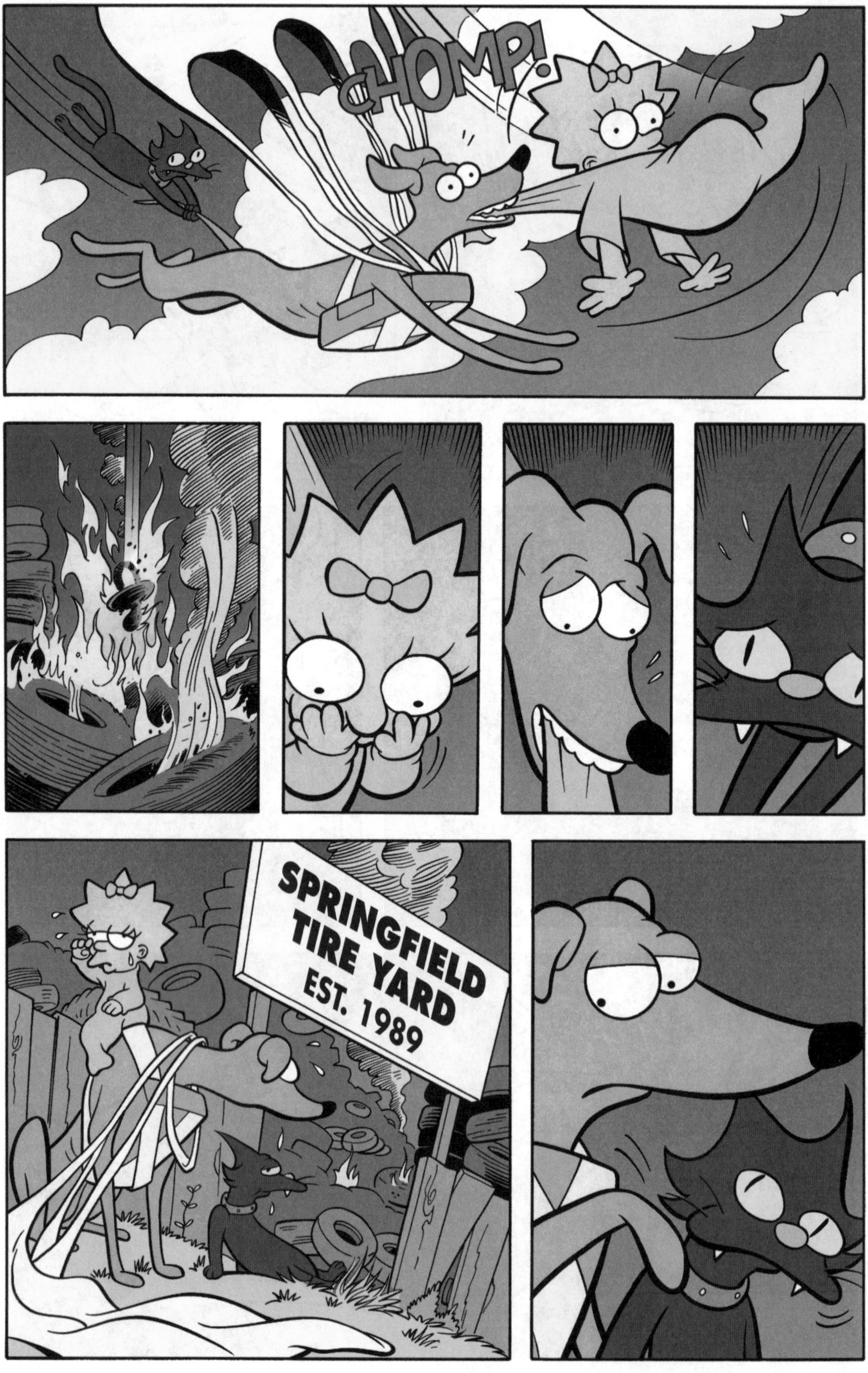
CHOMP!
SPRINGFIELD
TIRE YARD
EST. 1989

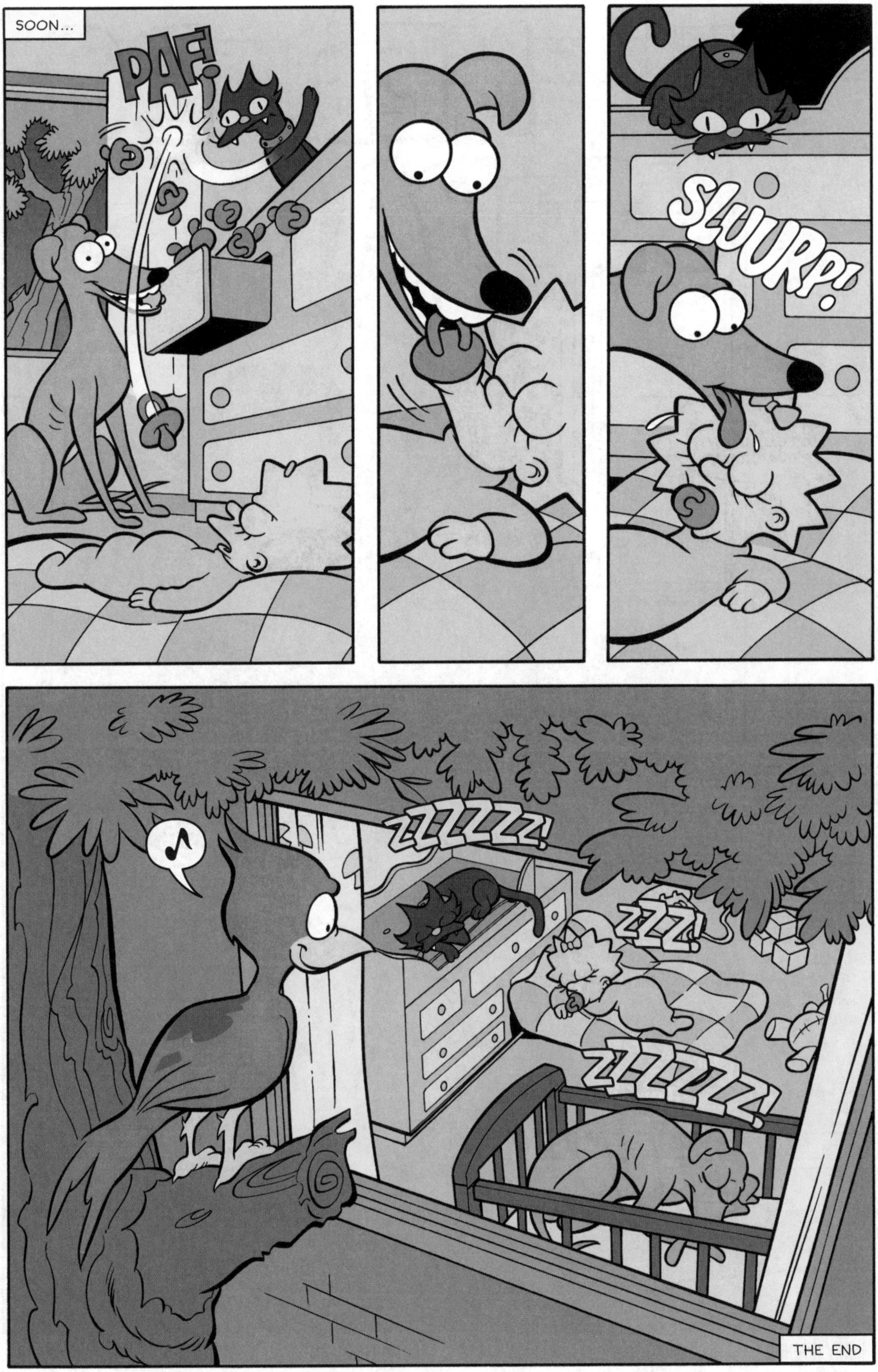
SOON...
PAF!
SLUURP!
ZZZZZZ!
ZZZ!
ZZZZZZ!
THE END

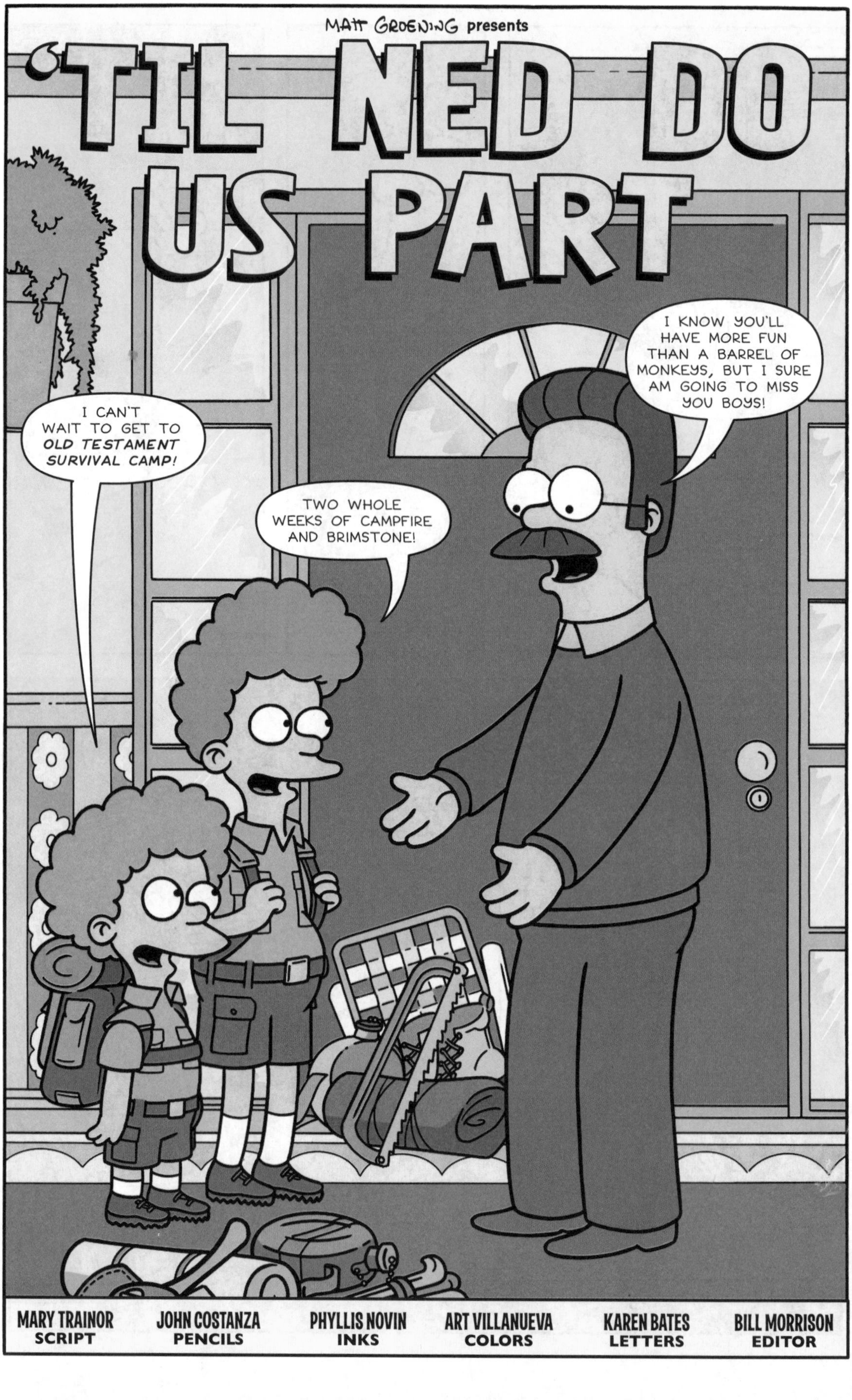

MATT GROENING presents
'TIL NED DO US PART
I CAN'T WAIT TO GET TO OLD TESTAMENT SURVIVAL CAMP!
TWO WHOLE WEEKS OF CAMPFIRE AND BRIMSTONE!
I KNOW YOU'LL HAVE MORE FUN THAN A BARREL OF MONKEYS, BUT I SURE AM GOING TO MISS YOU BOYS!
MARY TRAINOR SCRIPT
JOHN COSTANZA PENCILS
PHYLLIS NOVIN INKS
ART VILLANUEVA COLORS
KAREN BATES LETTERS
BILL MORRISON EDITOR

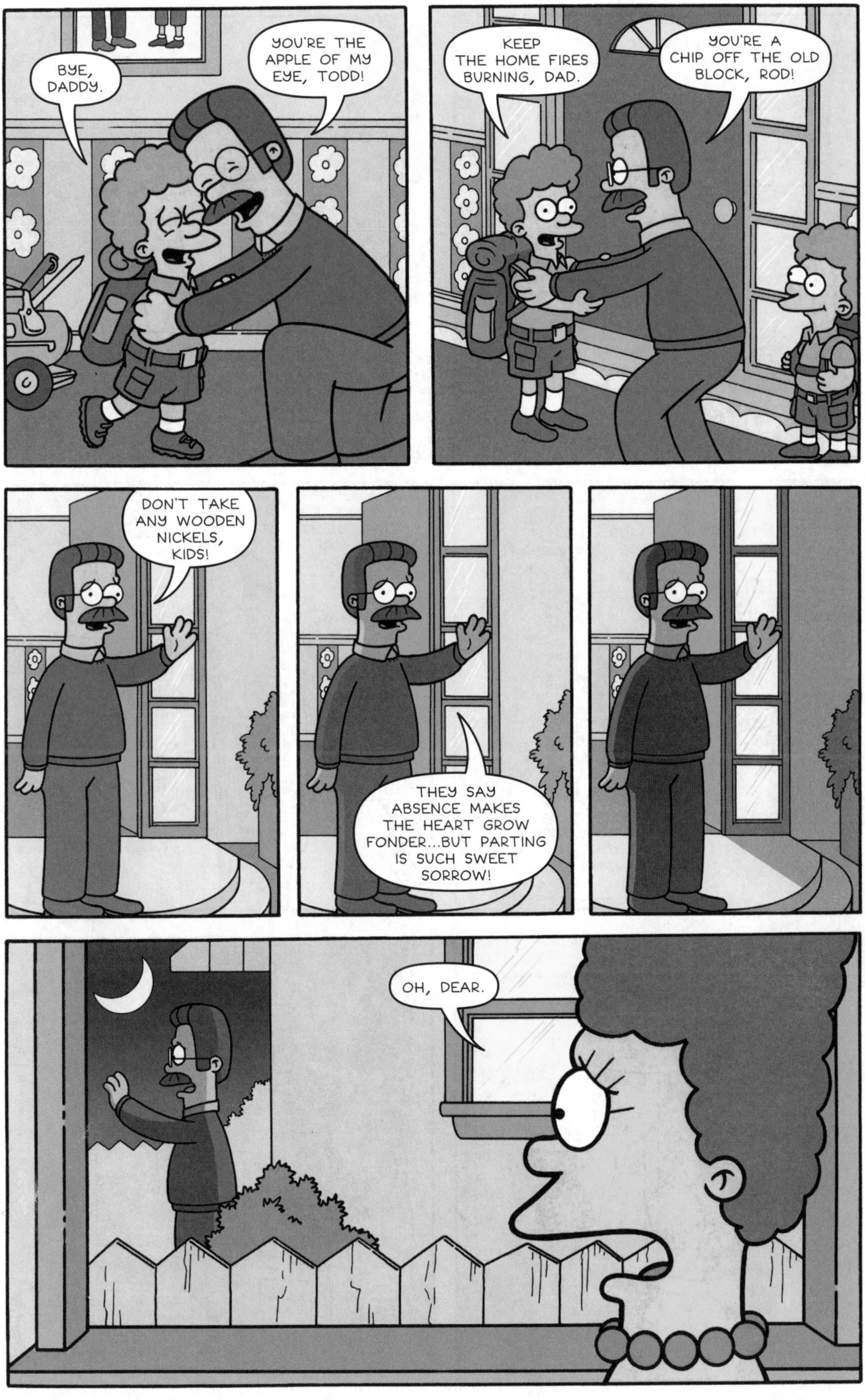
BYE, DADDY.
YOU'RE THE APPLE OF MY EYE, TODD!
KEEP THE HOME FIRES BURNING, DAD.
YOU'RE A CHIP OFF THE OLD BLOCK, ROD!
DON'T TAKE ANY WOODEN NICKELS, KIDS!
THEY SAY ABSENCE MAKES THE HEART GROW FONDER...BUT PARTING IS SUCH SWEET SORROW!
OH, DEAR.

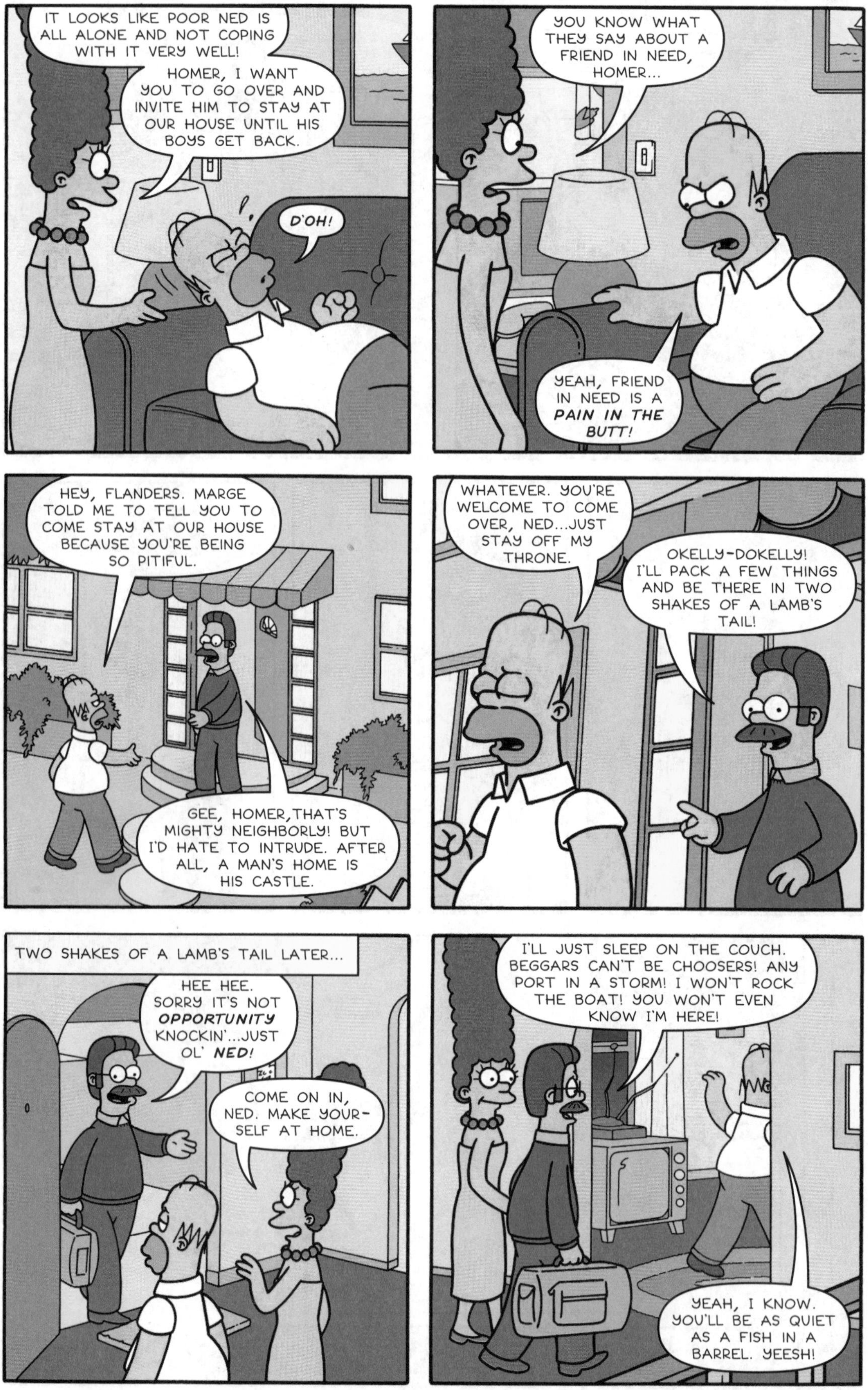
IT LOOKS LIKE POOR NED IS ALL ALONE AND NOT COPING WITH IT VERY WELL!
HOMER, I WANT YOU TO GO OVER AND INVITE HIM TO STAY AT OUR HOUSE UNTIL HIS BOYS GET BACK.
D'OH!
YOU KNOW WHAT THEY SAY ABOUT A FRIEND IN NEED, HOMER...
YEAH, FRIEND IN NEED IS A ***PAIN IN THE BUTT!***
HEY, FLANDERS. MARGE TOLD ME TO TELL YOU TO COME STAY AT OUR HOUSE BECAUSE YOU'RE BEING SO PITIFUL.
GEE, HOMER, THAT'S MIGHTY NEIGHBORLY! BUT I'D HATE TO INTRUDE. AFTER ALL, A MAN'S HOME IS HIS CASTLE.
WHATEVER. YOU'RE WELCOME TO COME OVER, NED...JUST STAY OFF MY THRONE.
OKELLY-DOKELLY! I'LL PACK A FEW THINGS AND BE THERE IN TWO SHAKES OF A LAMB'S TAIL!
TWO SHAKES OF A LAMB'S TAIL LATER...
HEE HEE. SORRY IT'S NOT ***OPPORTUNITY*** KNOCKIN'...JUST OL' ***NED!***
COME ON IN, NED. MAKE YOURSELF AT HOME.
I'LL JUST SLEEP ON THE COUCH. BEGGARS CAN'T BE CHOOSERS! ANY PORT IN A STORM! I WON'T ROCK THE BOAT! YOU WON'T EVEN KNOW I'M HERE!
YEAH, I KNOW. YOU'LL BE AS QUIET AS A FISH IN A BARREL. YEESH!

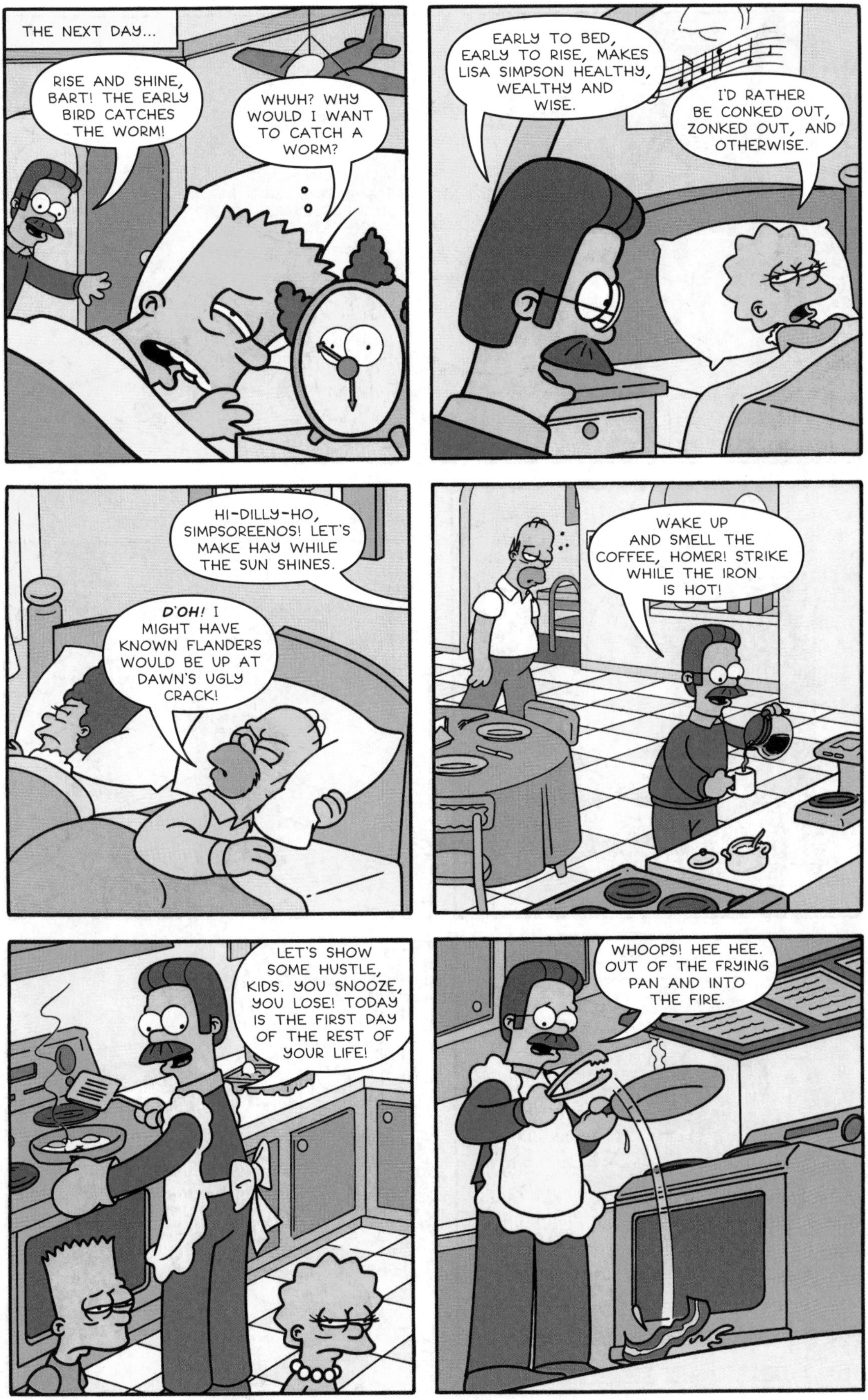
THE NEXT DAY...
RISE AND SHINE, BART! THE EARLY BIRD CATCHES THE WORM!
WHUH? WHY WOULD I WANT TO CATCH A WORM?
EARLY TO BED, EARLY TO RISE, MAKES LISA SIMPSON HEALTHY, WEALTHY AND WISE.
I'D RATHER BE CONKED OUT, ZONKED OUT, AND OTHERWISE.
HI-DILLY-HO, SIMPSOREENOS! LET'S MAKE HAY WHILE THE SUN SHINES.
D'OH! I MIGHT HAVE KNOWN FLANDERS WOULD BE UP AT DAWN'S UGLY CRACK!
WAKE UP AND SMELL THE COFFEE, HOMER! STRIKE WHILE THE IRON IS HOT!
LET'S SHOW SOME HUSTLE, KIDS. YOU SNOOZE, YOU LOSE! TODAY IS THE FIRST DAY OF THE REST OF YOUR LIFE!
WHOOPS! HEE HEE. OUT OF THE FRYING PAN AND INTO THE FIRE.

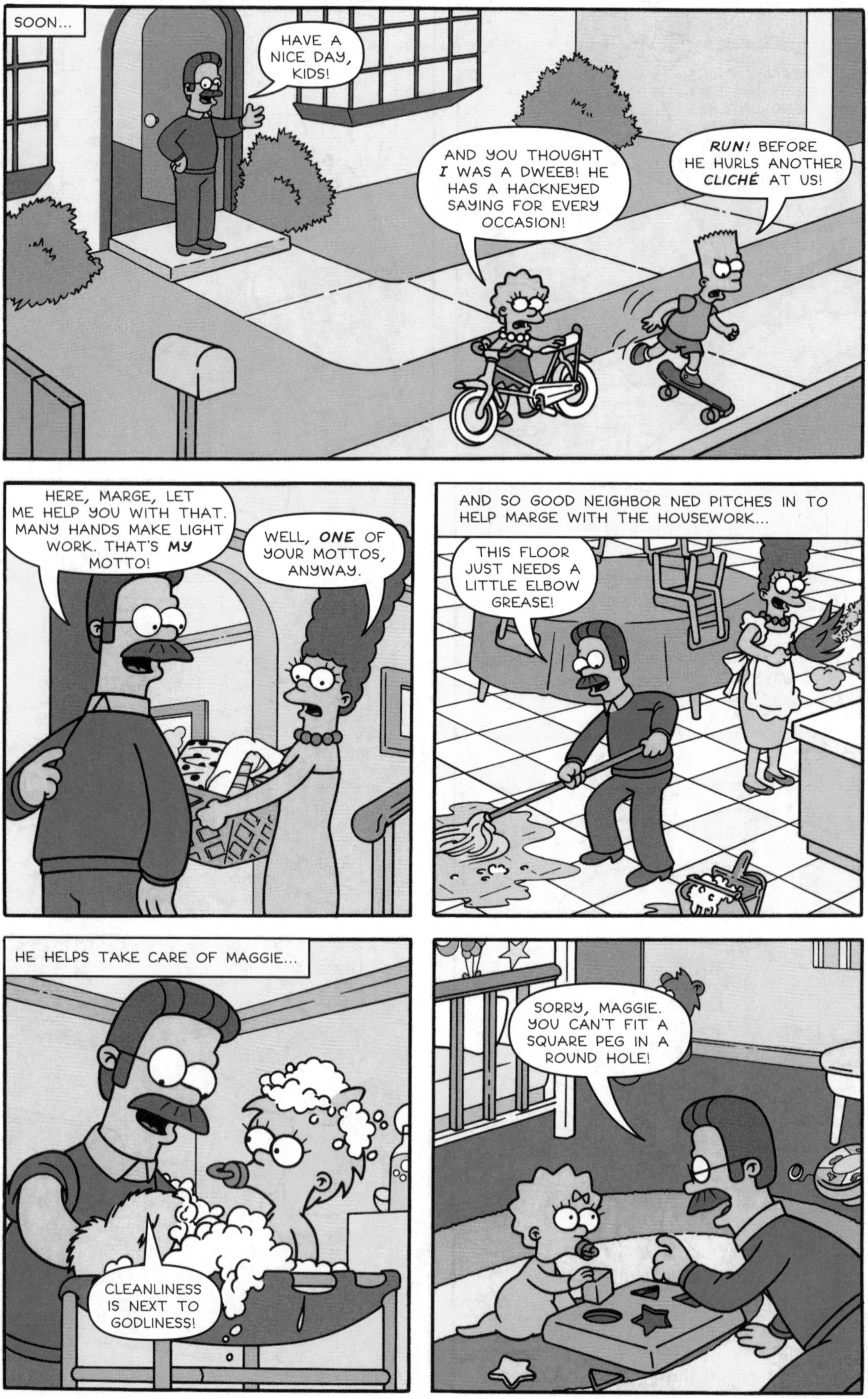
SOON...
HAVE A NICE DAY, KIDS!
AND YOU THOUGHT I WAS A DWEEB! HE HAS A HACKNEYED SAYING FOR EVERY OCCASION!
RUN! BEFORE HE HURLS ANOTHER CLICHÉ AT US!
HERE, MARGE, LET ME HELP YOU WITH THAT. MANY HANDS MAKE LIGHT WORK. THAT'S MY MOTTO!
WELL, ONE OF YOUR MOTTOS, ANYWAY.
AND SO GOOD NEIGHBOR NED PITCHES IN TO HELP MARGE WITH THE HOUSEWORK...
THIS FLOOR JUST NEEDS A LITTLE ELBOW GREASE!
HE HELPS TAKE CARE OF MAGGIE...
CLEANLINESS IS NEXT TO GODLINESS!
SORRY, MAGGIE. YOU CAN'T FIT A SQUARE PEG IN A ROUND HOLE!

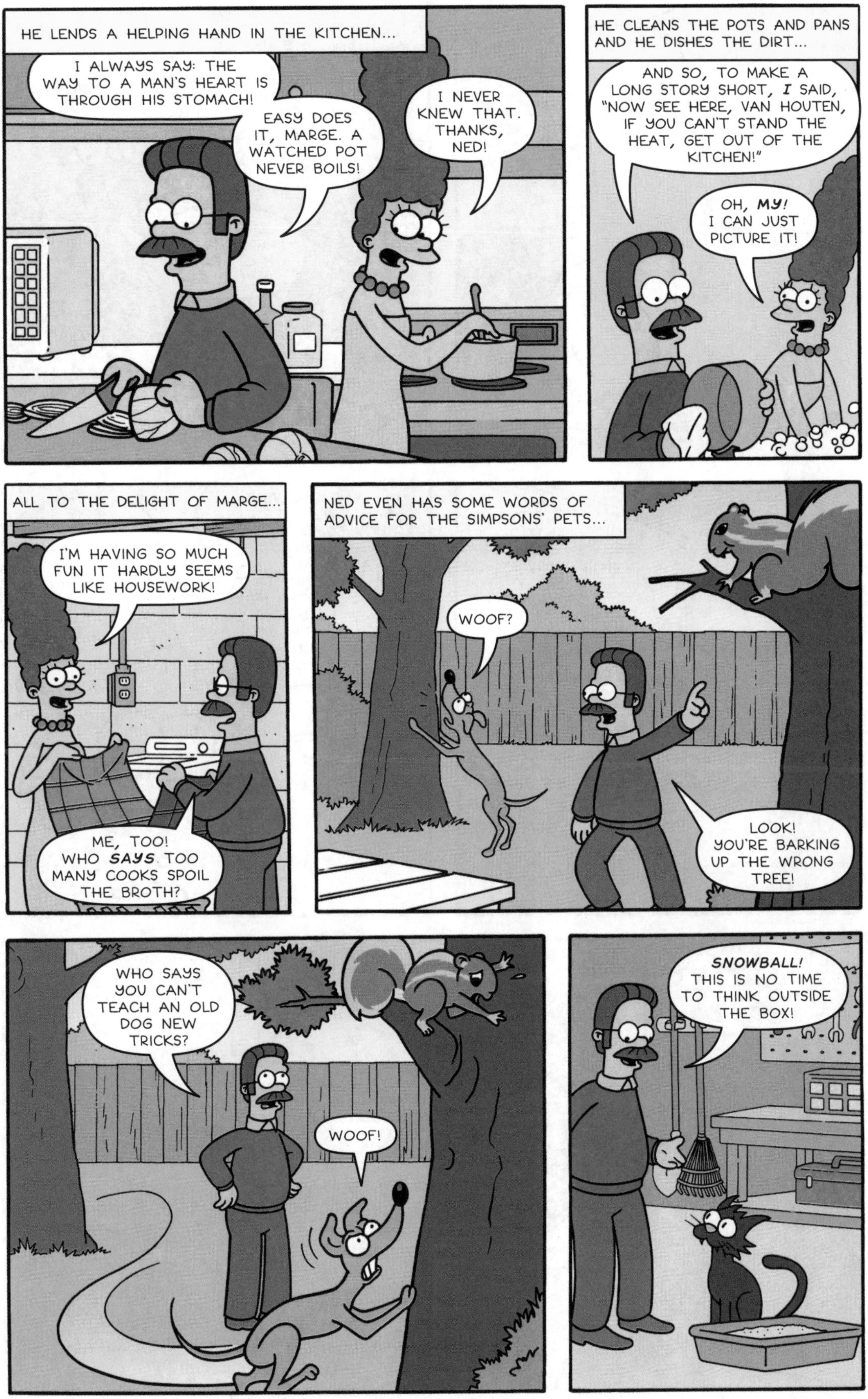
HE LENDS A HELPING HAND IN THE KITCHEN...
I ALWAYS SAY: THE WAY TO A MAN'S HEART IS THROUGH HIS STOMACH!
EASY DOES IT, MARGE. A WATCHED POT NEVER BOILS!
I NEVER KNEW THAT. THANKS, NED!
HE CLEANS THE POTS AND PANS AND HE DISHES THE DIRT...
AND SO, TO MAKE A LONG STORY SHORT, *I* SAID, "NOW SEE HERE, VAN HOUTEN, IF YOU CAN'T STAND THE HEAT, GET OUT OF THE KITCHEN!"
OH, **MY!** I CAN JUST PICTURE IT!
ALL TO THE DELIGHT OF MARGE...
I'M HAVING SO MUCH FUN IT HARDLY SEEMS LIKE HOUSEWORK!
ME, TOO! WHO ***SAYS*** TOO MANY COOKS SPOIL THE BROTH?
NED EVEN HAS SOME WORDS OF ADVICE FOR THE SIMPSONS' PETS...
WOOF?
LOOK! YOU'RE BARKING UP THE WRONG TREE!
WHO SAYS YOU CAN'T TEACH AN OLD DOG NEW TRICKS?
WOOF!
SNOWBALL! THIS IS NO TIME TO THINK OUTSIDE THE BOX!

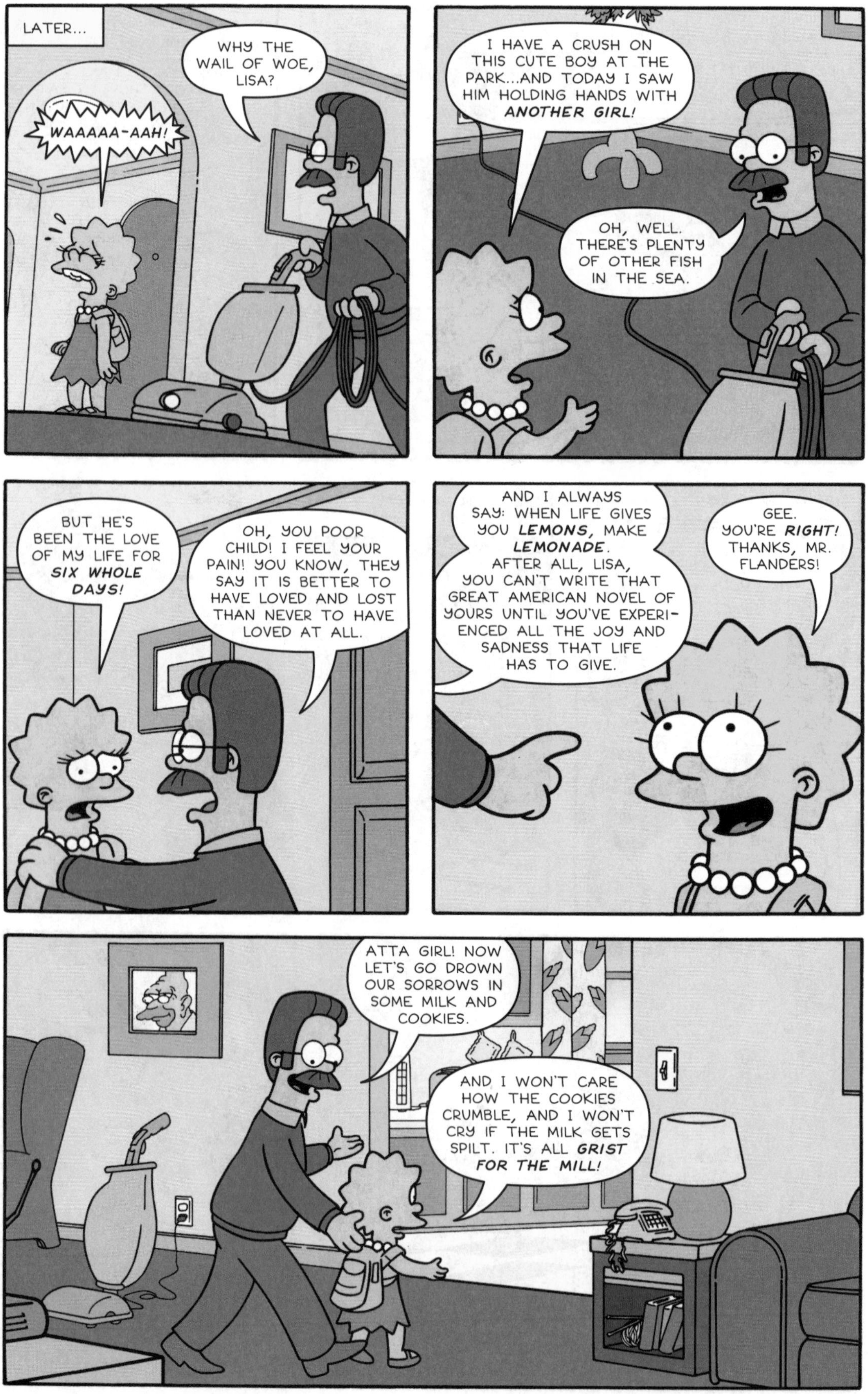

LATER...
WAAAAA-AAH!
WHY THE WAIL OF WOE, LISA?
I HAVE A CRUSH ON THIS CUTE BOY AT THE PARK...AND TODAY I SAW HIM HOLDING HANDS WITH ANOTHER GIRL!
OH, WELL. THERE'S PLENTY OF OTHER FISH IN THE SEA.
BUT HE'S BEEN THE LOVE OF MY LIFE FOR SIX WHOLE DAYS!
OH, YOU POOR CHILD! I FEEL YOUR PAIN! YOU KNOW, THEY SAY IT IS BETTER TO HAVE LOVED AND LOST THAN NEVER TO HAVE LOVED AT ALL.
AND I ALWAYS SAY: WHEN LIFE GIVES YOU LEMONS, MAKE LEMONADE. AFTER ALL, LISA, YOU CAN'T WRITE THAT GREAT AMERICAN NOVEL OF YOURS UNTIL YOU'VE EXPERIENCED ALL THE JOY AND SADNESS THAT LIFE HAS TO GIVE.
GEE. YOU'RE RIGHT! THANKS, MR. FLANDERS!
ATTA GIRL! NOW LET'S GO DROWN OUR SORROWS IN SOME MILK AND COOKIES.
AND I WON'T CARE HOW THE COOKIES CRUMBLE, AND I WON'T CRY IF THE MILK GETS SPILT. IT'S ALL GRIST FOR THE MILL!

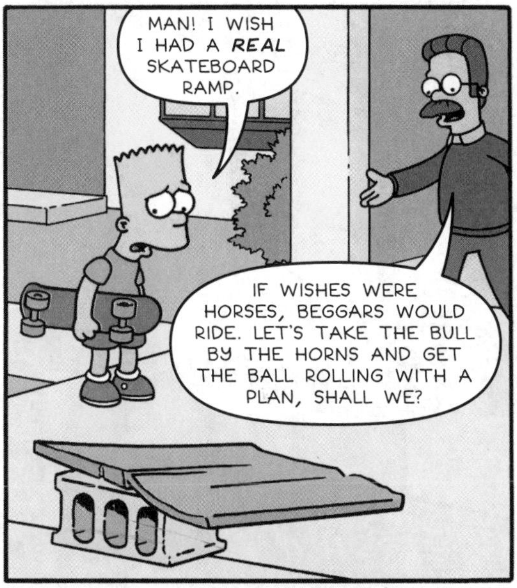
MAN! I WISH I HAD A ***REAL*** SKATEBOARD RAMP.
IF WISHES WERE HORSES, BEGGARS WOULD RIDE. LET'S TAKE THE BULL BY THE HORNS AND GET THE BALL ROLLING WITH A PLAN, SHALL WE?

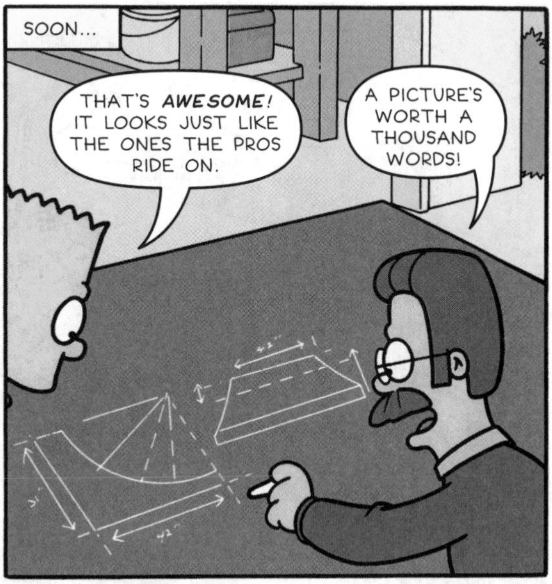
SOON...
THAT'S ***AWESOME!*** IT LOOKS JUST LIKE THE ONES THE PROS RIDE ON.
A PICTURE'S WORTH A THOUSAND WORDS!

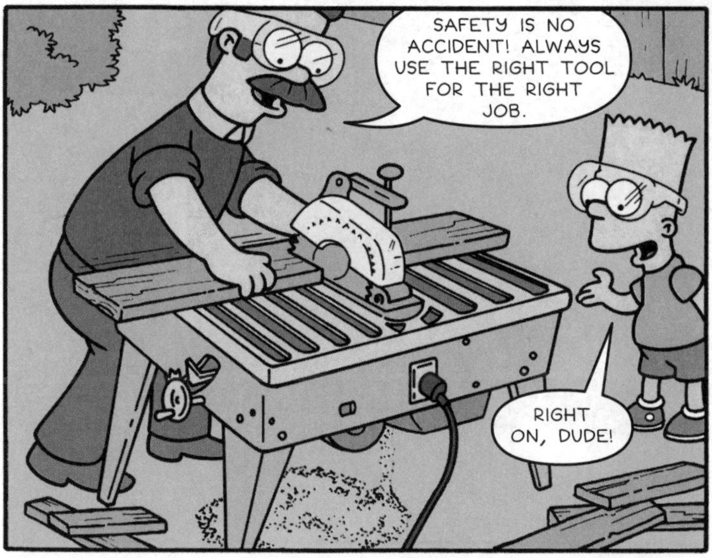
SAFETY IS NO ACCIDENT! ALWAYS USE THE RIGHT TOOL FOR THE RIGHT JOB.
RIGHT ON, DUDE!

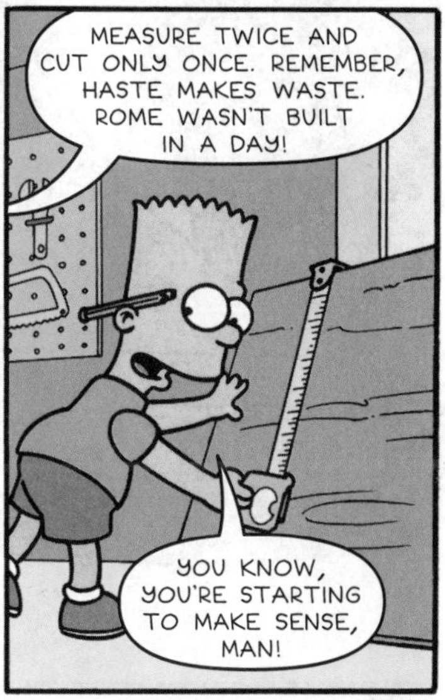
MEASURE TWICE AND CUT ONLY ONCE. REMEMBER, HASTE MAKES WASTE. ROME WASN'T BUILT IN A DAY!
YOU KNOW, YOU'RE STARTING TO MAKE SENSE, MAN!

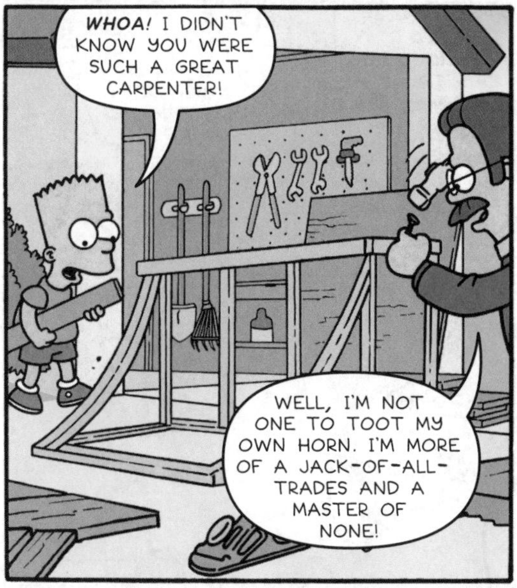
WHOA! I DIDN'T KNOW YOU WERE SUCH A GREAT CARPENTER!
WELL, I'M NOT ONE TO TOOT MY OWN HORN. I'M MORE OF A JACK-OF-ALL-TRADES AND A MASTER OF NONE!

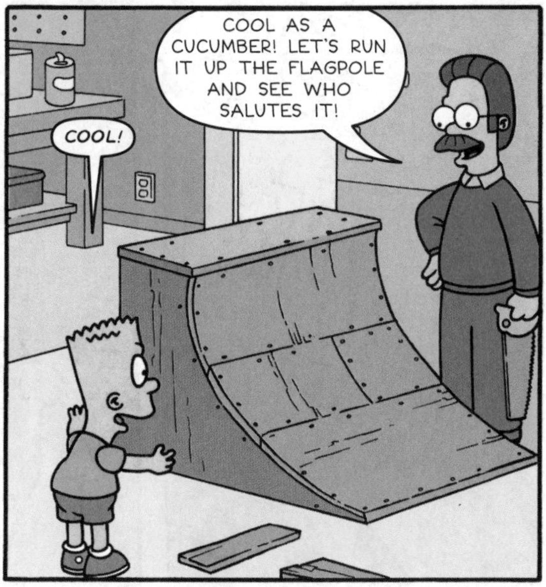
COOL AS A CUCUMBER! LET'S RUN IT UP THE FLAGPOLE AND SEE WHO SALUTES IT!
COOL!

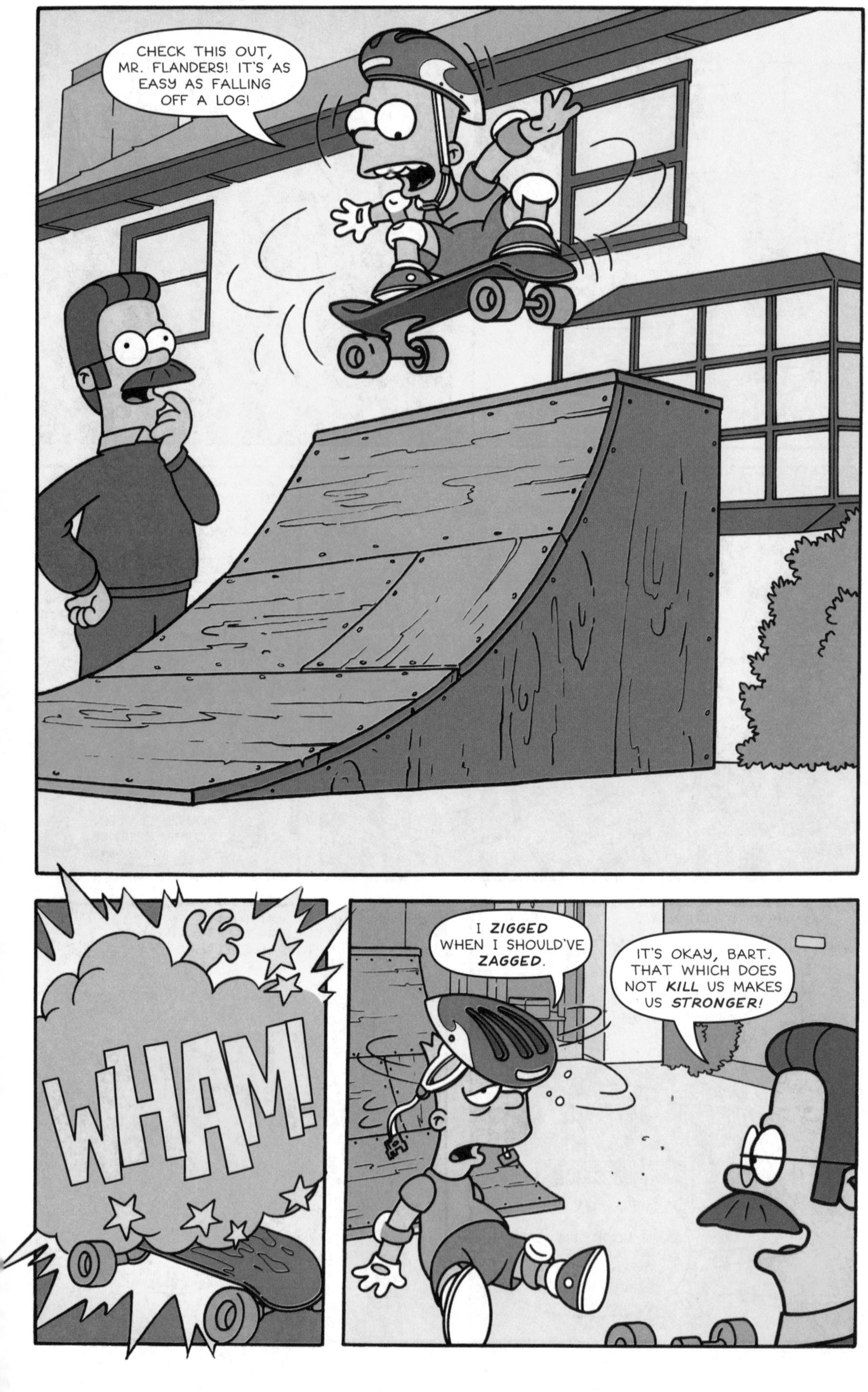
CHECK THIS OUT, MR. FLANDERS! IT'S AS EASY AS FALLING OFF A LOG!
WHAM!
I *ZIGGED* WHEN I SHOULD'VE *ZAGGED*.
IT'S OKAY, BART. THAT WHICH DOES NOT *KILL* US MAKES US *STRONGER!*

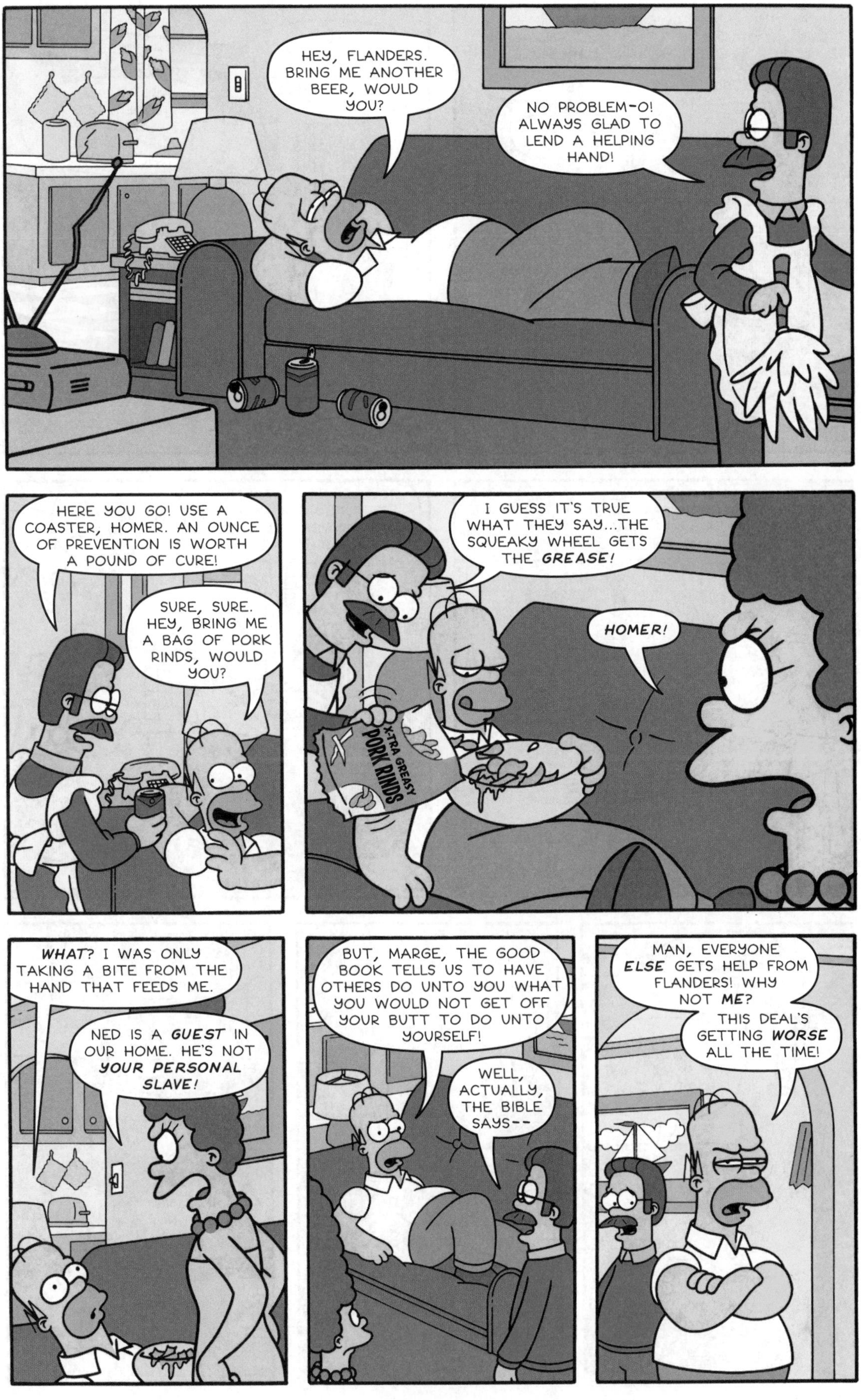
HEY, FLANDERS. BRING ME ANOTHER BEER, WOULD YOU?
NO PROBLEM-O! ALWAYS GLAD TO LEND A HELPING HAND!
HERE YOU GO! USE A COASTER, HOMER. AN OUNCE OF PREVENTION IS WORTH A POUND OF CURE!
SURE, SURE. HEY, BRING ME A BAG OF PORK RINDS, WOULD YOU?
I GUESS IT'S TRUE WHAT THEY SAY...THE SQUEAKY WHEEL GETS THE *GREASE!*
X-TRA GREASY PORK RINDS
HOMER!
WHAT? I WAS ONLY TAKING A BITE FROM THE HAND THAT FEEDS ME.
NED IS A *GUEST* IN OUR HOME. HE'S NOT *YOUR PERSONAL SLAVE!*
BUT, MARGE, THE GOOD BOOK TELLS US TO HAVE OTHERS DO UNTO YOU WHAT YOU WOULD NOT GET OFF YOUR BUTT TO DO UNTO YOURSELF!
WELL, ACTUALLY, THE BIBLE SAYS--
MAN, EVERYONE *ELSE* GETS HELP FROM FLANDERS! WHY NOT *ME*?
THIS DEAL'S GETTING *WORSE* ALL THE TIME!

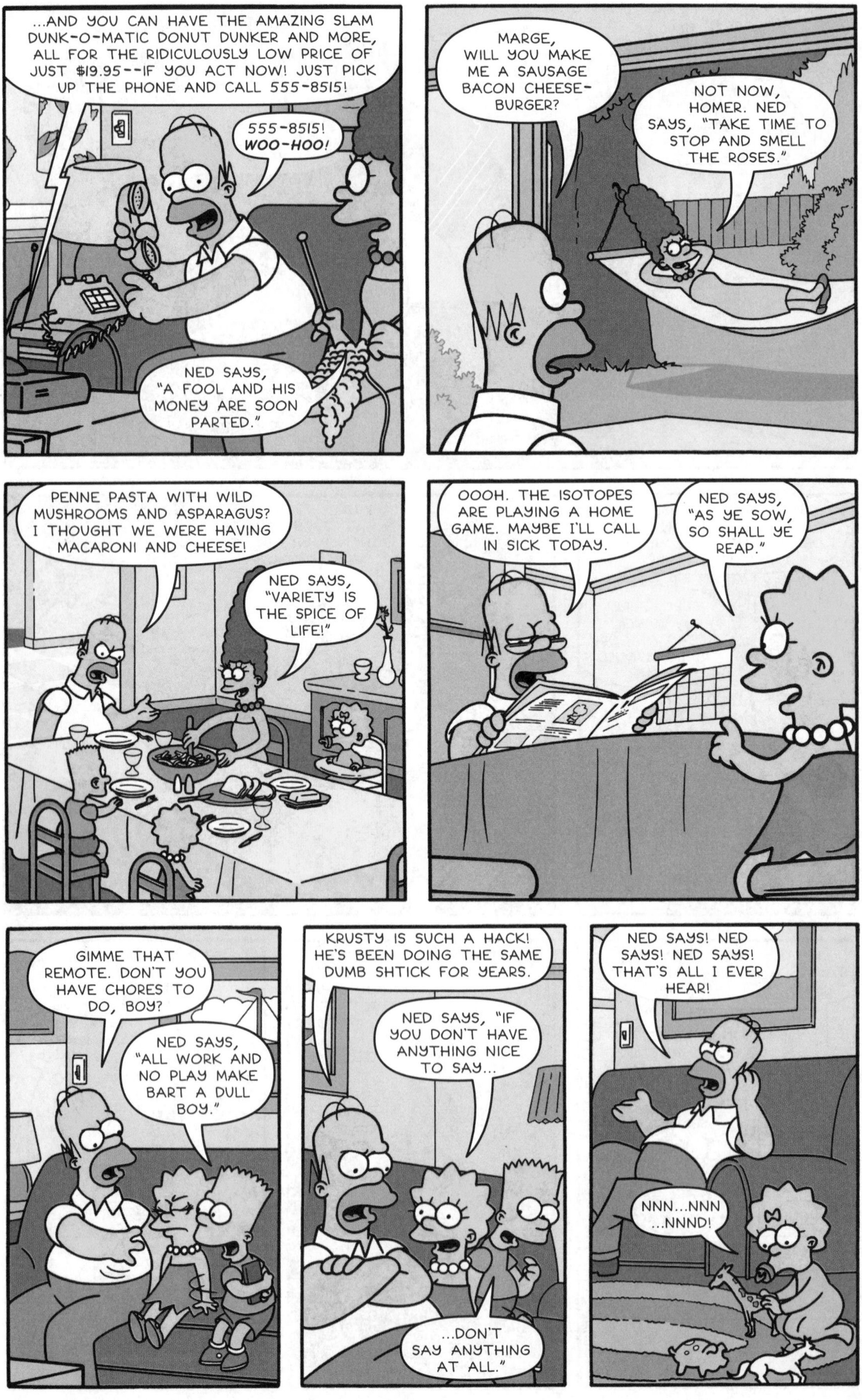

...AND YOU CAN HAVE THE AMAZING SLAM DUNK-O-MATIC DONUT DUNKER AND MORE, ALL FOR THE RIDICULOUSLY LOW PRICE OF JUST $19.95--IF YOU ACT NOW! JUST PICK UP THE PHONE AND CALL 555-8515!
555-8515! WOO-HOO!
NED SAYS, "A FOOL AND HIS MONEY ARE SOON PARTED."
MARGE, WILL YOU MAKE ME A SAUSAGE BACON CHEESE-BURGER?
NOT NOW, HOMER. NED SAYS, "TAKE TIME TO STOP AND SMELL THE ROSES."
PENNE PASTA WITH WILD MUSHROOMS AND ASPARAGUS? I THOUGHT WE WERE HAVING MACARONI AND CHEESE!
NED SAYS, "VARIETY IS THE SPICE OF LIFE!"
OOOH. THE ISOTOPES ARE PLAYING A HOME GAME. MAYBE I'LL CALL IN SICK TODAY.
NED SAYS, "AS YE SOW, SO SHALL YE REAP."
GIMME THAT REMOTE. DON'T YOU HAVE CHORES TO DO, BOY?
NED SAYS, "ALL WORK AND NO PLAY MAKE BART A DULL BOY."
KRUSTY IS SUCH A HACK! HE'S BEEN DOING THE SAME DUMB SHTICK FOR YEARS.
NED SAYS, "IF YOU DON'T HAVE ANYTHING NICE TO SAY...
...DON'T SAY ANYTHING AT ALL."
NED SAYS! NED SAYS! NED SAYS! THAT'S ALL I EVER HEAR!
NNN...NNN ...NNND!

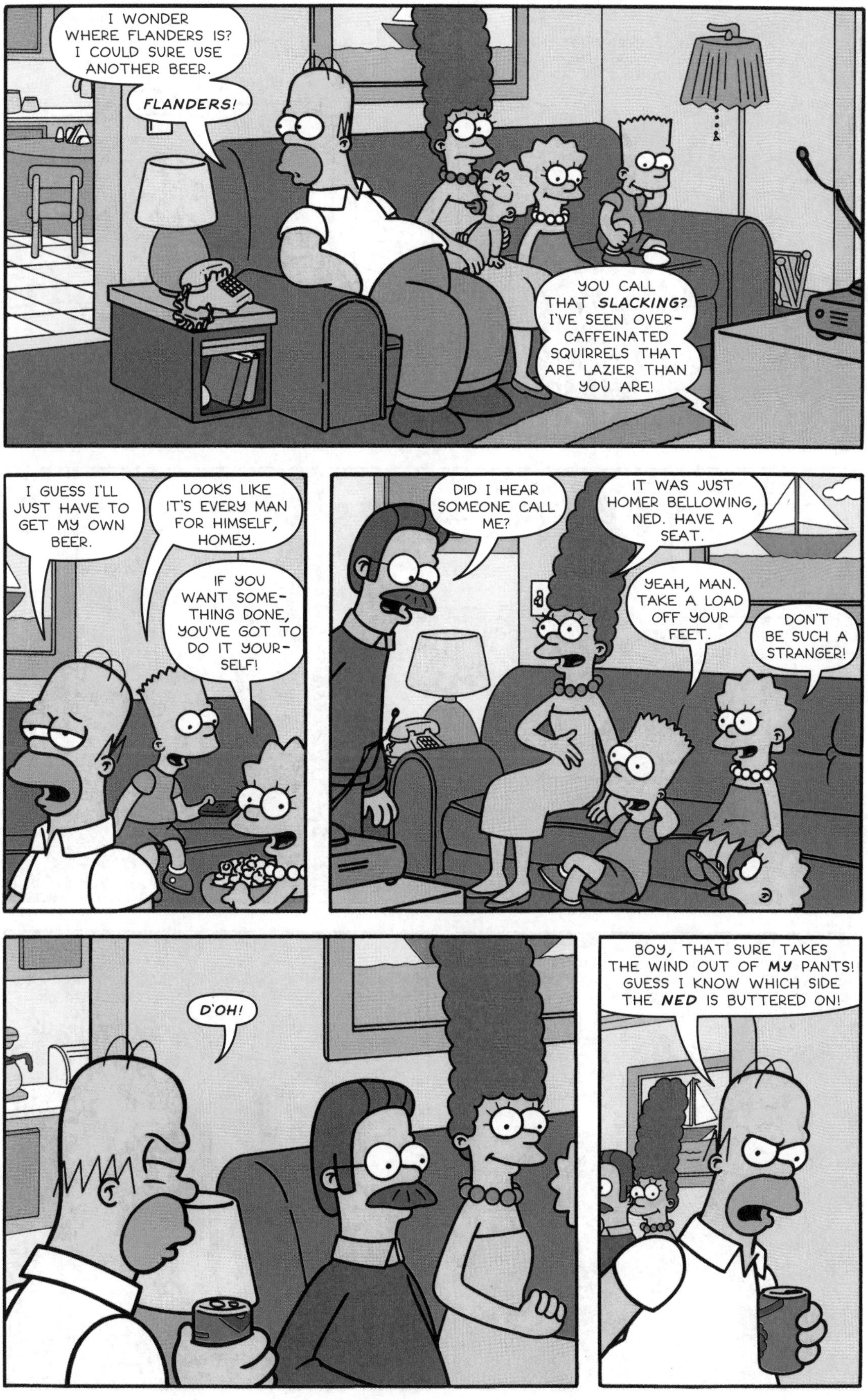
I WONDER WHERE FLANDERS IS? I COULD SURE USE ANOTHER BEER.
FLANDERS!
YOU CALL THAT SLACKING? I'VE SEEN OVER-CAFFEINATED SQUIRRELS THAT ARE LAZIER THAN YOU ARE!
I GUESS I'LL JUST HAVE TO GET MY OWN BEER.
LOOKS LIKE IT'S EVERY MAN FOR HIMSELF, HOMEY.
IF YOU WANT SOME-THING DONE, YOU'VE GOT TO DO IT YOUR-SELF!
DID I HEAR SOMEONE CALL ME?
IT WAS JUST HOMER BELLOWING, NED. HAVE A SEAT.
YEAH, MAN. TAKE A LOAD OFF YOUR FEET.
DON'T BE SUCH A STRANGER!
D'OH!
BOY, THAT SURE TAKES THE WIND OUT OF MY PANTS! GUESS I KNOW WHICH SIDE THE NED IS BUTTERED ON!

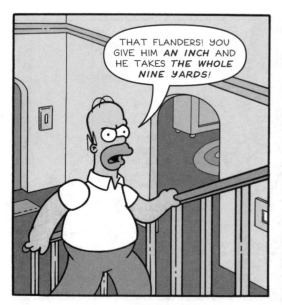

THAT FLANDERS! YOU GIVE HIM *AN INCH* AND HE TAKES *THE WHOLE NINE YARDS!*

WELL, HE ATE CRACKERS IN MY BED, AND NOW I HAVE TO LIE IN IT.

TWO WEEKS PASS AND TODD AND ROD RETURN FROM CAMP...

MY SONS! MY PRIDE AND JOY! COME! LET'S FLOCK TOGETHER LIKE BIRDS OF A FEATHER!

WE HAD A DIVINE TIME AT OLD TESTAMENT SURVIVAL CAMP!

BUT WE SURE MISSED YOU, DAD!

LOOK, DAD! I SAVED UP ALL MY SUMMER ALLOWANCE TO BUY NEW SCHOOL CLOTHES. AFTER ALL, MONEY DOESN'T GROW ON TREES!

HA HA. LIKE FATHER, LIKE SON!

AND I ATE ALL MY VEGETABLES, SO I'LL BE BIG AND STRONG LIKE YOU AND ROD. THE FLANDERS CHAIN IS ONLY AS STRONG AS ITS WEAKEST LINK, YOU KNOW!

OUT OF THE MOUTHS OF BABES! YOU BOYS ARE LIKE TWO PEAS IN A POD!

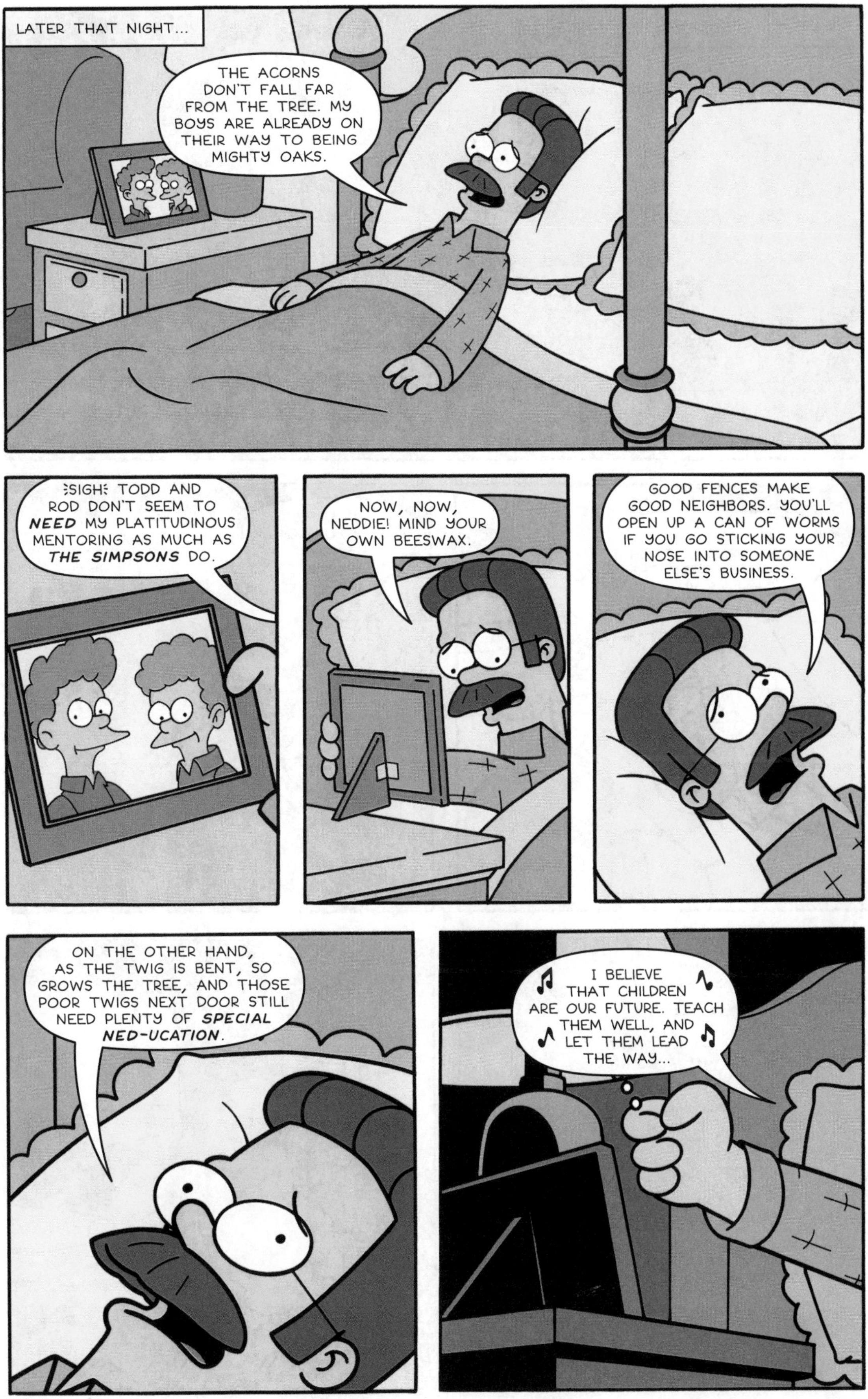
LATER THAT NIGHT...
THE ACORNS DON'T FALL FAR FROM THE TREE. MY BOYS ARE ALREADY ON THEIR WAY TO BEING MIGHTY OAKS.
:SIGH: TODD AND ROD DON'T SEEM TO **NEED** MY PLATITUDINOUS MENTORING AS MUCH AS ***THE SIMPSONS*** DO.
NOW, NOW, NEDDIE! MIND YOUR OWN BEESWAX.
GOOD FENCES MAKE GOOD NEIGHBORS. YOU'LL OPEN UP A CAN OF WORMS IF YOU GO STICKING YOUR NOSE INTO SOMEONE ELSE'S BUSINESS.
ON THE OTHER HAND, AS THE TWIG IS BENT, SO GROWS THE TREE, AND THOSE POOR TWIGS NEXT DOOR STILL NEED PLENTY OF ***SPECIAL NED-UCATION***.
♪ I BELIEVE THAT CHILDREN ARE OUR FUTURE. TEACH THEM WELL, AND LET THEM LEAD THE WAY... ♪

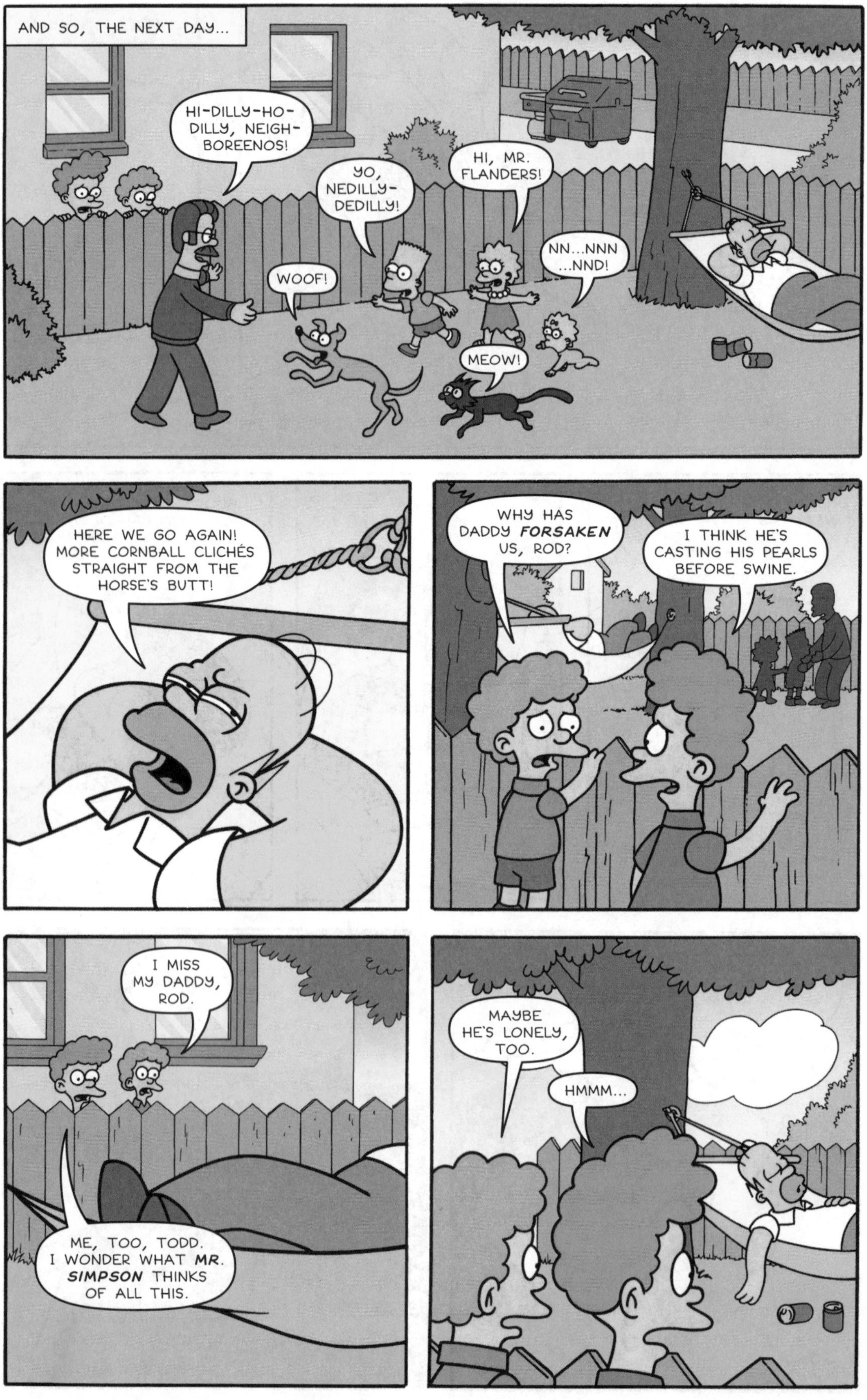

AND SO, THE NEXT DAY...
HI-DILLY-HO-DILLY, NEIGH-BOREENOS!
YO, NEDILLY-DEDILLY!
HI, MR. FLANDERS!
WOOF!
NN...NNN ...NND!
MEOW!
HERE WE GO AGAIN! MORE CORNBALL CLICHÉS STRAIGHT FROM THE HORSE'S BUTT!
WHY HAS DADDY **FORSAKEN** US, ROD?
I THINK HE'S CASTING HIS PEARLS BEFORE SWINE.
I MISS MY DADDY, ROD.
ME, TOO, TODD. I WONDER WHAT **MR. SIMPSON** THINKS OF ALL THIS.
MAYBE HE'S LONELY, TOO.
HMMM...

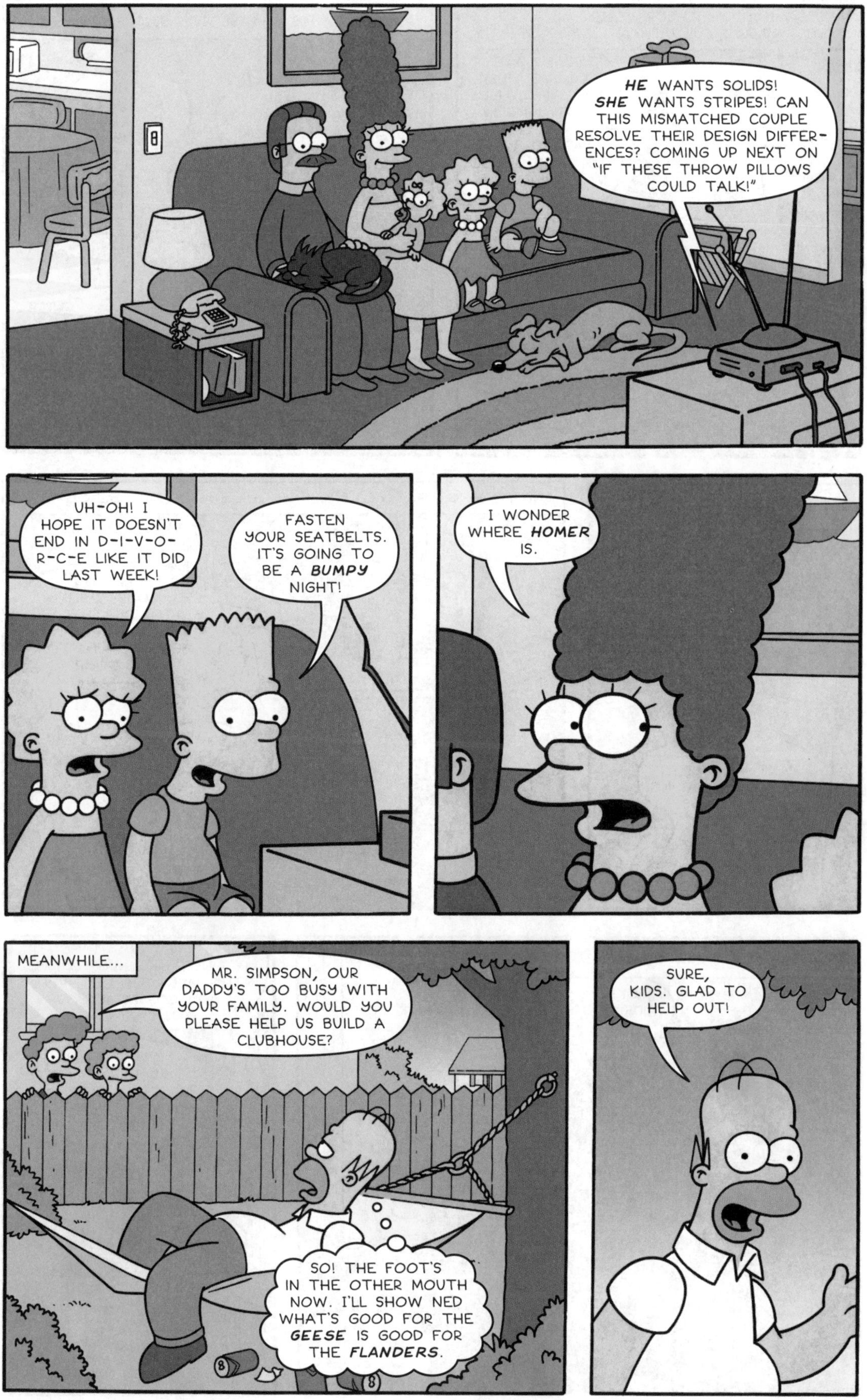
HE WANTS SOLIDS! SHE WANTS STRIPES! CAN THIS MISMATCHED COUPLE RESOLVE THEIR DESIGN DIFFERENCES? COMING UP NEXT ON "IF THESE THROW PILLOWS COULD TALK!"
UH-OH! I HOPE IT DOESN'T END IN D-I-V-O-R-C-E LIKE IT DID LAST WEEK!
FASTEN YOUR SEATBELTS. IT'S GOING TO BE A BUMPY NIGHT!
I WONDER WHERE HOMER IS.
MEANWHILE...
MR. SIMPSON, OUR DADDY'S TOO BUSY WITH YOUR FAMILY. WOULD YOU PLEASE HELP US BUILD A CLUBHOUSE?
SO! THE FOOT'S IN THE OTHER MOUTH NOW. I'LL SHOW NED WHAT'S GOOD FOR THE GEESE IS GOOD FOR THE FLANDERS.
SURE, KIDS. GLAD TO HELP OUT!

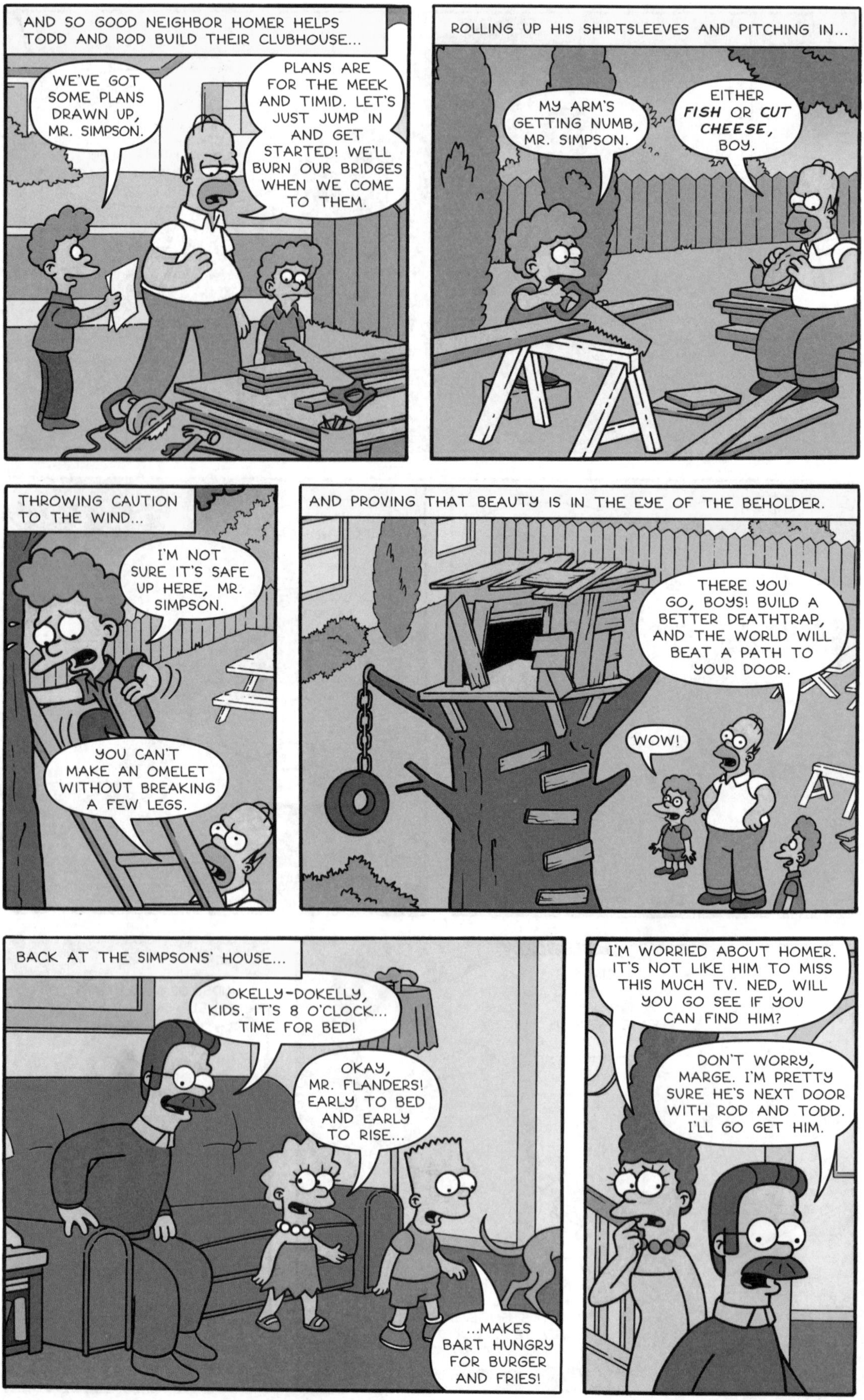
AND SO GOOD NEIGHBOR HOMER HELPS TODD AND ROD BUILD THEIR CLUBHOUSE...
WE'VE GOT SOME PLANS DRAWN UP, MR. SIMPSON.
PLANS ARE FOR THE MEEK AND TIMID. LET'S JUST JUMP IN AND GET STARTED! WE'LL BURN OUR BRIDGES WHEN WE COME TO THEM.
ROLLING UP HIS SHIRTSLEEVES AND PITCHING IN...
MY ARM'S GETTING NUMB, MR. SIMPSON.
EITHER **FISH** OR **CUT CHEESE,** BOY.
THROWING CAUTION TO THE WIND...
I'M NOT SURE IT'S SAFE UP HERE, MR. SIMPSON.
YOU CAN'T MAKE AN OMELET WITHOUT BREAKING A FEW LEGS.
AND PROVING THAT BEAUTY IS IN THE EYE OF THE BEHOLDER.
THERE YOU GO, BOYS! BUILD A BETTER DEATHTRAP, AND THE WORLD WILL BEAT A PATH TO YOUR DOOR.
WOW!
BACK AT THE SIMPSONS' HOUSE...
OKELLY-DOKELLY, KIDS. IT'S 8 O'CLOCK... TIME FOR BED!
OKAY, MR. FLANDERS! EARLY TO BED AND EARLY TO RISE...
...MAKES BART HUNGRY FOR BURGER AND FRIES!
I'M WORRIED ABOUT HOMER. IT'S NOT LIKE HIM TO MISS THIS MUCH TV. NED, WILL YOU GO SEE IF YOU CAN FIND HIM?
DON'T WORRY, MARGE. I'M PRETTY SURE HE'S NEXT DOOR WITH ROD AND TODD. I'LL GO GET HIM.

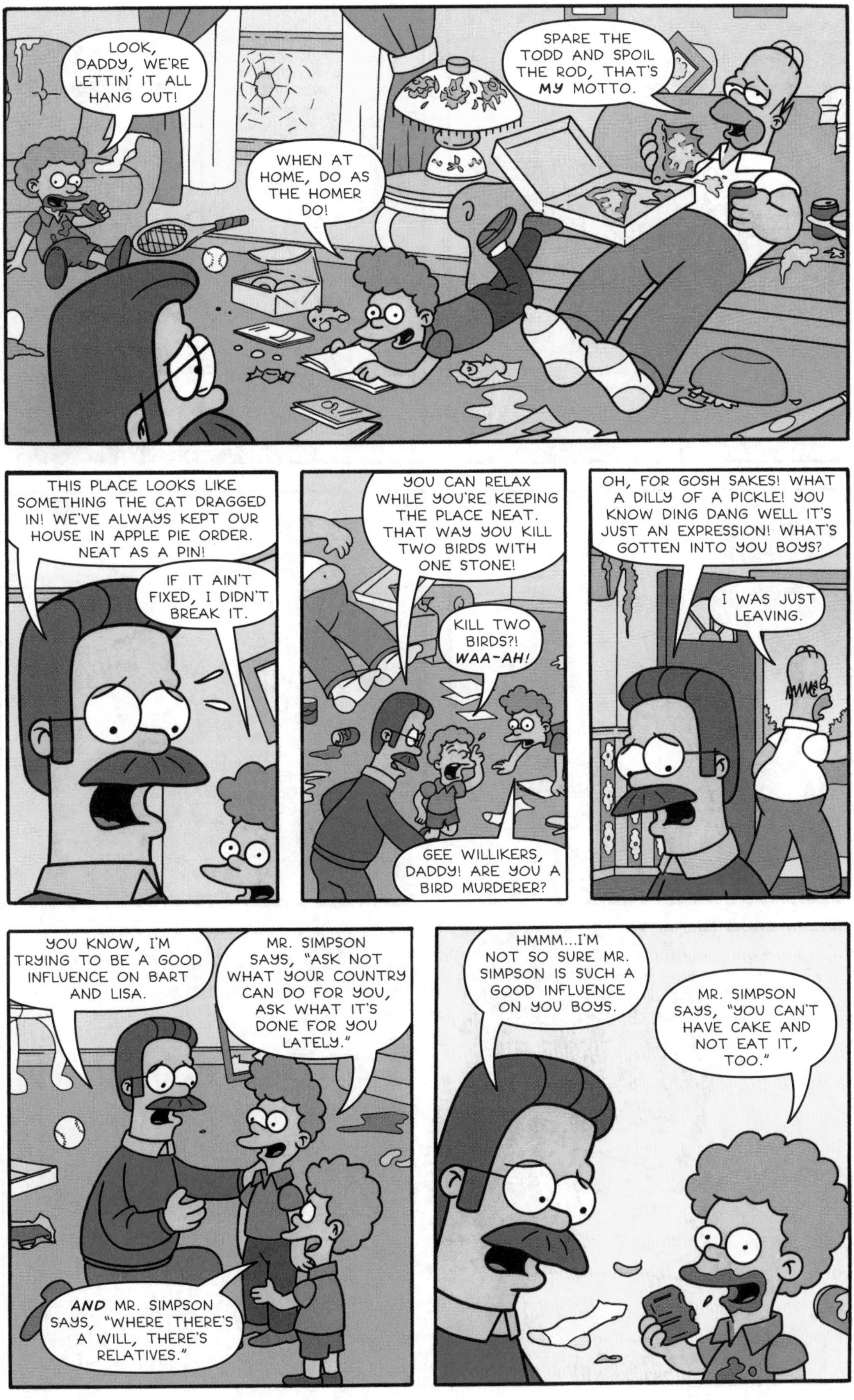
LOOK, DADDY, WE'RE LETTIN' IT ALL HANG OUT!
WHEN AT HOME, DO AS THE HOMER DO!
SPARE THE TODD AND SPOIL THE ROD, THAT'S MY MOTTO.
THIS PLACE LOOKS LIKE SOMETHING THE CAT DRAGGED IN! WE'VE ALWAYS KEPT OUR HOUSE IN APPLE PIE ORDER. NEAT AS A PIN!
IF IT AIN'T FIXED, I DIDN'T BREAK IT.
YOU CAN RELAX WHILE YOU'RE KEEPING THE PLACE NEAT. THAT WAY YOU KILL TWO BIRDS WITH ONE STONE!
KILL TWO BIRDS?! WAA-AH!
GEE WILLIKERS, DADDY! ARE YOU A BIRD MURDERER?
OH, FOR GOSH SAKES! WHAT A DILLY OF A PICKLE! YOU KNOW DING DANG WELL IT'S JUST AN EXPRESSION! WHAT'S GOTTEN INTO YOU BOYS?
I WAS JUST LEAVING.
YOU KNOW, I'M TRYING TO BE A GOOD INFLUENCE ON BART AND LISA.
MR. SIMPSON SAYS, "ASK NOT WHAT YOUR COUNTRY CAN DO FOR YOU, ASK WHAT IT'S DONE FOR YOU LATELY."
AND MR. SIMPSON SAYS, "WHERE THERE'S A WILL, THERE'S RELATIVES."
HMMM...I'M NOT SO SURE MR. SIMPSON IS SUCH A GOOD INFLUENCE ON YOU BOYS.
MR. SIMPSON SAYS, "YOU CAN'T HAVE CAKE AND NOT EAT IT, TOO."

LATER THAT NIGHT...

MR. SIMPSON SAYS, "IT'S ALWAYS DARKEST JUST BEFORE DAYLIGHT SAVINGS TIME."

MR. SIMPSON SAYS, "PEOPLE WHO LIVE IN GLASS HOUSES SHOULDN'T WALK AROUND IN THEIR UNDERWEAR."

≡SIGH≡ LITTLE PITCHERS HAVE SUCH BIG EARS.

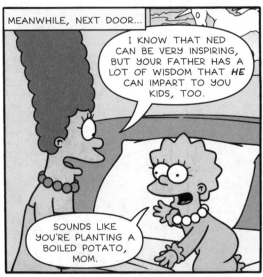

MEANWHILE, NEXT DOOR...

I KNOW THAT NED CAN BE VERY INSPIRING, BUT YOUR FATHER HAS A LOT OF WISDOM THAT *HE* CAN IMPART TO YOU KIDS, TOO.

SOUNDS LIKE YOU'RE PLANTING A BOILED POTATO, MOM.

I KNOW THAT NED IS ONLY TRYING TO BE A GOOD INFLUENCE ON YOU AND LISA, BUT HE'S JUST YOUR NEIGHBOR...HE'S NOT YOUR FATHER.

DON'T LOOK A GIFT HORSE IN THE MOUTH, MOM.

THAT DOES IT.

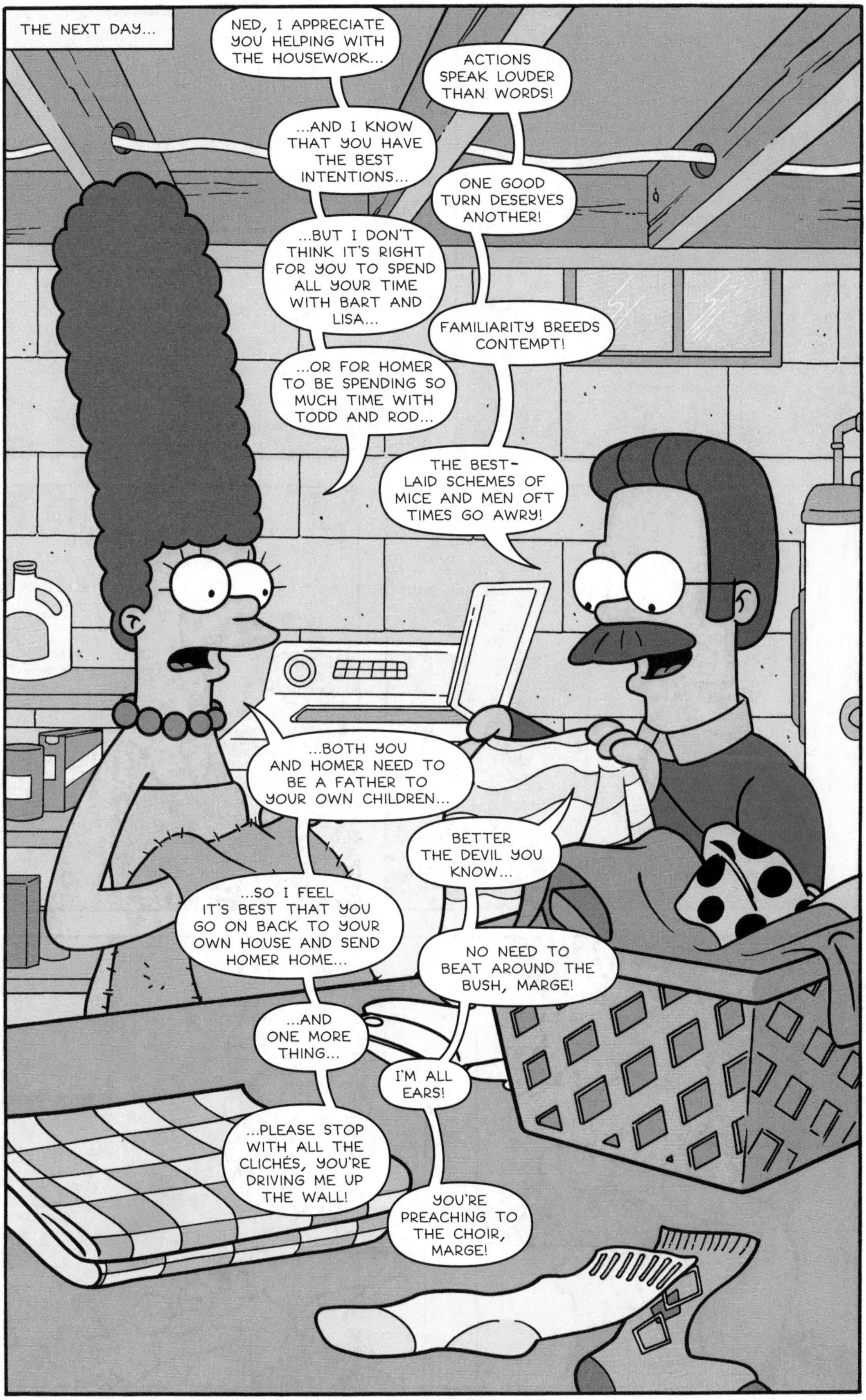
THE NEXT DAY...
NED, I APPRECIATE YOU HELPING WITH THE HOUSEWORK...
...AND I KNOW THAT YOU HAVE THE BEST INTENTIONS...
...BUT I DON'T THINK IT'S RIGHT FOR YOU TO SPEND ALL YOUR TIME WITH BART AND LISA...
...OR FOR HOMER TO BE SPENDING SO MUCH TIME WITH TODD AND ROD...
ACTIONS SPEAK LOUDER THAN WORDS!
ONE GOOD TURN DESERVES ANOTHER!
FAMILIARITY BREEDS CONTEMPT!
THE BEST-LAID SCHEMES OF MICE AND MEN OFT TIMES GO AWRY!
...BOTH YOU AND HOMER NEED TO BE A FATHER TO YOUR OWN CHILDREN...
BETTER THE DEVIL YOU KNOW...
...SO I FEEL IT'S BEST THAT YOU GO ON BACK TO YOUR OWN HOUSE AND SEND HOMER HOME...
NO NEED TO BEAT AROUND THE BUSH, MARGE!
...AND ONE MORE THING...
I'M ALL EARS!
...PLEASE STOP WITH ALL THE CLICHÉS, YOU'RE DRIVING ME UP THE WALL!
YOU'RE PREACHING TO THE CHOIR, MARGE!

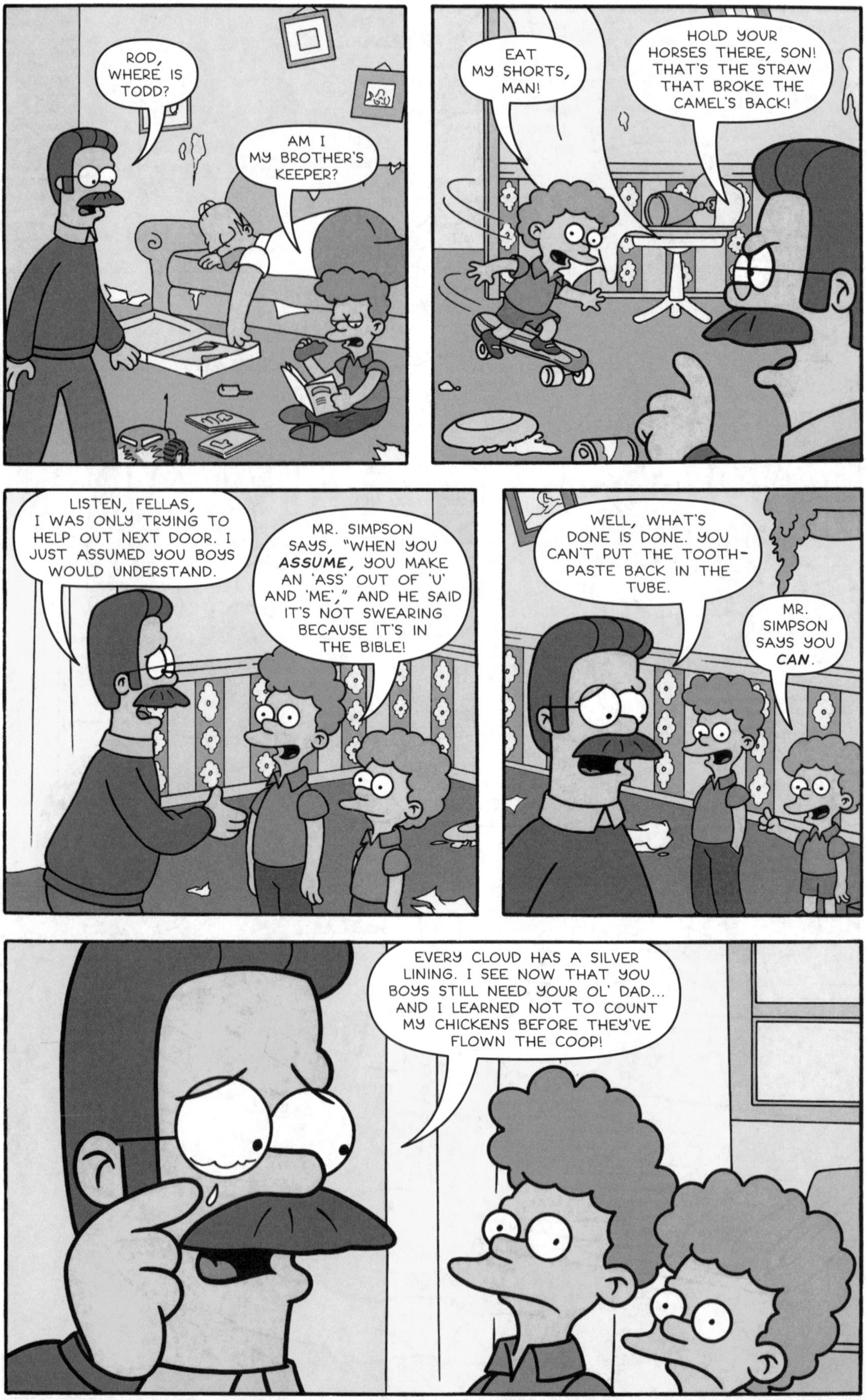
ROD, WHERE IS TODD?
AM I MY BROTHER'S KEEPER?
EAT MY SHORTS, MAN!
HOLD YOUR HORSES THERE, SON! THAT'S THE STRAW THAT BROKE THE CAMEL'S BACK!
LISTEN, FELLAS, I WAS ONLY TRYING TO HELP OUT NEXT DOOR. I JUST ASSUMED YOU BOYS WOULD UNDERSTAND.
MR. SIMPSON SAYS, "WHEN YOU ***ASSUME***, YOU MAKE AN 'ASS' OUT OF 'U' AND 'ME'," AND HE SAID IT'S NOT SWEARING BECAUSE IT'S IN THE BIBLE!
WELL, WHAT'S DONE IS DONE. YOU CAN'T PUT THE TOOTH-PASTE BACK IN THE TUBE.
MR. SIMPSON SAYS YOU ***CAN***.
EVERY CLOUD HAS A SILVER LINING. I SEE NOW THAT YOU BOYS STILL NEED YOUR OL' DAD... AND I LEARNED NOT TO COUNT MY CHICKENS BEFORE THEY'VE FLOWN THE COOP!

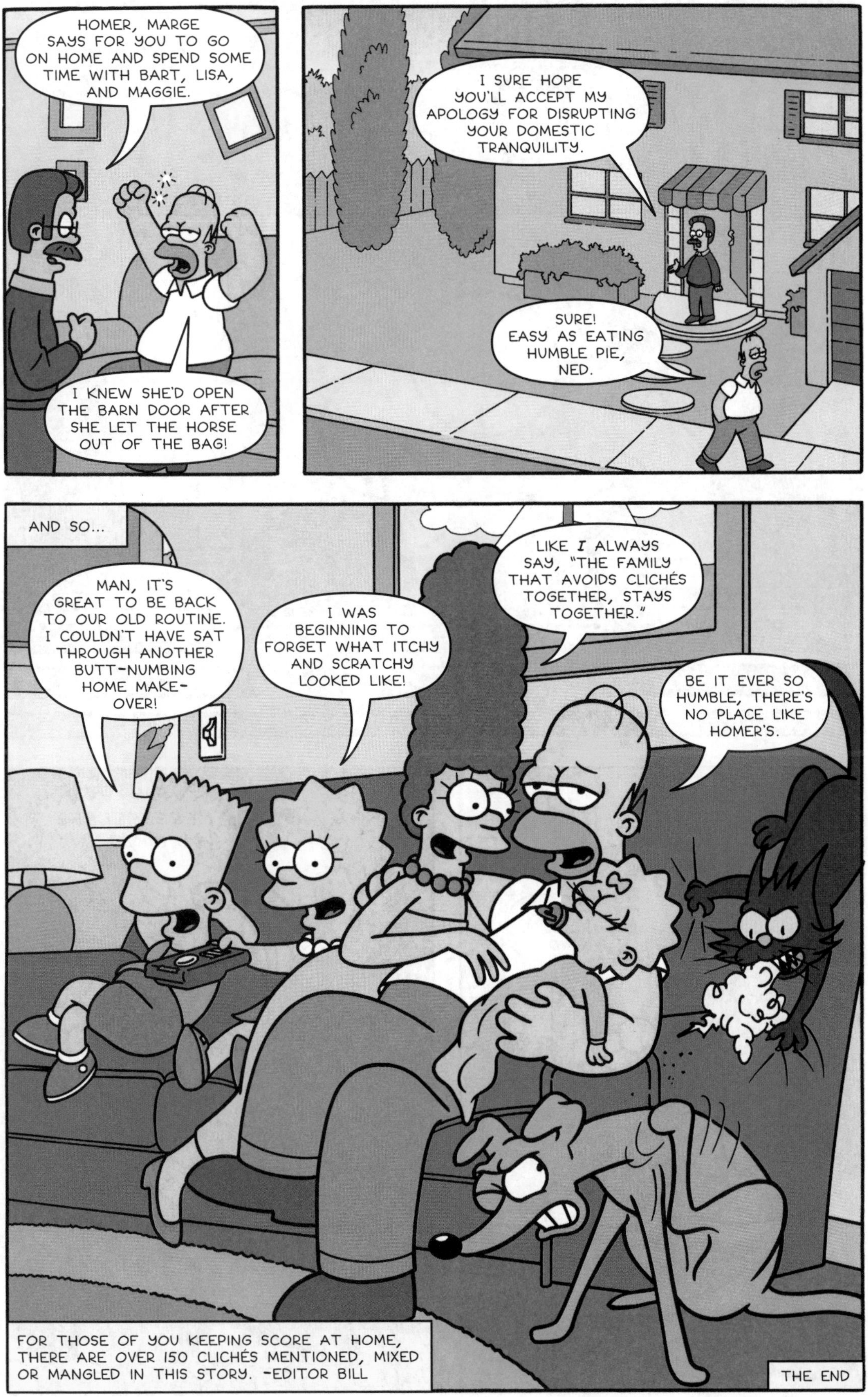
HOMER, MARGE SAYS FOR YOU TO GO ON HOME AND SPEND SOME TIME WITH BART, LISA, AND MAGGIE.
I KNEW SHE'D OPEN THE BARN DOOR AFTER SHE LET THE HORSE OUT OF THE BAG!
I SURE HOPE YOU'LL ACCEPT MY APOLOGY FOR DISRUPTING YOUR DOMESTIC TRANQUILITY.
SURE! EASY AS EATING HUMBLE PIE, NED.
AND SO...
MAN, IT'S GREAT TO BE BACK TO OUR OLD ROUTINE. I COULDN'T HAVE SAT THROUGH ANOTHER BUTT-NUMBING HOME MAKE-OVER!
I WAS BEGINNING TO FORGET WHAT ITCHY AND SCRATCHY LOOKED LIKE!
LIKE *I* ALWAYS SAY, "THE FAMILY THAT AVOIDS CLICHÉS TOGETHER, STAYS TOGETHER."
BE IT EVER SO HUMBLE, THERE'S NO PLACE LIKE HOMER'S.
FOR THOSE OF YOU KEEPING SCORE AT HOME, THERE ARE OVER 150 CLICHÉS MENTIONED, MIXED OR MANGLED IN THIS STORY. -EDITOR BILL
THE END

MATT GROENING presents

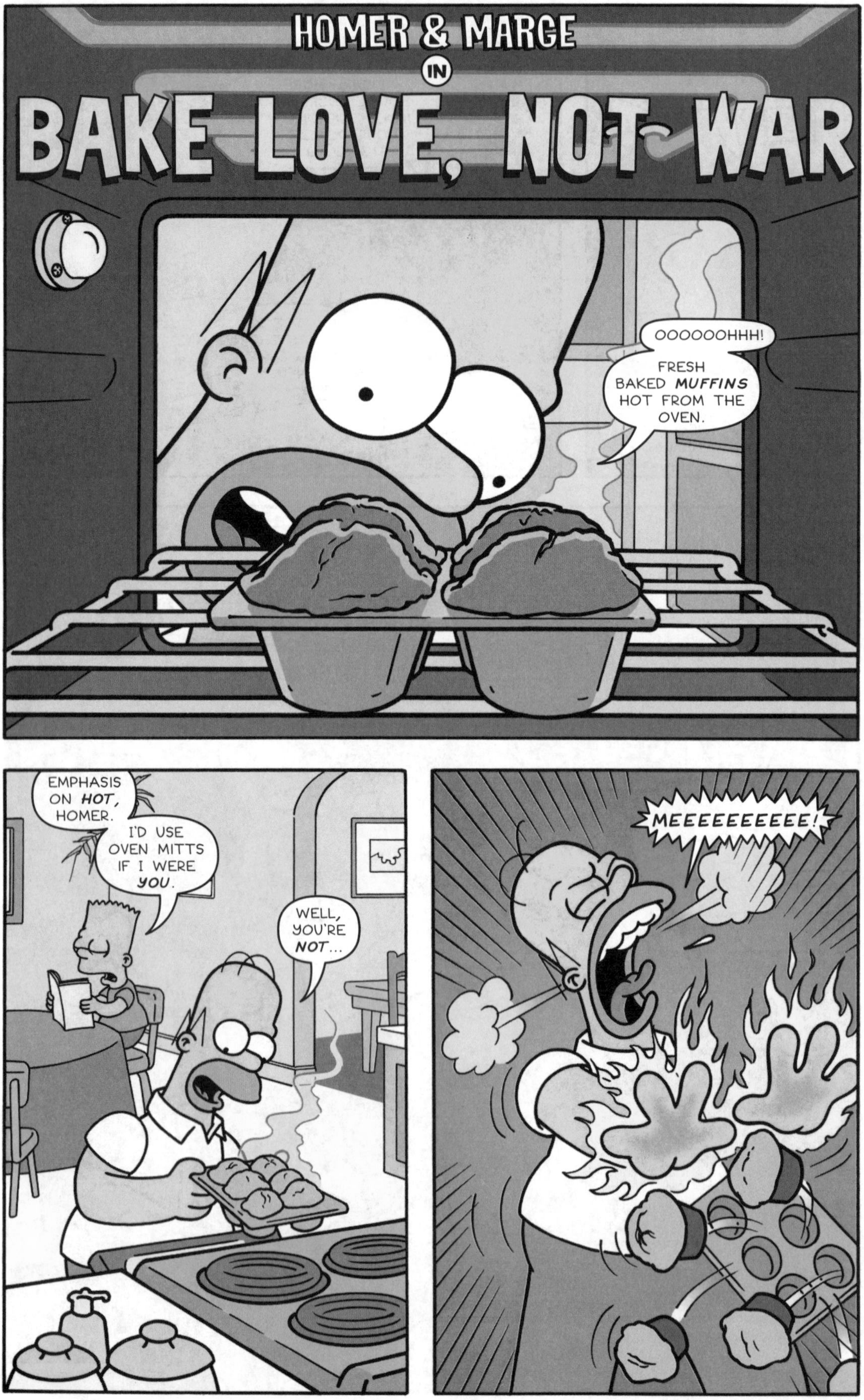
HOMER & MARGE
IN
BAKE LOVE, NOT WAR
OOOOOOHHH!
FRESH BAKED MUFFINS HOT FROM THE OVEN.
EMPHASIS ON HOT, HOMER.
I'D USE OVEN MITTS IF I WERE YOU.
WELL, YOU'RE NOT...
MEEEEEEEEEE!

CHUCK DIXON SCRIPT | *JOHN COSTANZA* PENCILS | *PHYLLIS NOVIN* INKS | *ART VILLANUEVA* COLORS | *KAREN BATES* LETTERS | *BILL MORRISON* EDITOR

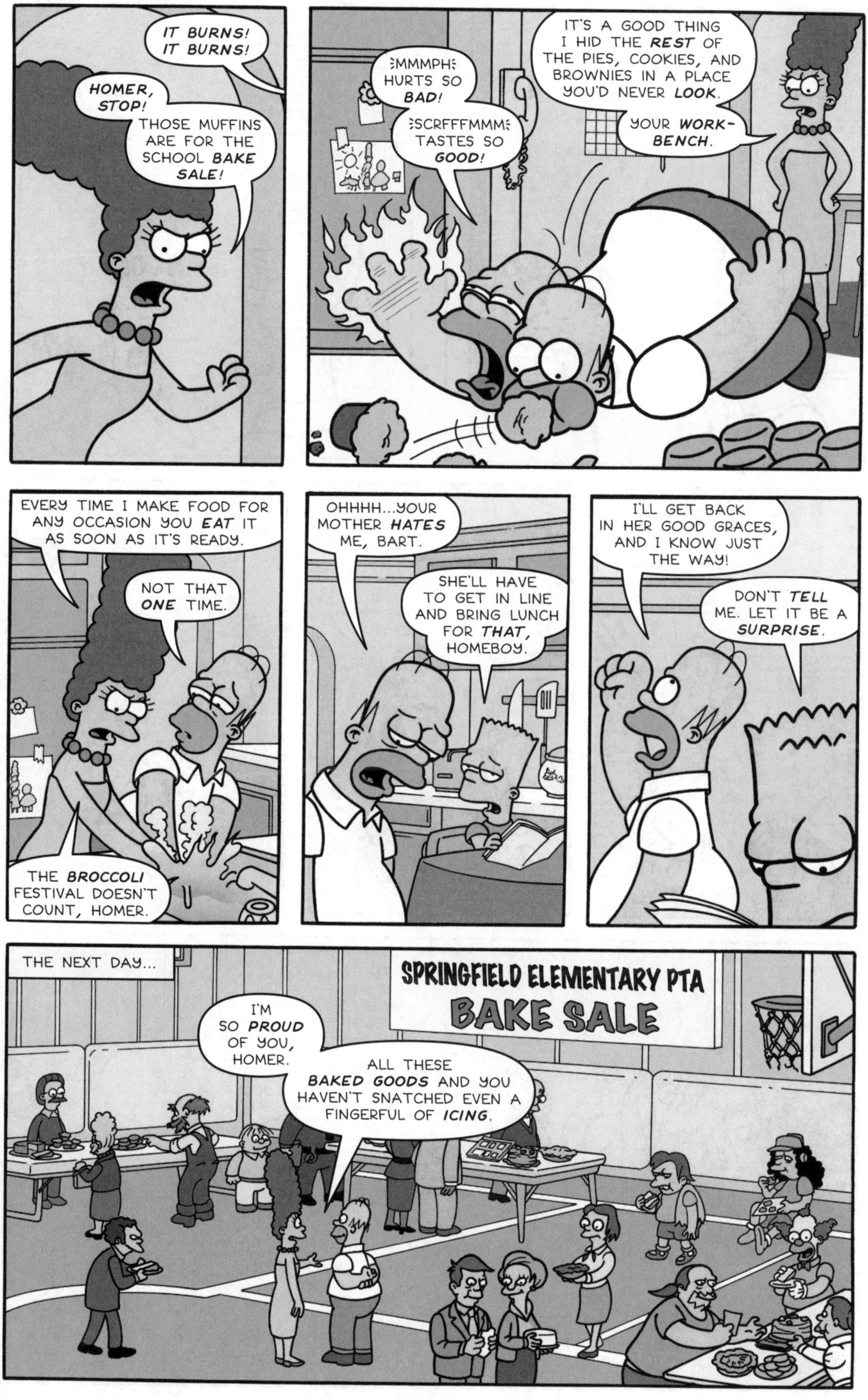
IT BURNS! IT BURNS!
HOMER, STOP!
THOSE MUFFINS ARE FOR THE SCHOOL BAKE SALE!
MMMPH HURTS SO BAD!
SCRFFFMMM TASTES SO GOOD!
IT'S A GOOD THING I HID THE REST OF THE PIES, COOKIES, AND BROWNIES IN A PLACE YOU'D NEVER LOOK.
YOUR WORK-BENCH.
EVERY TIME I MAKE FOOD FOR ANY OCCASION YOU EAT IT AS SOON AS IT'S READY.
NOT THAT ONE TIME.
THE BROCCOLI FESTIVAL DOESN'T COUNT, HOMER.
OHHHH...YOUR MOTHER HATES ME, BART.
SHE'LL HAVE TO GET IN LINE AND BRING LUNCH FOR THAT, HOMEBOY.
I'LL GET BACK IN HER GOOD GRACES, AND I KNOW JUST THE WAY!
DON'T TELL ME. LET IT BE A SURPRISE.
THE NEXT DAY...
SPRINGFIELD ELEMENTARY PTA
BAKE SALE
I'M SO PROUD OF YOU, HOMER.
ALL THESE BAKED GOODS AND YOU HAVEN'T SNATCHED EVEN A FINGERFUL OF ICING.

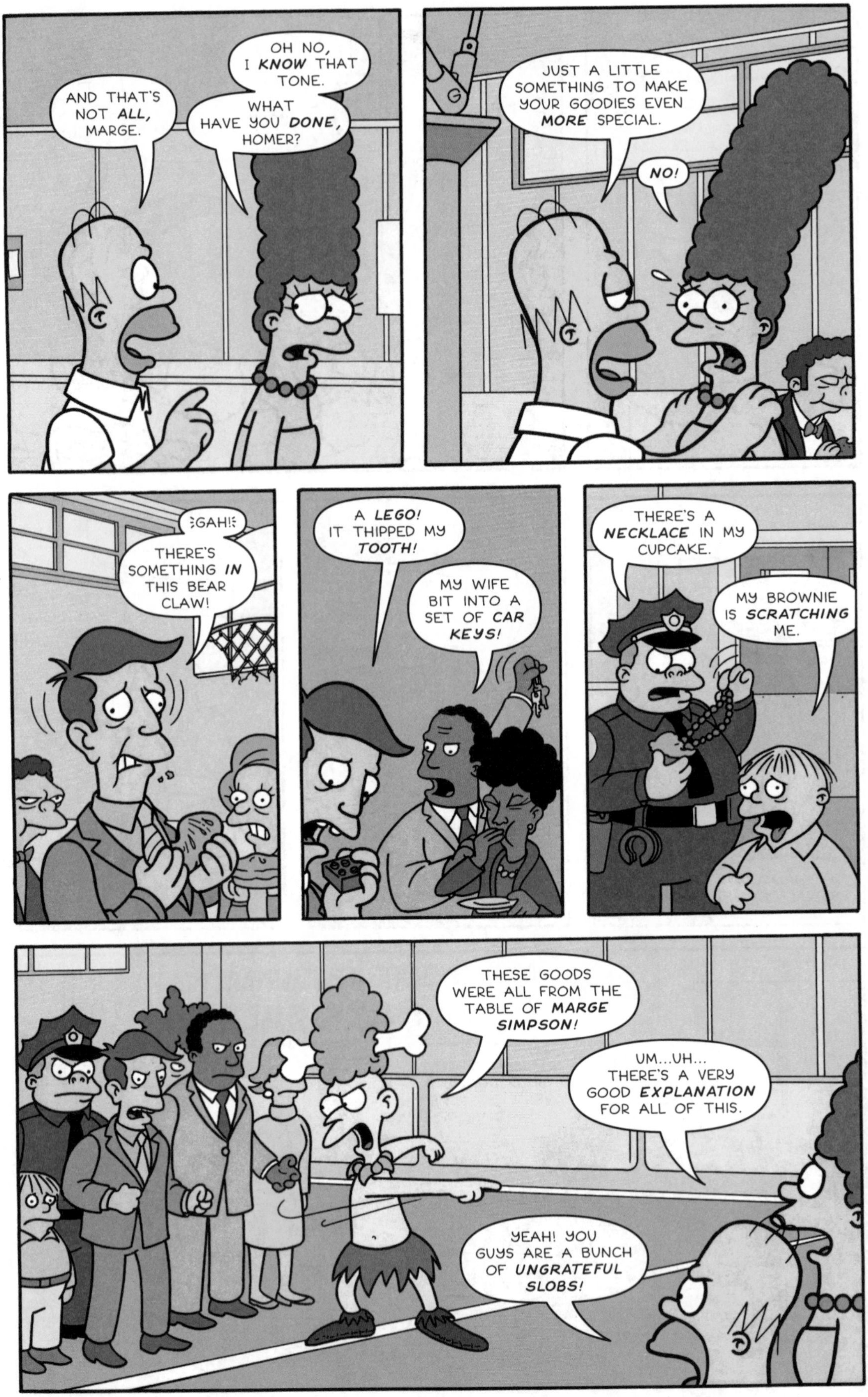
AND THAT'S NOT ALL, MARGE.
OH NO, I KNOW THAT TONE.
WHAT HAVE YOU DONE, HOMER?
JUST A LITTLE SOMETHING TO MAKE YOUR GOODIES EVEN MORE SPECIAL.
NO!
GAH!
THERE'S SOMETHING IN THIS BEAR CLAW!
A LEGO! IT THIPPED MY TOOTH!
MY WIFE BIT INTO A SET OF CAR KEYS!
THERE'S A NECKLACE IN MY CUPCAKE.
MY BROWNIE IS SCRATCHING ME.
THESE GOODS WERE ALL FROM THE TABLE OF MARGE SIMPSON!
UM...UH... THERE'S A VERY GOOD EXPLANATION FOR ALL OF THIS.
YEAH! YOU GUYS ARE A BUNCH OF UNGRATEFUL SLOBS!

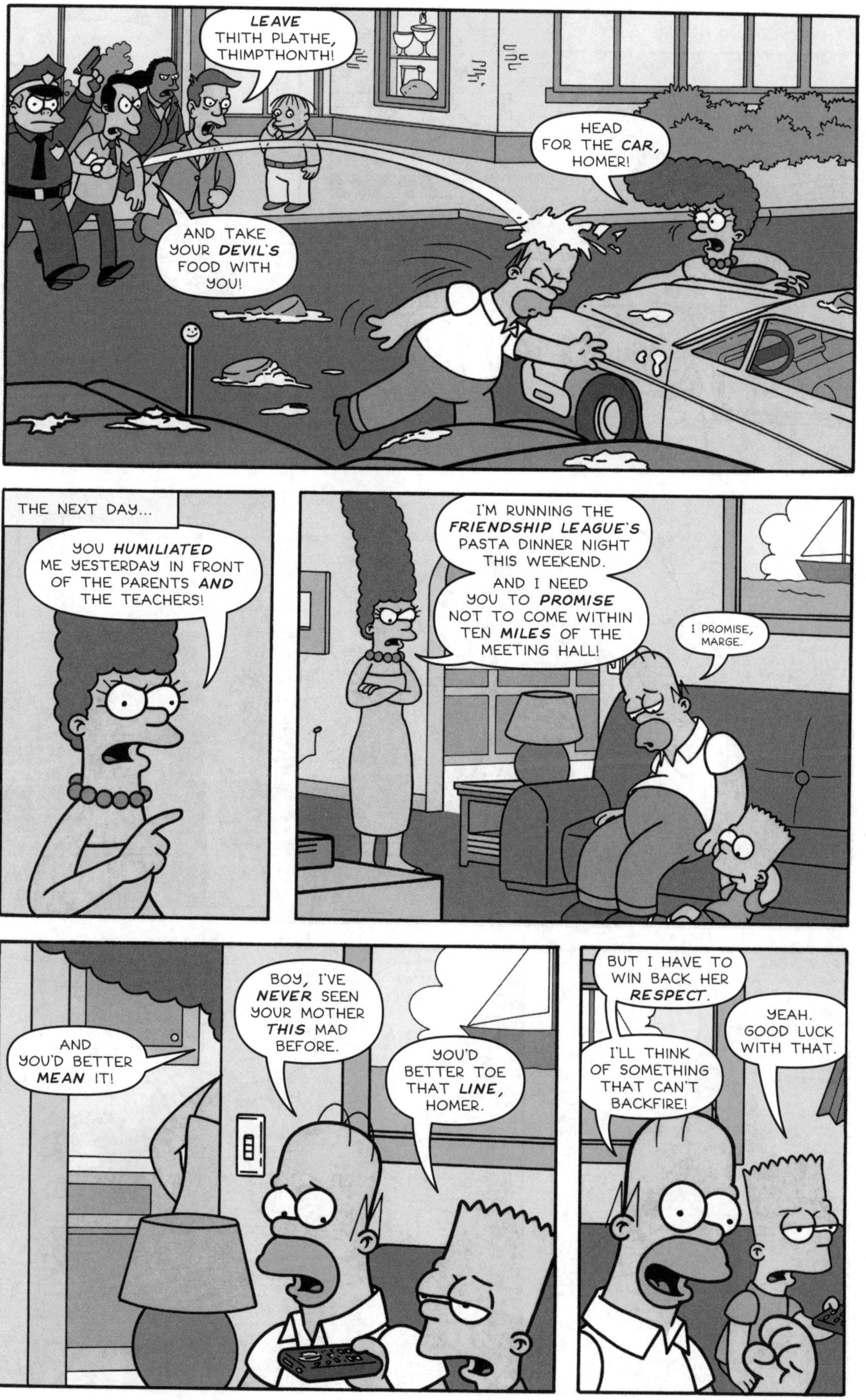
LEAVE THITH PLATHE, THIMPTHONTH!
AND TAKE YOUR DEVIL'S FOOD WITH YOU!
HEAD FOR THE CAR, HOMER!
THE NEXT DAY...
YOU HUMILIATED ME YESTERDAY IN FRONT OF THE PARENTS AND THE TEACHERS!
I'M RUNNING THE FRIENDSHIP LEAGUE'S PASTA DINNER NIGHT THIS WEEKEND.
AND I NEED YOU TO PROMISE NOT TO COME WITHIN TEN MILES OF THE MEETING HALL!
I PROMISE, MARGE.
AND YOU'D BETTER MEAN IT!
BOY, I'VE NEVER SEEN YOUR MOTHER THIS MAD BEFORE.
YOU'D BETTER TOE THAT LINE, HOMER.
BUT I HAVE TO WIN BACK HER RESPECT.
I'LL THINK OF SOMETHING THAT CAN'T BACKFIRE!
YEAH. GOOD LUCK WITH THAT.

THAT WEEKEND AT THE MEETING HALL...

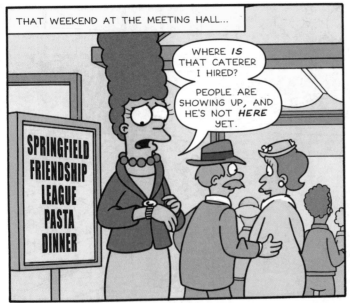

WHERE *IS* THAT CATERER I HIRED?

PEOPLE ARE SHOWING UP, AND HE'S NOT *HERE* YET.

SPRINGFIELD FRIENDSHIP LEAGUE PASTA DINNER

SIGNORS AND SIGNORINIS!

NO...

IT'S-A YOUR OLD-A PAISANO, *SPAGHETTI JOE!*

HERE TO SERVE-A YOU SOME-A *HOT AND SPICY MEATBALLS!*

PASTAFAZOOL! HE'S-A AN ETHNIC *STEREOTYPE!*

SOMEBODY SHOULD TAKE THAT LOUSE FOR A *RIDE.*

IT'S PLUMB PO-LITICALLY *ON*CORRECT, I RECKON!

HOMER! HOW *COULD* YOU?

WELL, RENTING THE *MONKEY* WASN'T AS HARD AS I THOUGHT.

BUT I WAS UP ALL *NIGHT* SEWING HIS GONDOLIER OUTFIT.

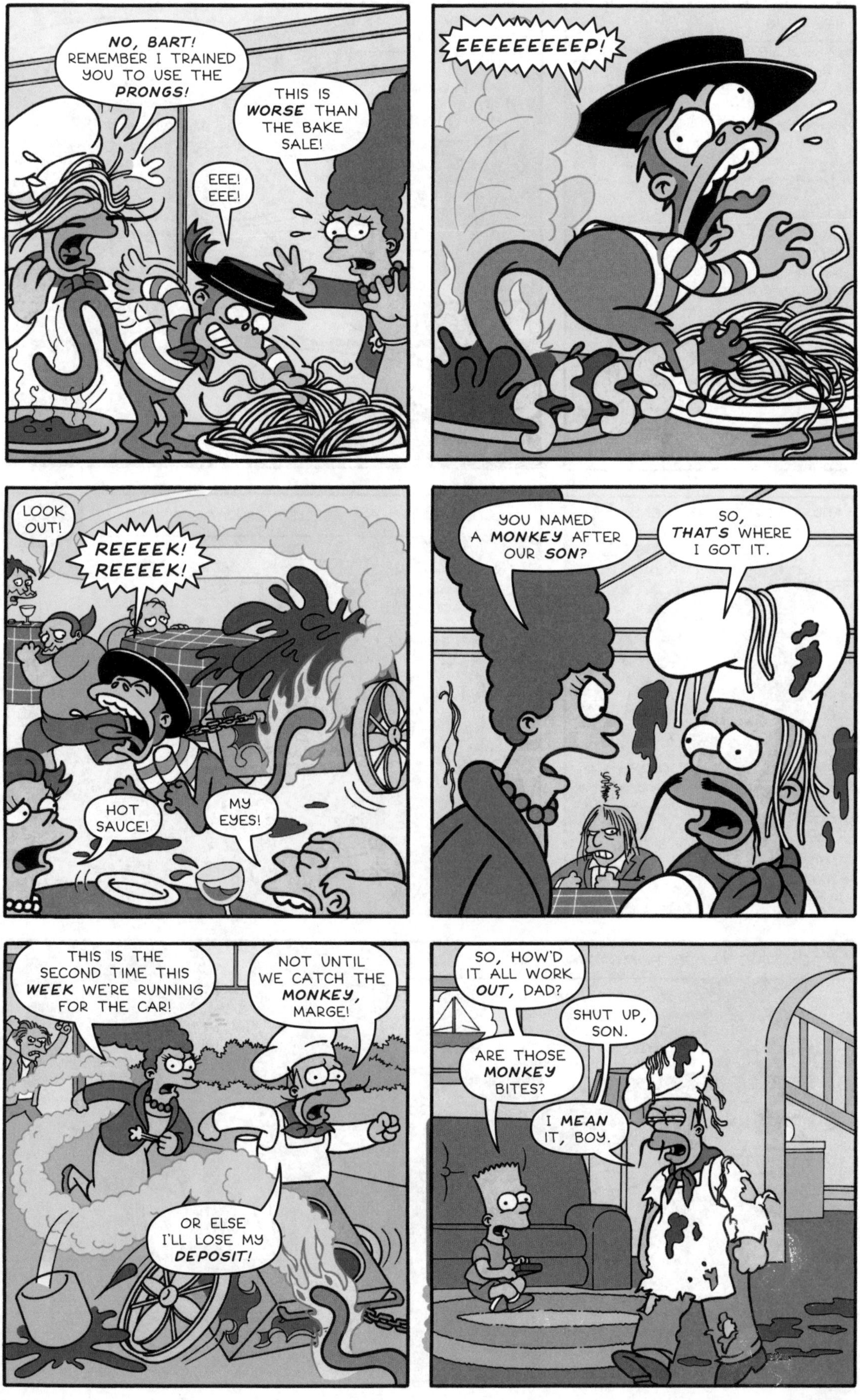
NO, BART! REMEMBER I TRAINED YOU TO USE THE PRONGS!
THIS IS WORSE THAN THE BAKE SALE!
EEE! EEE!
EEEEEEEEEP!
SSSSS
LOOK OUT!
REEEEK! REEEEK!
HOT SAUCE!
MY EYES!
YOU NAMED A MONKEY AFTER OUR SON?
SO, THAT'S WHERE I GOT IT.
THIS IS THE SECOND TIME THIS WEEK WE'RE RUNNING FOR THE CAR!
NOT UNTIL WE CATCH THE MONKEY, MARGE!
OR ELSE I'LL LOSE MY DEPOSIT!
SO, HOW'D IT ALL WORK OUT, DAD?
ARE THOSE MONKEY BITES?
SHUT UP, SON.
I MEAN IT, BOY.

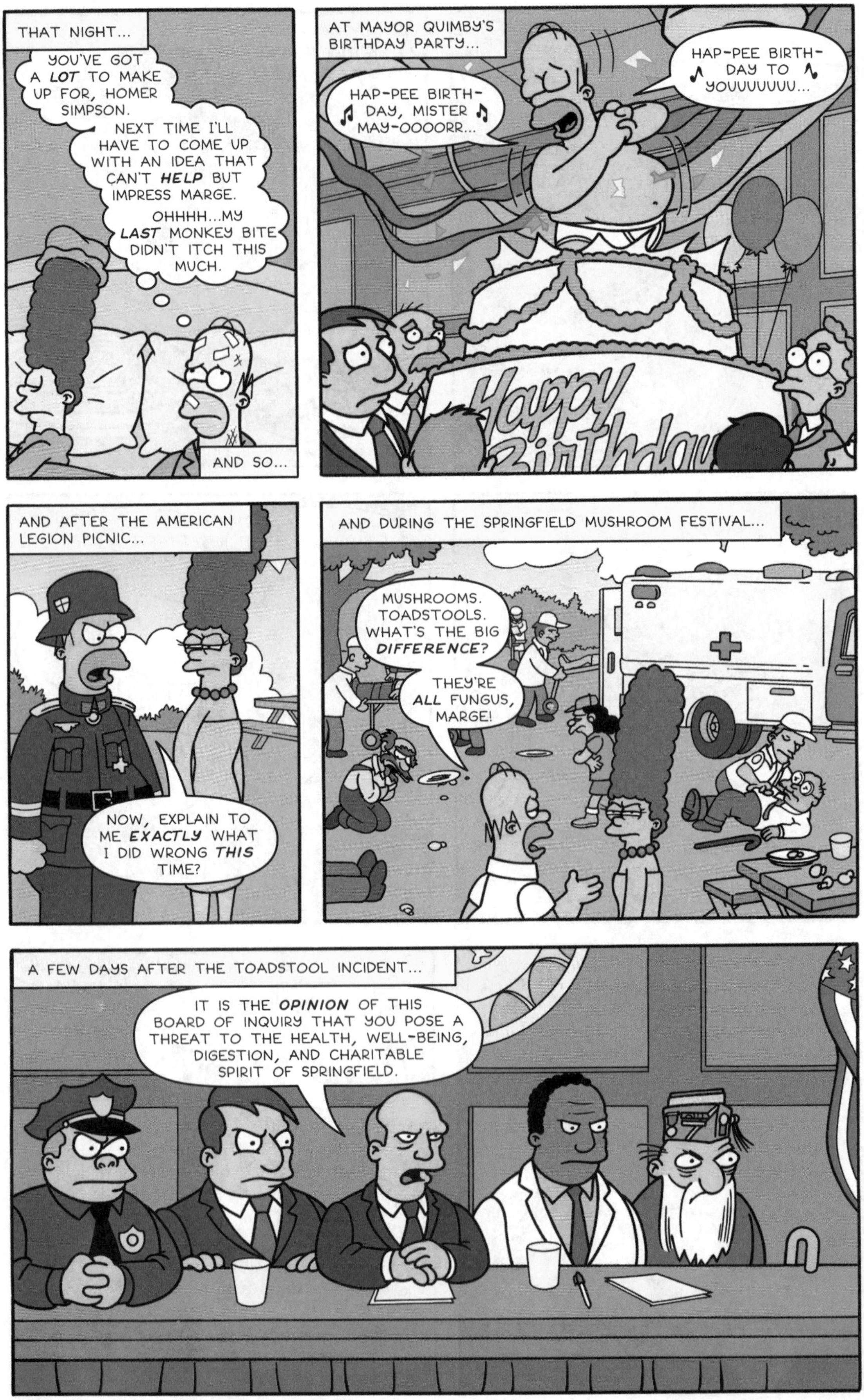
THAT NIGHT...
YOU'VE GOT A LOT TO MAKE UP FOR, HOMER SIMPSON.
NEXT TIME I'LL HAVE TO COME UP WITH AN IDEA THAT CAN'T HELP BUT IMPRESS MARGE.
OHHHH...MY LAST MONKEY BITE DIDN'T ITCH THIS MUCH.
AND SO...
AT MAYOR QUIMBY'S BIRTHDAY PARTY...
HAP-PEE BIRTH-DAY, MISTER MAY-OOOORR...
HAP-PEE BIRTH-DAY TO YOUUUUUUU...
Happy
AND AFTER THE AMERICAN LEGION PICNIC...
NOW, EXPLAIN TO ME EXACTLY WHAT I DID WRONG THIS TIME?
AND DURING THE SPRINGFIELD MUSHROOM FESTIVAL...
MUSHROOMS. TOADSTOOLS. WHAT'S THE BIG DIFFERENCE?
THEY'RE ALL FUNGUS, MARGE!
A FEW DAYS AFTER THE TOADSTOOL INCIDENT...
IT IS THE OPINION OF THIS BOARD OF INQUIRY THAT YOU POSE A THREAT TO THE HEALTH, WELL-BEING, DIGESTION, AND CHARITABLE SPIRIT OF SPRINGFIELD.

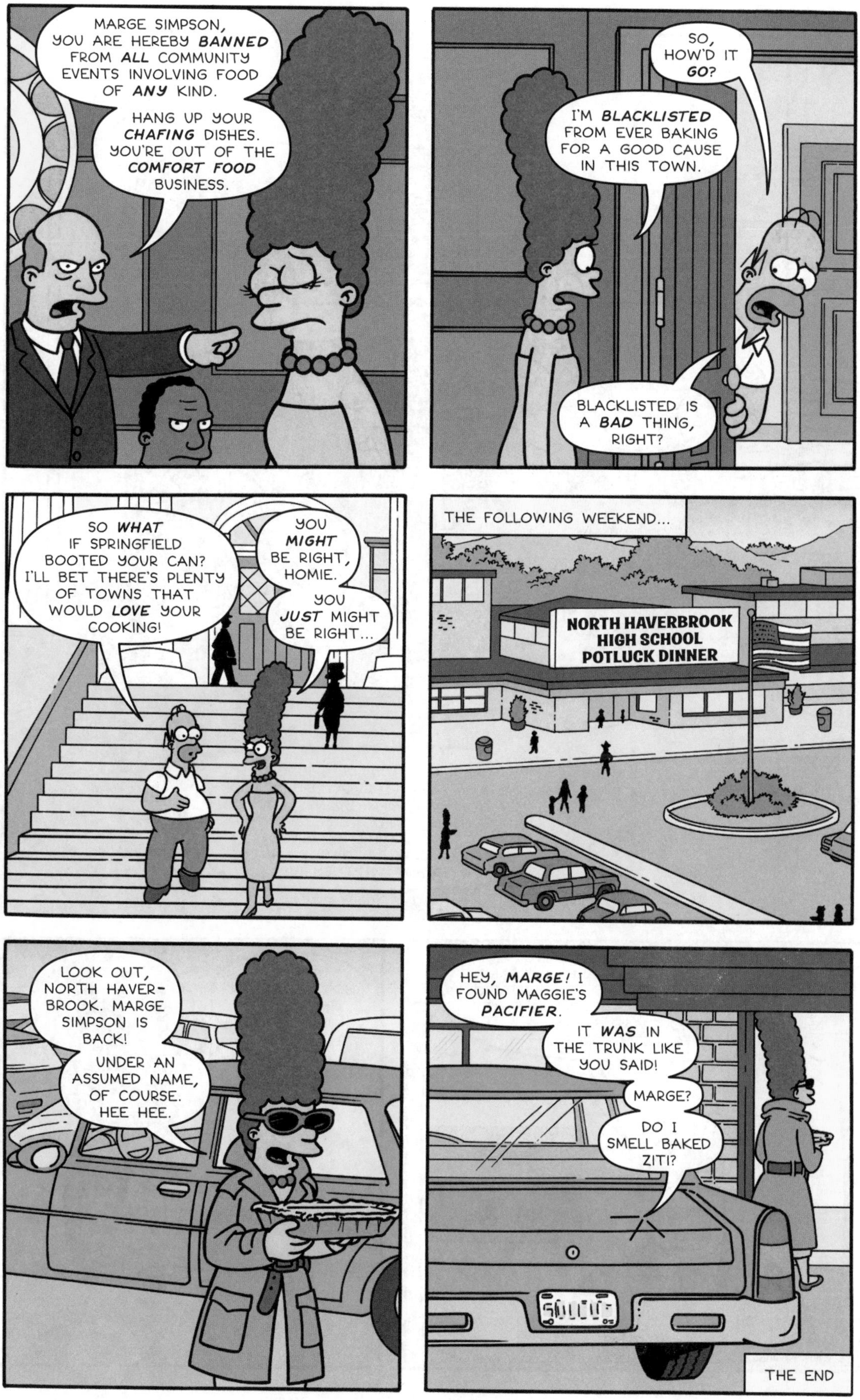
MARGE SIMPSON, YOU ARE HEREBY BANNED FROM ALL COMMUNITY EVENTS INVOLVING FOOD OF ANY KIND.
HANG UP YOUR CHAFING DISHES. YOU'RE OUT OF THE COMFORT FOOD BUSINESS.
SO, HOW'D IT GO?
I'M BLACKLISTED FROM EVER BAKING FOR A GOOD CAUSE IN THIS TOWN.
BLACKLISTED IS A BAD THING, RIGHT?
SO WHAT IF SPRINGFIELD BOOTED YOUR CAN? I'LL BET THERE'S PLENTY OF TOWNS THAT WOULD LOVE YOUR COOKING!
YOU MIGHT BE RIGHT, HOMIE.
YOU JUST MIGHT BE RIGHT...
THE FOLLOWING WEEKEND...
NORTH HAVERBROOK HIGH SCHOOL POTLUCK DINNER
LOOK OUT, NORTH HAVER-BROOK. MARGE SIMPSON IS BACK!
UNDER AN ASSUMED NAME, OF COURSE. HEE HEE.
HEY, MARGE! I FOUND MAGGIE'S PACIFIER.
IT WAS IN THE TRUNK LIKE YOU SAID!
MARGE?
DO I SMELL BAKED ZITI?
THE END

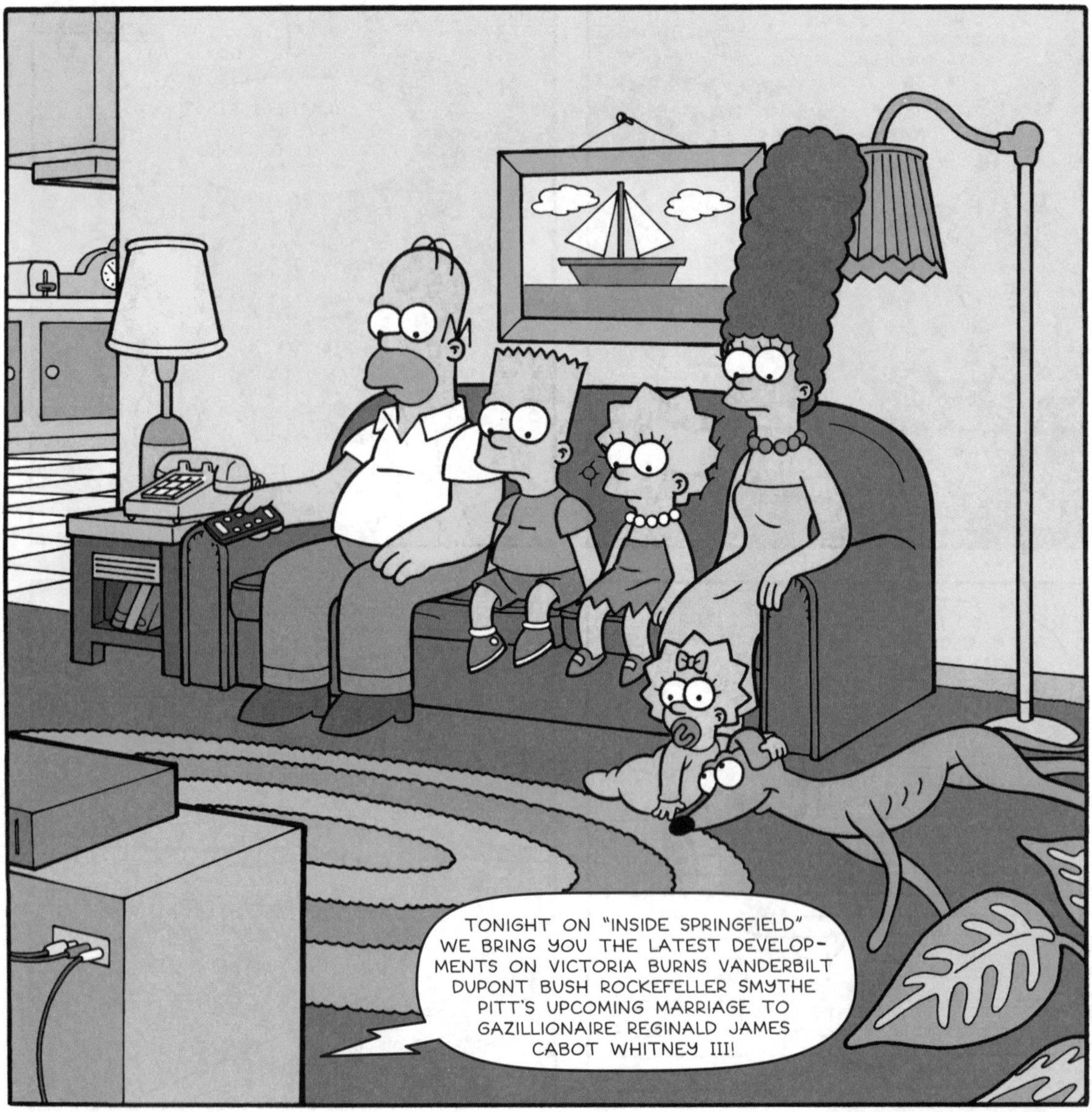
TONIGHT ON "INSIDE SPRINGFIELD" WE BRING YOU THE LATEST DEVELOPMENTS ON VICTORIA BURNS VANDERBILT DUPONT BUSH ROCKEFELLER SMYTHE PITT'S UPCOMING MARRIAGE TO GAZILLIONAIRE REGINALD JAMES CABOT WHITNEY III!
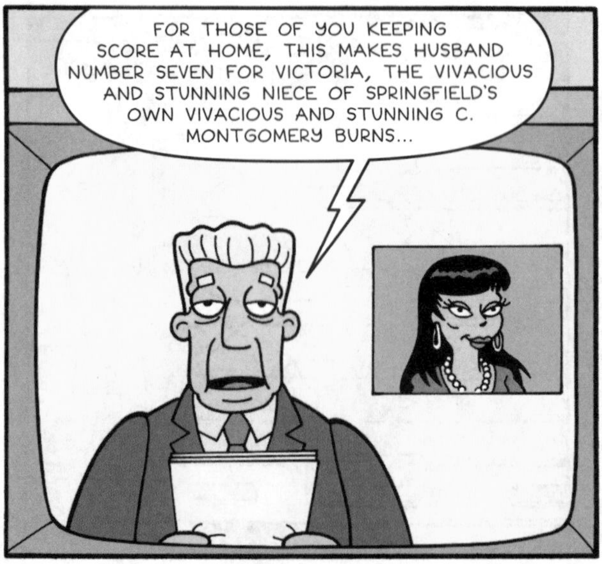
FOR THOSE OF YOU KEEPING SCORE AT HOME, THIS MAKES HUSBAND NUMBER SEVEN FOR VICTORIA, THE VIVACIOUS AND STUNNING NIECE OF SPRINGFIELD'S OWN VIVACIOUS AND STUNNING C. MONTGOMERY BURNS...
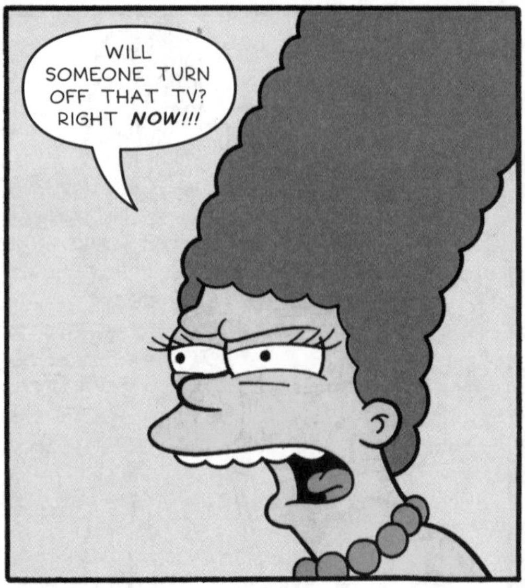
WILL SOMEONE TURN OFF THAT TV? RIGHT ***NOW!!!***

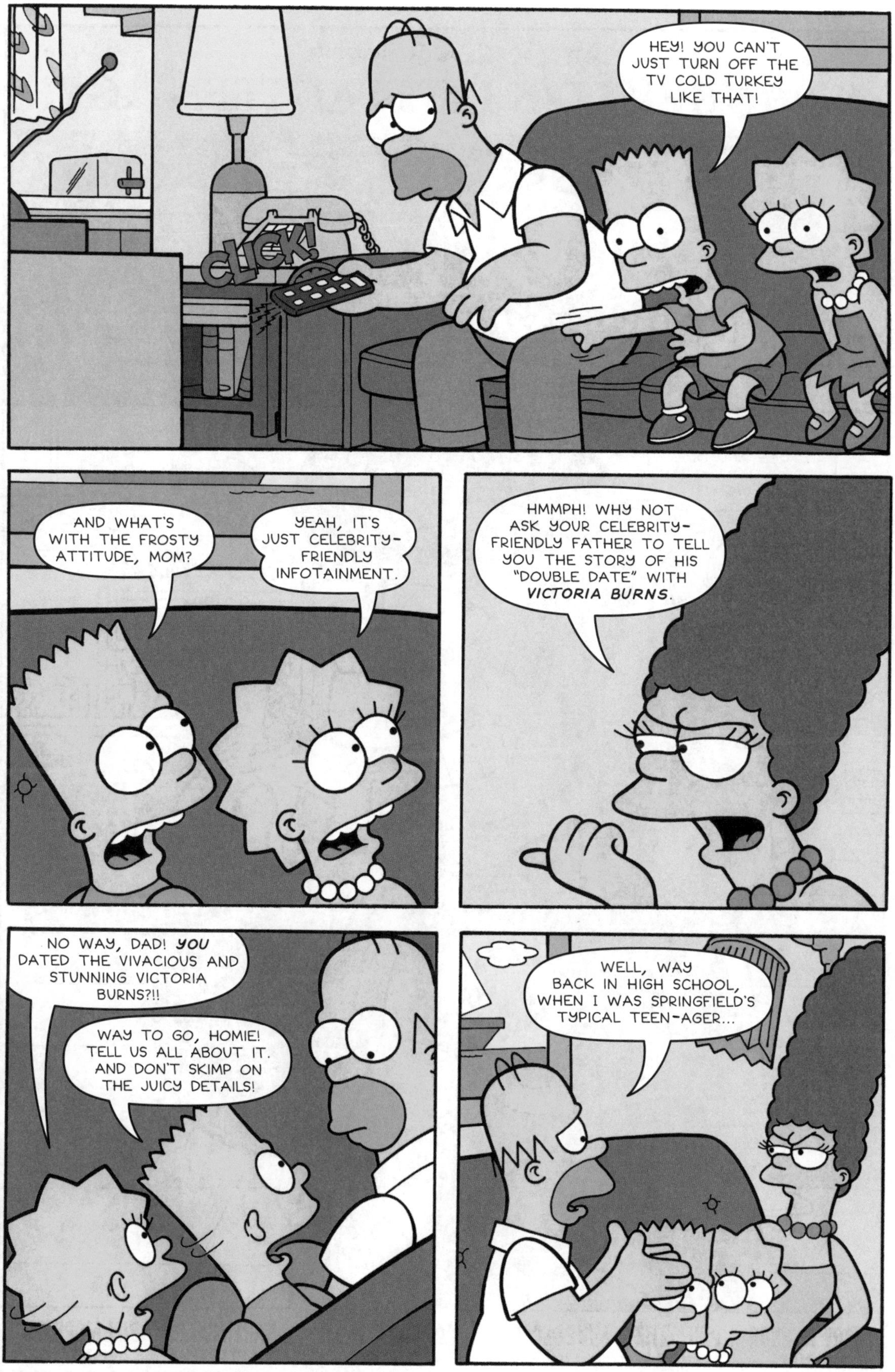
HEY! YOU CAN'T JUST TURN OFF THE TV COLD TURKEY LIKE THAT!
CLICK!
AND WHAT'S WITH THE FROSTY ATTITUDE, MOM?
YEAH, IT'S JUST CELEBRITY-FRIENDLY INFOTAINMENT.
HMMPH! WHY NOT ASK YOUR CELEBRITY-FRIENDLY FATHER TO TELL YOU THE STORY OF HIS "DOUBLE DATE" WITH VICTORIA BURNS.
NO WAY, DAD! YOU DATED THE VIVACIOUS AND STUNNING VICTORIA BURNS?!!
WAY TO GO, HOMIE! TELL US ALL ABOUT IT. AND DON'T SKIMP ON THE JUICY DETAILS!
WELL, WAY BACK IN HIGH SCHOOL, WHEN I WAS SPRINGFIELD'S TYPICAL TEEN-AGER...

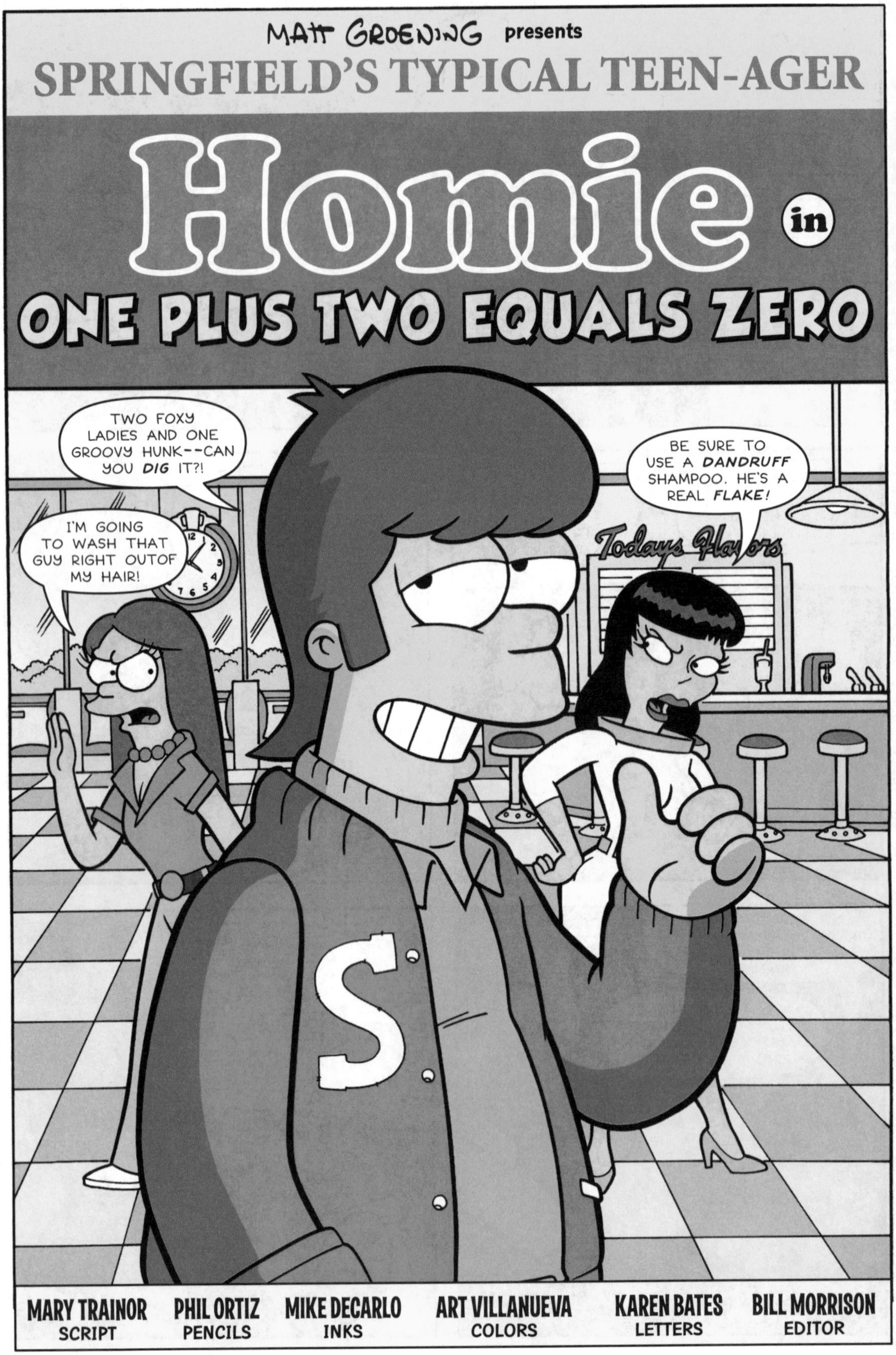

MATT GROENING presents
SPRINGFIELD'S TYPICAL TEEN-AGER
Homie in
ONE PLUS TWO EQUALS ZERO
TWO FOXY LADIES AND ONE GROOVY HUNK--CAN YOU DIG IT?!
I'M GOING TO WASH THAT GUY RIGHT OUTOF MY HAIR!
BE SURE TO USE A DANDRUFF SHAMPOO. HE'S A REAL FLAKE!
Todays Flavors
S
MARY TRAINOR SCRIPT
PHIL ORTIZ PENCILS
MIKE DECARLO INKS
ART VILLANUEVA COLORS
KAREN BATES LETTERS
BILL MORRISON EDITOR

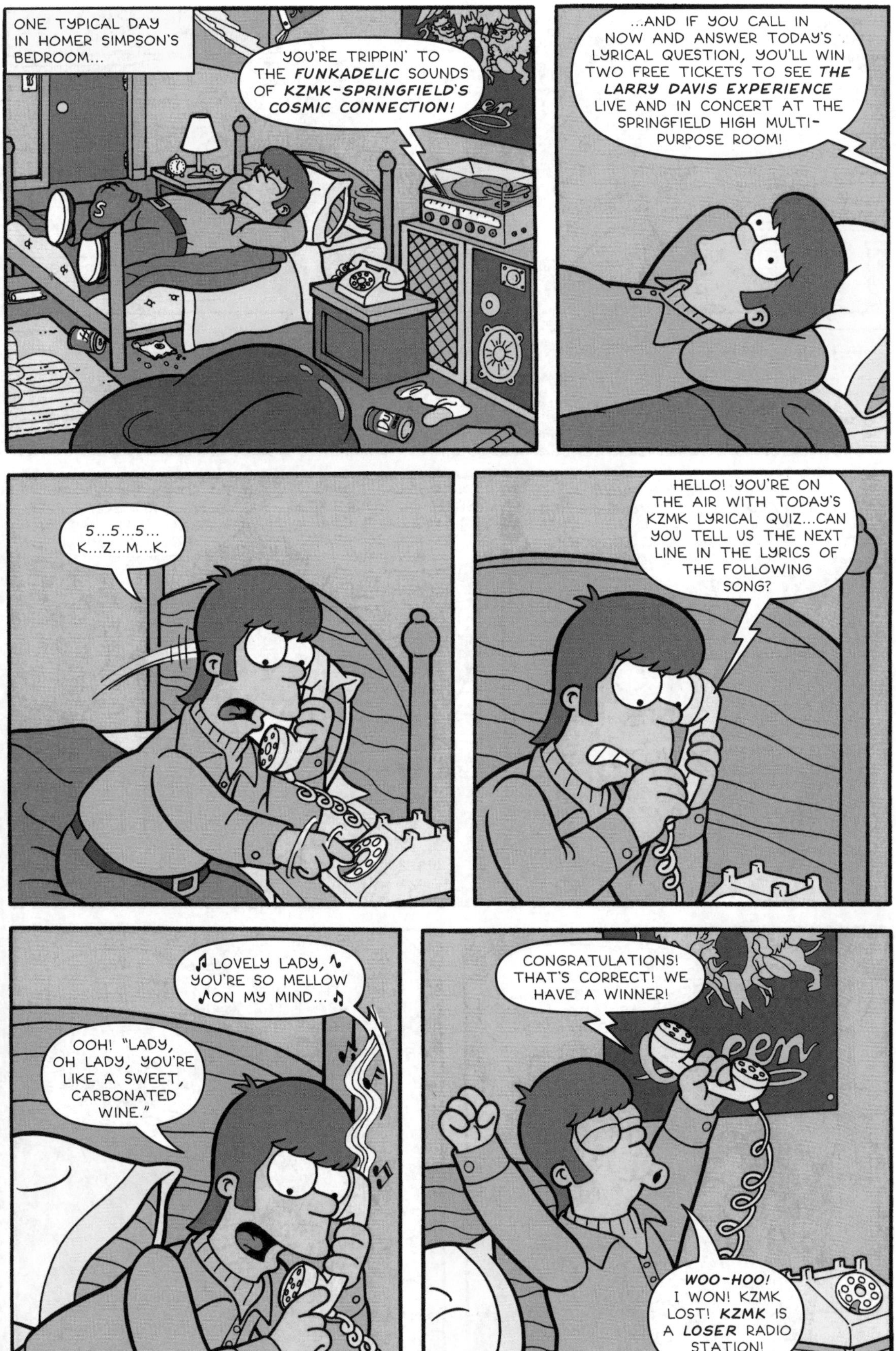
ONE TYPICAL DAY IN HOMER SIMPSON'S BEDROOM...
YOU'RE TRIPPIN' TO THE FUNKADELIC SOUNDS OF KZMK-SPRINGFIELD'S COSMIC CONNECTION!
...AND IF YOU CALL IN NOW AND ANSWER TODAY'S LYRICAL QUESTION, YOU'LL WIN TWO FREE TICKETS TO SEE THE LARRY DAVIS EXPERIENCE LIVE AND IN CONCERT AT THE SPRINGFIELD HIGH MULTI-PURPOSE ROOM!
5...5...5... K...Z...M...K.
HELLO! YOU'RE ON THE AIR WITH TODAY'S KZMK LYRICAL QUIZ...CAN YOU TELL US THE NEXT LINE IN THE LYRICS OF THE FOLLOWING SONG?
♫ LOVELY LADY, ♪ YOU'RE SO MELLOW ♪ ON MY MIND... ♫
OOH! "LADY, OH LADY, YOU'RE LIKE A SWEET, CARBONATED WINE."
CONGRATULATIONS! THAT'S CORRECT! WE HAVE A WINNER!
WOO-HOO! I WON! KZMK LOST! KZMK IS A LOSER RADIO STATION!

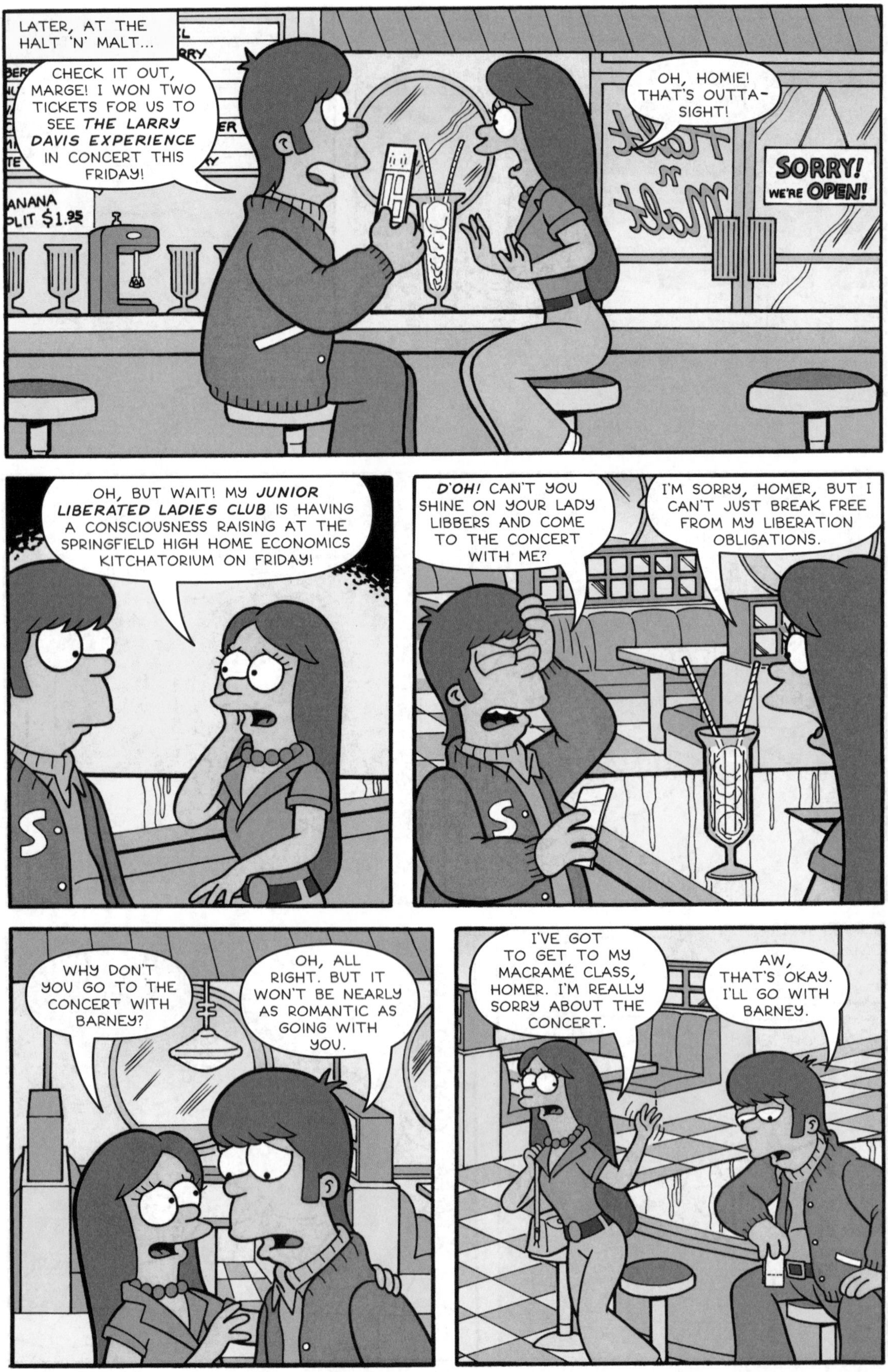
LATER, AT THE HALT 'N' MALT...
CHECK IT OUT, MARGE! I WON TWO TICKETS FOR US TO SEE THE LARRY DAVIS EXPERIENCE IN CONCERT THIS FRIDAY!
OH, HOMIE! THAT'S OUTTA-SIGHT!
SORRY! WE'RE OPEN!
OH, BUT WAIT! MY JUNIOR LIBERATED LADIES CLUB IS HAVING A CONSCIOUSNESS RAISING AT THE SPRINGFIELD HIGH HOME ECONOMICS KITCHATORIUM ON FRIDAY!
D'OH! CAN'T YOU SHINE ON YOUR LADY LIBBERS AND COME TO THE CONCERT WITH ME?
I'M SORRY, HOMER, BUT I CAN'T JUST BREAK FREE FROM MY LIBERATION OBLIGATIONS.
WHY DON'T YOU GO TO THE CONCERT WITH BARNEY?
OH, ALL RIGHT. BUT IT WON'T BE NEARLY AS ROMANTIC AS GOING WITH YOU.
I'VE GOT TO GET TO MY MACRAMÉ CLASS, HOMER. I'M REALLY SORRY ABOUT THE CONCERT.
AW, THAT'S OKAY. I'LL GO WITH BARNEY.

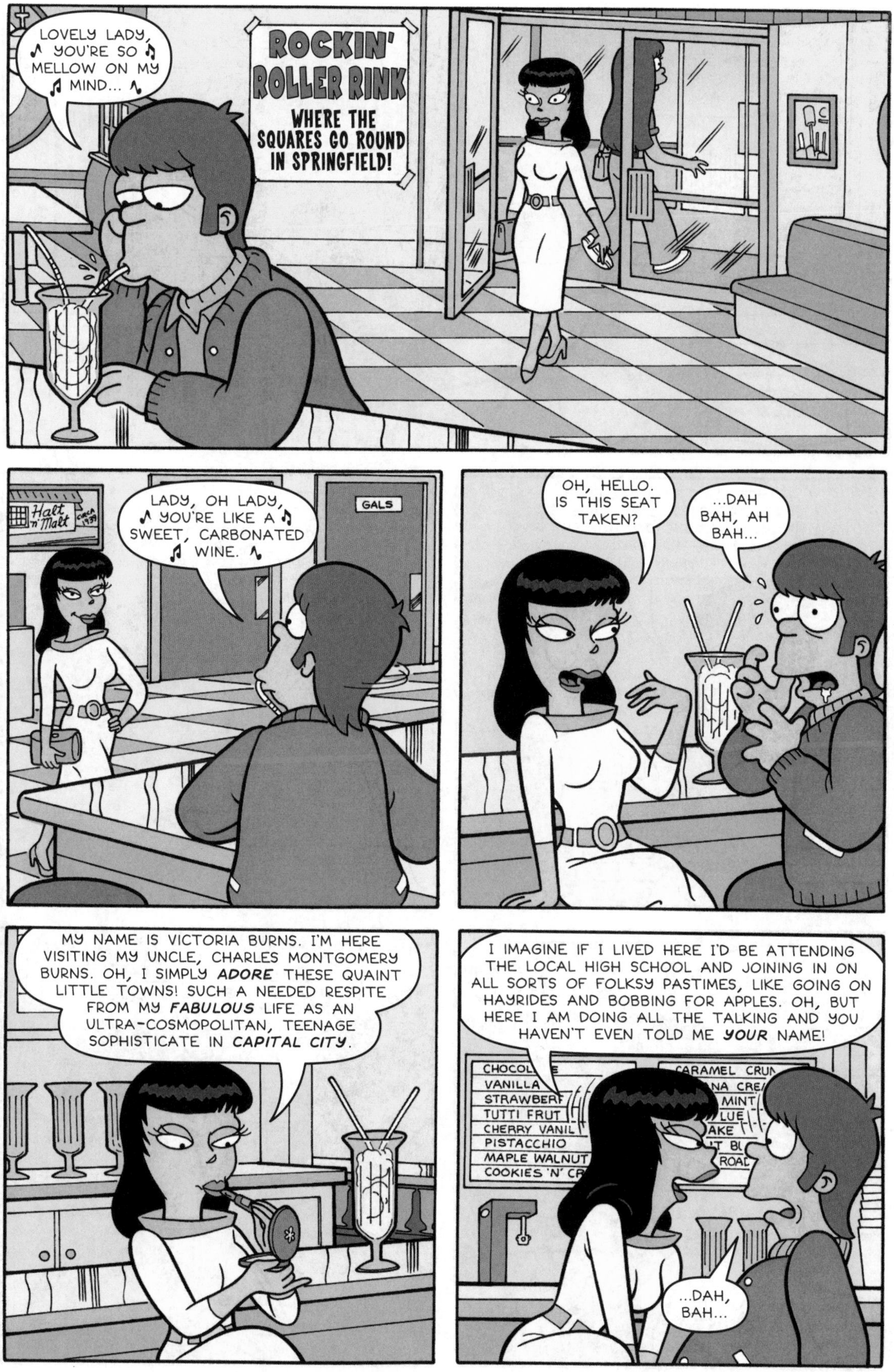
LOVELY LADY, YOU'RE SO MELLOW ON MY MIND...
ROCKIN' ROLLER RINK
WHERE THE SQUARES GO ROUND IN SPRINGFIELD!
Halt 'n' Malt
CIRCA 1939
GALS
LADY, OH LADY, YOU'RE LIKE A SWEET, CARBONATED WINE.
OH, HELLO. IS THIS SEAT TAKEN?
...DAH BAH, AH BAH...
MY NAME IS VICTORIA BURNS. I'M HERE VISITING MY UNCLE, CHARLES MONTGOMERY BURNS. OH, I SIMPLY **ADORE** THESE QUAINT LITTLE TOWNS! SUCH A NEEDED RESPITE FROM MY **FABULOUS** LIFE AS AN ULTRA-COSMOPOLITAN, TEENAGE SOPHISTICATE IN **CAPITAL CITY**.
I IMAGINE IF I LIVED HERE I'D BE ATTENDING THE LOCAL HIGH SCHOOL AND JOINING IN ON ALL SORTS OF FOLKSY PASTIMES, LIKE GOING ON HAYRIDES AND BOBBING FOR APPLES. OH, BUT HERE I AM DOING ALL THE TALKING AND YOU HAVEN'T EVEN TOLD ME **YOUR** NAME!
VANILLA
PISTACCHIO
MAPLE WALNUT
...DAH, BAH...

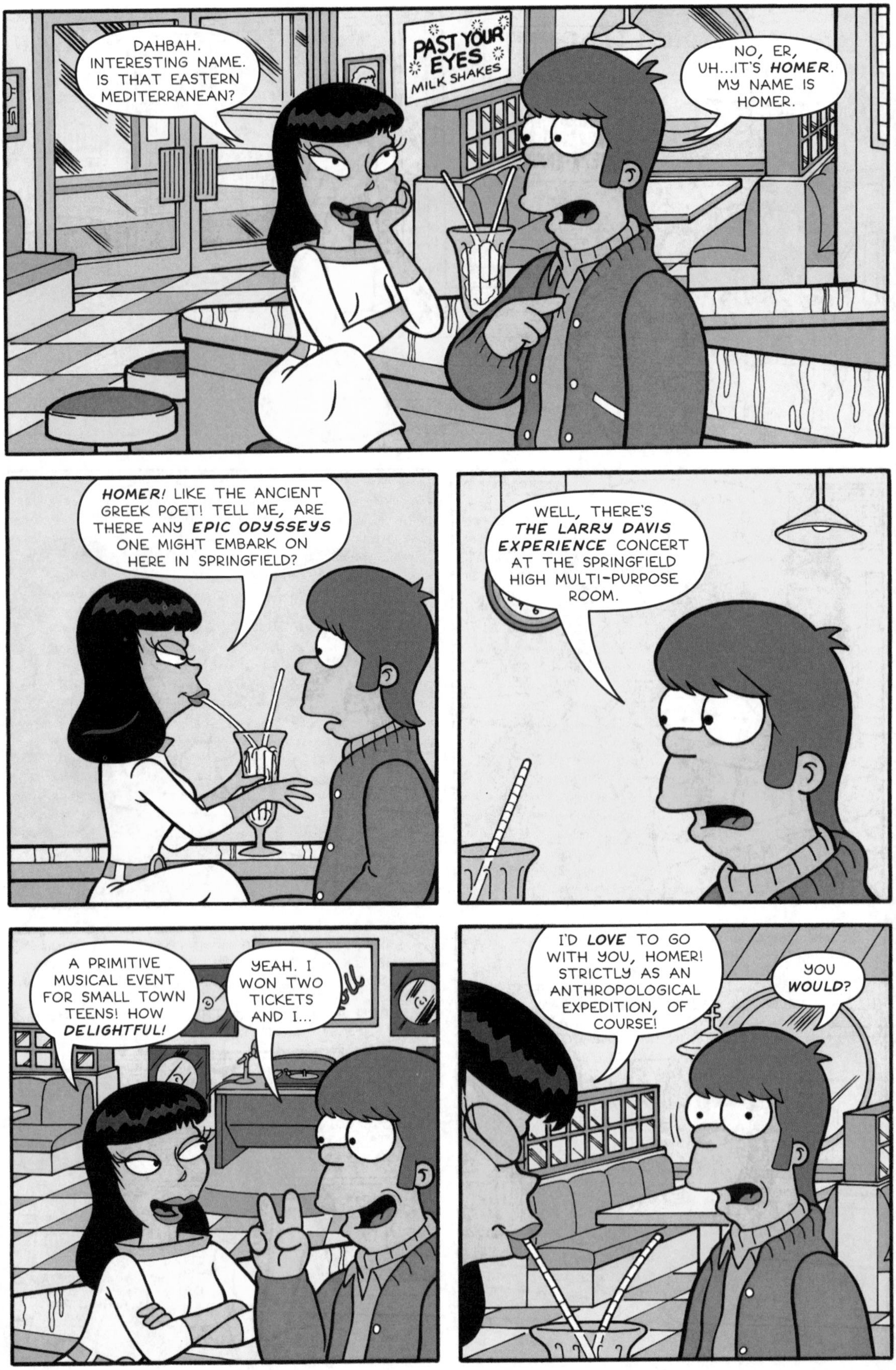
DAHBAH. INTERESTING NAME. IS THAT EASTERN MEDITERRANEAN?
PAST YOUR EYES MILK SHAKES
NO, ER, UH...IT'S **HOMER**. MY NAME IS HOMER.
HOMER! LIKE THE ANCIENT GREEK POET! TELL ME, ARE THERE ANY **EPIC ODYSSEYS** ONE MIGHT EMBARK ON HERE IN SPRINGFIELD?
WELL, THERE'S **THE LARRY DAVIS EXPERIENCE** CONCERT AT THE SPRINGFIELD HIGH MULTI-PURPOSE ROOM.
A PRIMITIVE MUSICAL EVENT FOR SMALL TOWN TEENS! HOW **DELIGHTFUL!**
YEAH. I WON TWO TICKETS AND I...
I'D **LOVE** TO GO WITH YOU, HOMER! STRICTLY AS AN ANTHROPOLOGICAL EXPEDITION, OF COURSE!
YOU **WOULD?**

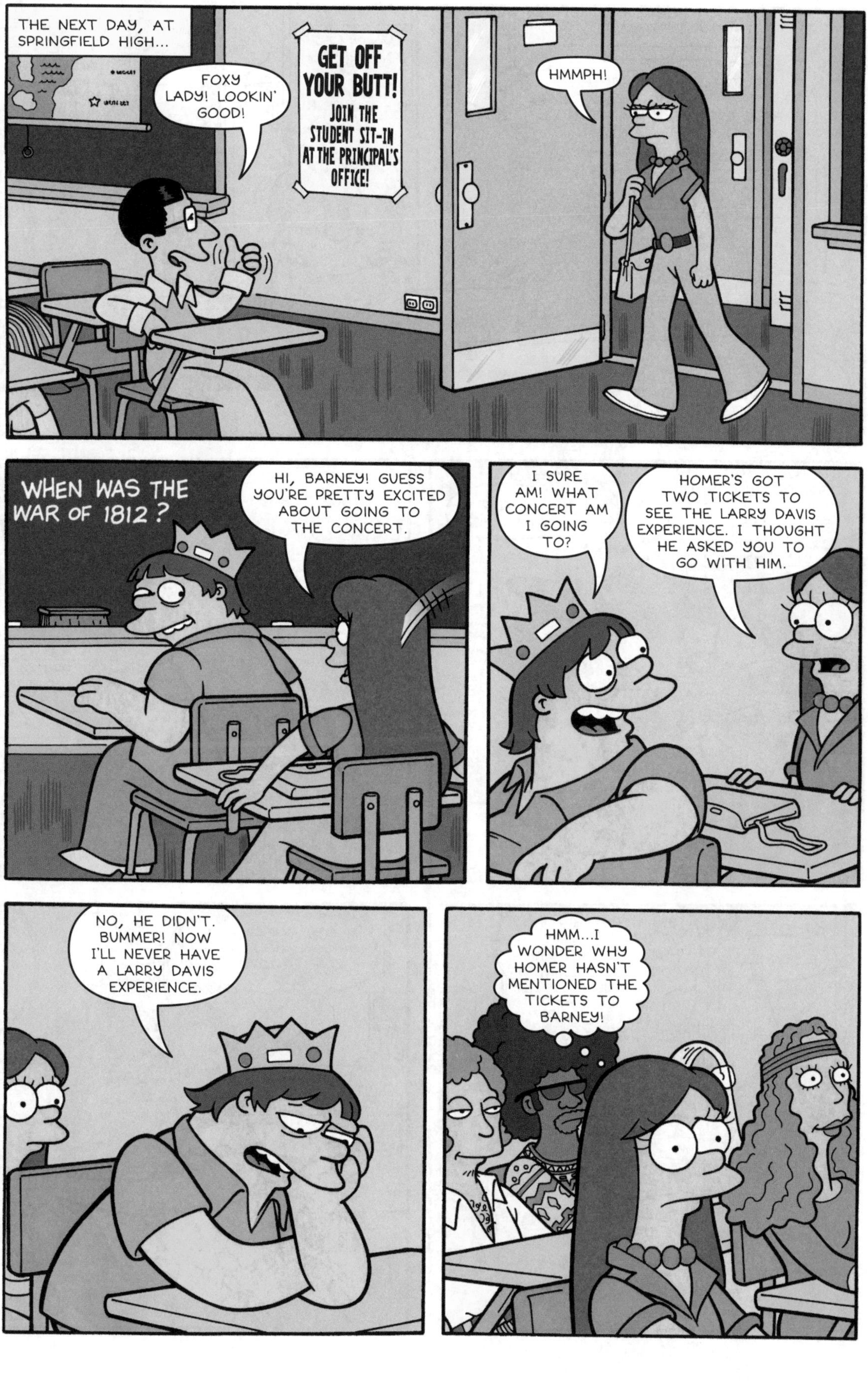

THE NEXT DAY, AT SPRINGFIELD HIGH...
FOXY LADY! LOOKIN' GOOD!
GET OFF YOUR BUTT! JOIN THE STUDENT SIT-IN AT THE PRINCIPAL'S OFFICE!
HMMPH!
WHEN WAS THE WAR OF 1812 ?
HI, BARNEY! GUESS YOU'RE PRETTY EXCITED ABOUT GOING TO THE CONCERT.
I SURE AM! WHAT CONCERT AM I GOING TO?
HOMER'S GOT TWO TICKETS TO SEE THE LARRY DAVIS EXPERIENCE. I THOUGHT HE ASKED YOU TO GO WITH HIM.
NO, HE DIDN'T. BUMMER! NOW I'LL NEVER HAVE A LARRY DAVIS EXPERIENCE.
HMM...I WONDER WHY HOMER HASN'T MENTIONED THE TICKETS TO BARNEY!

LATER, AT THE HALT 'N' MALT...

...AND SO I'M SITTING HERE AND THE MOST *BODACIOUS BABE* I HAVE EVER SEEN WALKS IN AND STARTS FLIRTING WITH *ME!*

FAR OUT! FIRST YOU GET MARGE BOUVIER TO GO STEADY WITH YOU, AND NOW YOU'VE GOT A DATE WITH A REAL, LIVE CAPITAL CITY DEBUTANTE! HOMER SIMPSON, YOU ARE ONE GROOVY GUY!

LOW ON CASH? DINE and DASH *at the* HALT 'N' MALT *home of the* KLEPTOBURGER!

OH, THERE YOU ARE, HOMER! SO, ARE YOU TAKING BARNEY TO THE CONCERT AFTER ALL?

CONCERT? *WHAT* CONCERT? NOBODY'S TAKING ANYBODY TO A CONCERT. NOPE. NO CONCERT-GOERS HERE!

GOTTA RUN. BYE BYE!

BUT I THOUGHT YOU WERE GOING TO THE CONCERT WITH BARNEY.

YES! NO! WELL...I'M THINKING OF GOING...UH... ELSEWHERE...

CHOCOLAT
VANILLA
STRAWBER
TUTTI FRU
CHERRY VA
PISTACCHIO
ORANGE S
NEAPP

ELSEWHERE?

YEAH. I'M THINKING OF GOING...UH...WITH YOU...TO GET MY CONSCIENCELESSNESS RAISED!

OH, HOMER SIMPSON, YOU ARE ONE GROOVY GUY!

D'OH!

AND THAT'S HOW I STUPIDLY SET MYSELF UP TO BE IN TWO PLACES WITH TWO DIFFERENT CHICKS AT THE SAME TIME!

WHOA! A LADIES' MAN! GET DOWN WITH YOUR BAD SELF, HOMIE!

GEE, DAD, IT SOUNDS LIKE YOU WERE A REAL NO-GOOD TWO-TIMER.

WELL, I NEVER QUITE GOT THE HANG OF IT, SO, TECHNICALLY, I WAS ONLY A ONE TIME TWO-TIMER.

SO THEN WHAT HAPPENED? WAS YOUR SHAMEFUL DUPLICITY EXPOSED? DID ONE OF THE DAMES HAVE A GUN? WERE YOU SHOT? WERE YOU KILLED? DID YOU DIE?

COOL IT, BART. THIS IS A LIGHTHEARTED TEENAGE FARCE, NOT FILM NOIR.

WELL, I HAD MADE MY BED, AND NOW I HAD TO LIE IN IT.

HAH! LIE IS RIGHT!

WOW. MOM SURE DOES HOLD A GRUDGE.

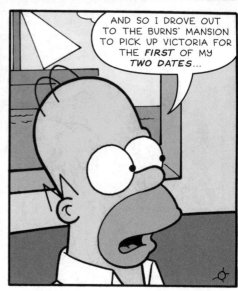

AND SO I DROVE OUT TO THE BURNS' MANSION TO PICK UP VICTORIA FOR THE FIRST OF MY TWO DATES...

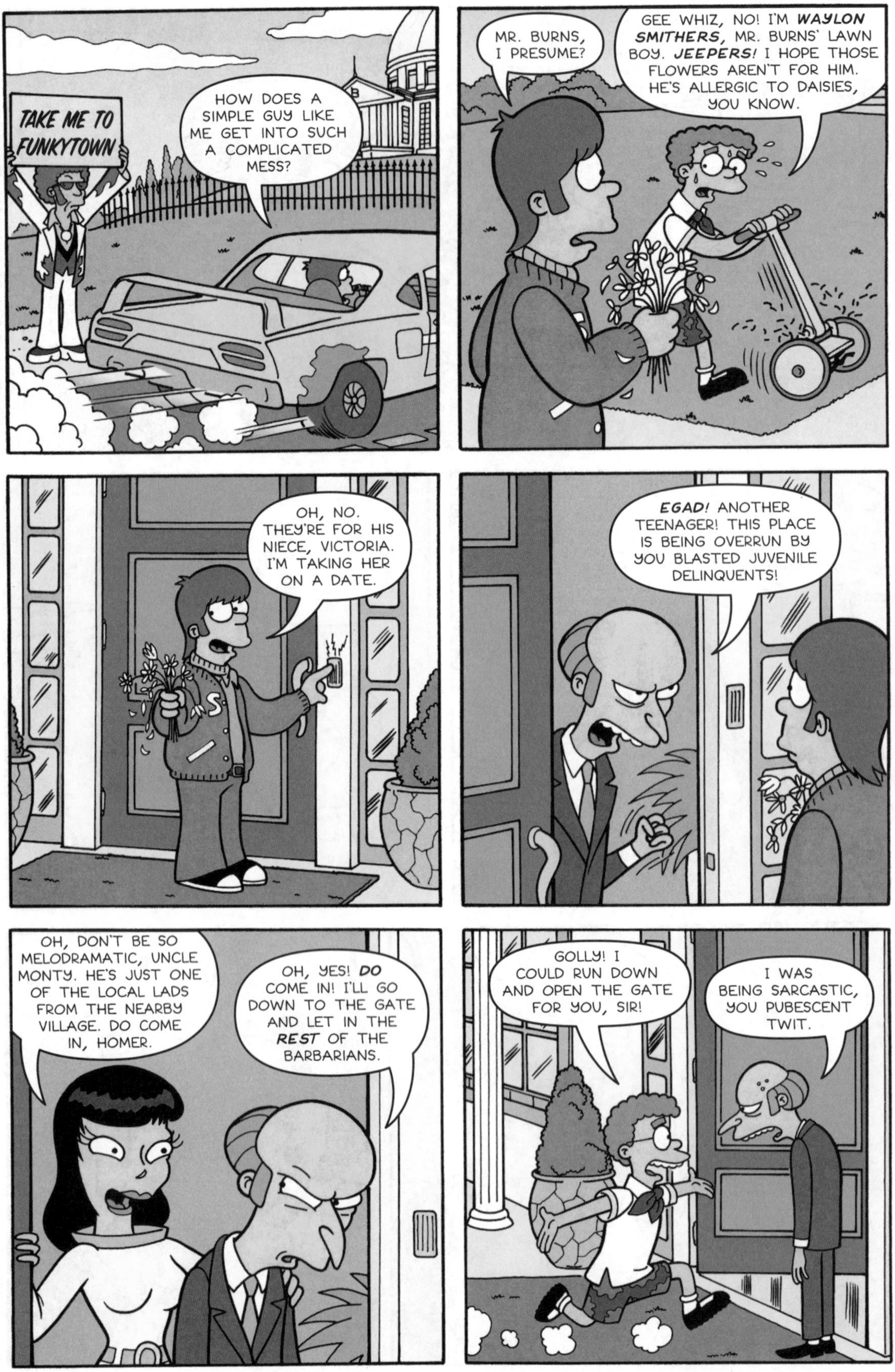

TAKE ME TO FUNKYTOWN
HOW DOES A SIMPLE GUY LIKE ME GET INTO SUCH A COMPLICATED MESS?
MR. BURNS, I PRESUME?
GEE WHIZ, NO! I'M **WAYLON SMITHERS,** MR. BURNS' LAWN BOY. **JEEPERS!** I HOPE THOSE FLOWERS AREN'T FOR HIM. HE'S ALLERGIC TO DAISIES, YOU KNOW.
OH, NO. THEY'RE FOR HIS NIECE, VICTORIA. I'M TAKING HER ON A DATE.
EGAD! ANOTHER TEENAGER! THIS PLACE IS BEING OVERRUN BY YOU BLASTED JUVENILE DELINQUENTS!
OH, DON'T BE SO MELODRAMATIC, UNCLE MONTY. HE'S JUST ONE OF THE LOCAL LADS FROM THE NEARBY VILLAGE. DO COME IN, HOMER.
OH, YES! **DO** COME IN! I'LL GO DOWN TO THE GATE AND LET IN THE **REST** OF THE BARBARIANS.
GOLLY! I COULD RUN DOWN AND OPEN THE GATE FOR YOU, SIR!
I WAS BEING SARCASTIC, YOU PUBESCENT TWIT.

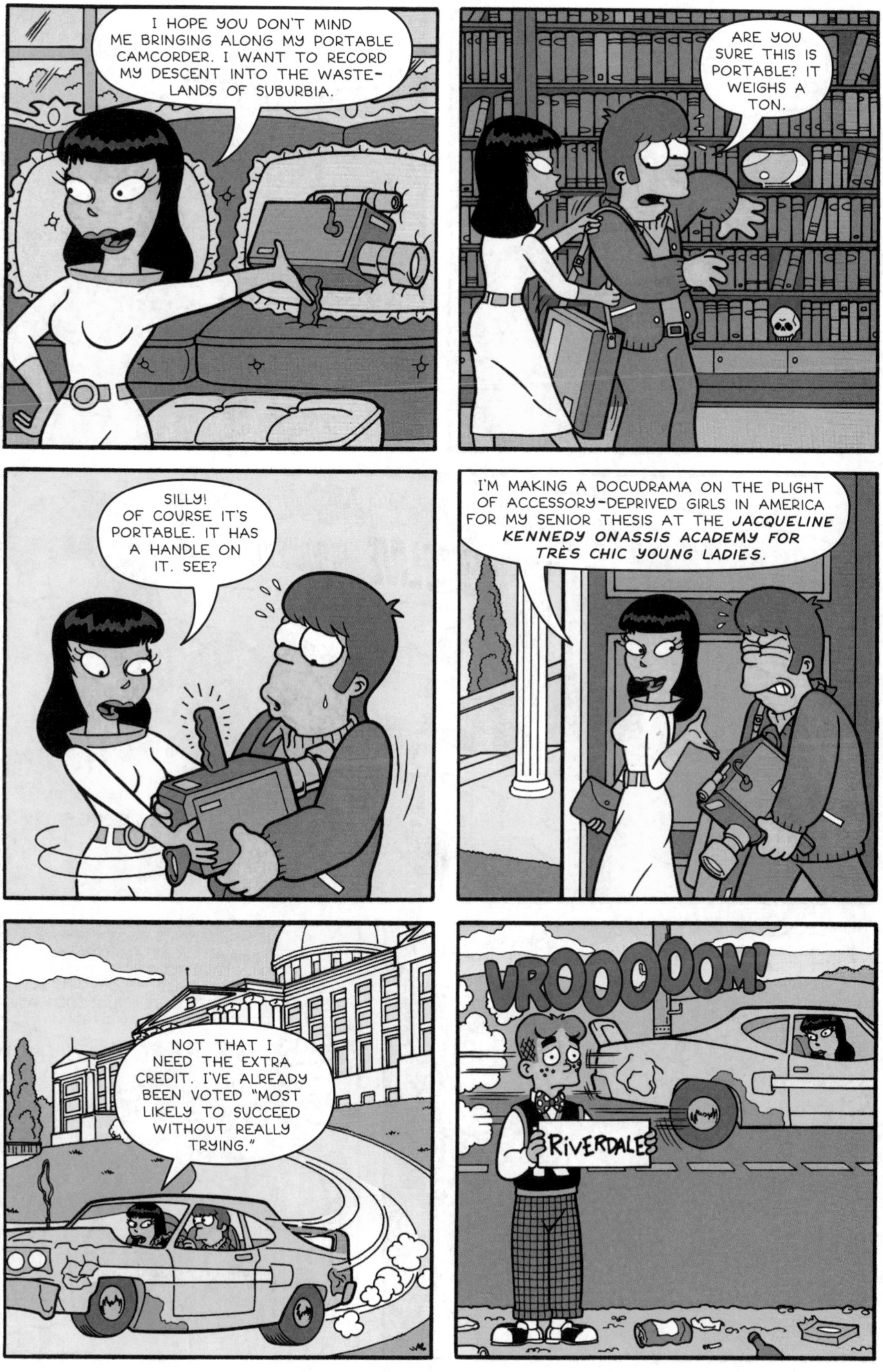
I HOPE YOU DON'T MIND ME BRINGING ALONG MY PORTABLE CAMCORDER. I WANT TO RECORD MY DESCENT INTO THE WASTE-LANDS OF SUBURBIA.
ARE YOU SURE THIS IS PORTABLE? IT WEIGHS A TON.
SILLY! OF COURSE IT'S PORTABLE. IT HAS A HANDLE ON IT. SEE?
I'M MAKING A DOCUDRAMA ON THE PLIGHT OF ACCESSORY-DEPRIVED GIRLS IN AMERICA FOR MY SENIOR THESIS AT THE *JACQUELINE KENNEDY ONASSIS ACADEMY FOR TRÈS CHIC YOUNG LADIES.*
NOT THAT I NEED THE EXTRA CREDIT. I'VE ALREADY BEEN VOTED "MOST LIKELY TO SUCCEED WITHOUT REALLY TRYING."
VROOOOOOM!
RIVERDALE

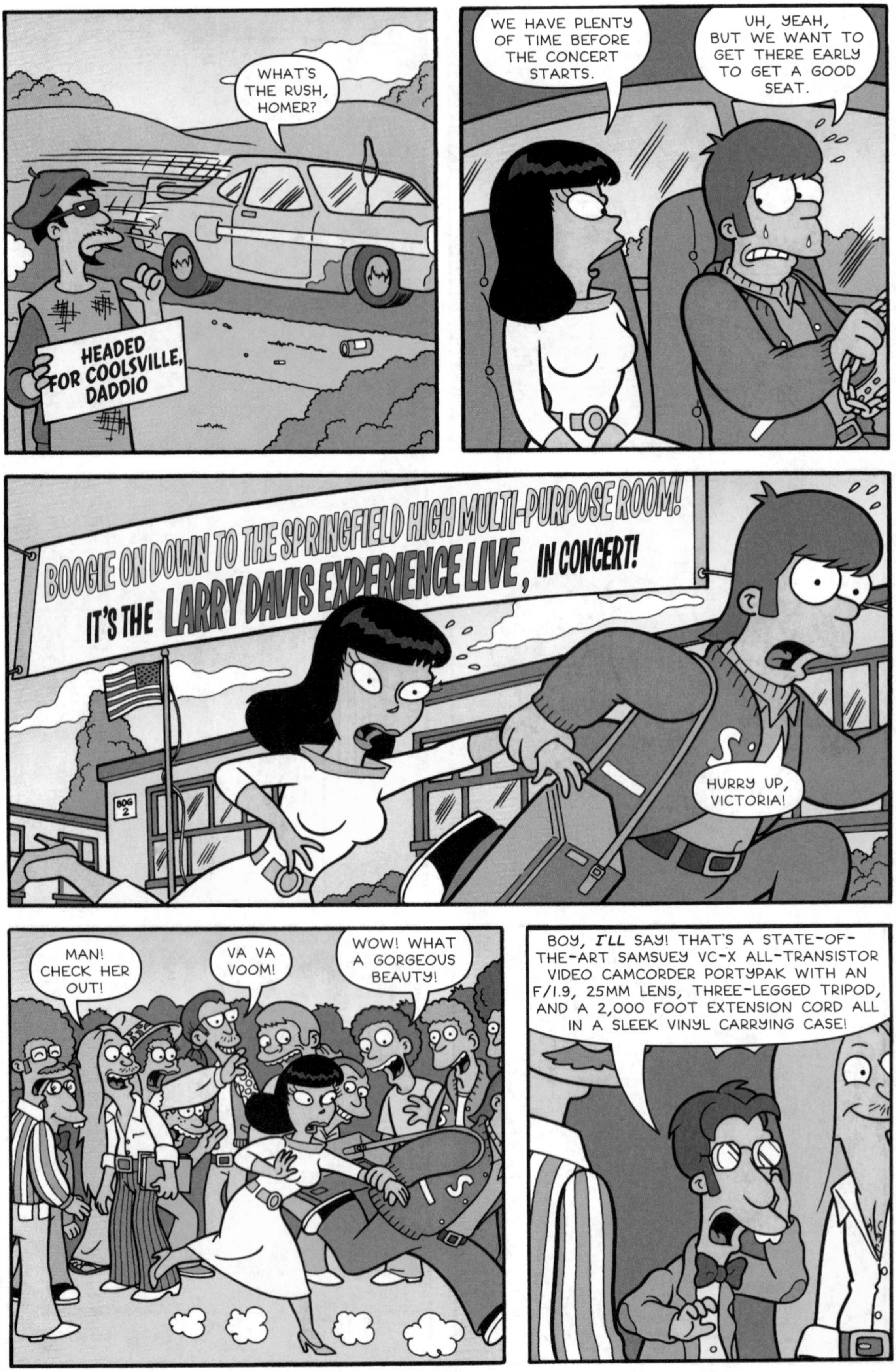
WHAT'S THE RUSH, HOMER?
HEADED FOR COOLSVILLE, DADDIO
WE HAVE PLENTY OF TIME BEFORE THE CONCERT STARTS.
UH, YEAH, BUT WE WANT TO GET THERE EARLY TO GET A GOOD SEAT.
BOOGIE ON DOWN TO THE SPRINGFIELD HIGH MULTI-PURPOSE ROOM!
IT'S THE LARRY DAVIS EXPERIENCE LIVE, IN CONCERT!
BOG 2
HURRY UP, VICTORIA!
MAN! CHECK HER OUT!
VA VA VOOM!
WOW! WHAT A GORGEOUS BEAUTY!
BOY, *I'LL* SAY! THAT'S A STATE-OF-THE-ART SAMSUEY VC-X ALL-TRANSISTOR VIDEO CAMCORDER PORTYPAK WITH AN F/1.9, 25MM LENS, THREE-LEGGED TRIPOD, AND A 2,000 FOOT EXTENSION CORD ALL IN A SLEEK VINYL CARRYING CASE!

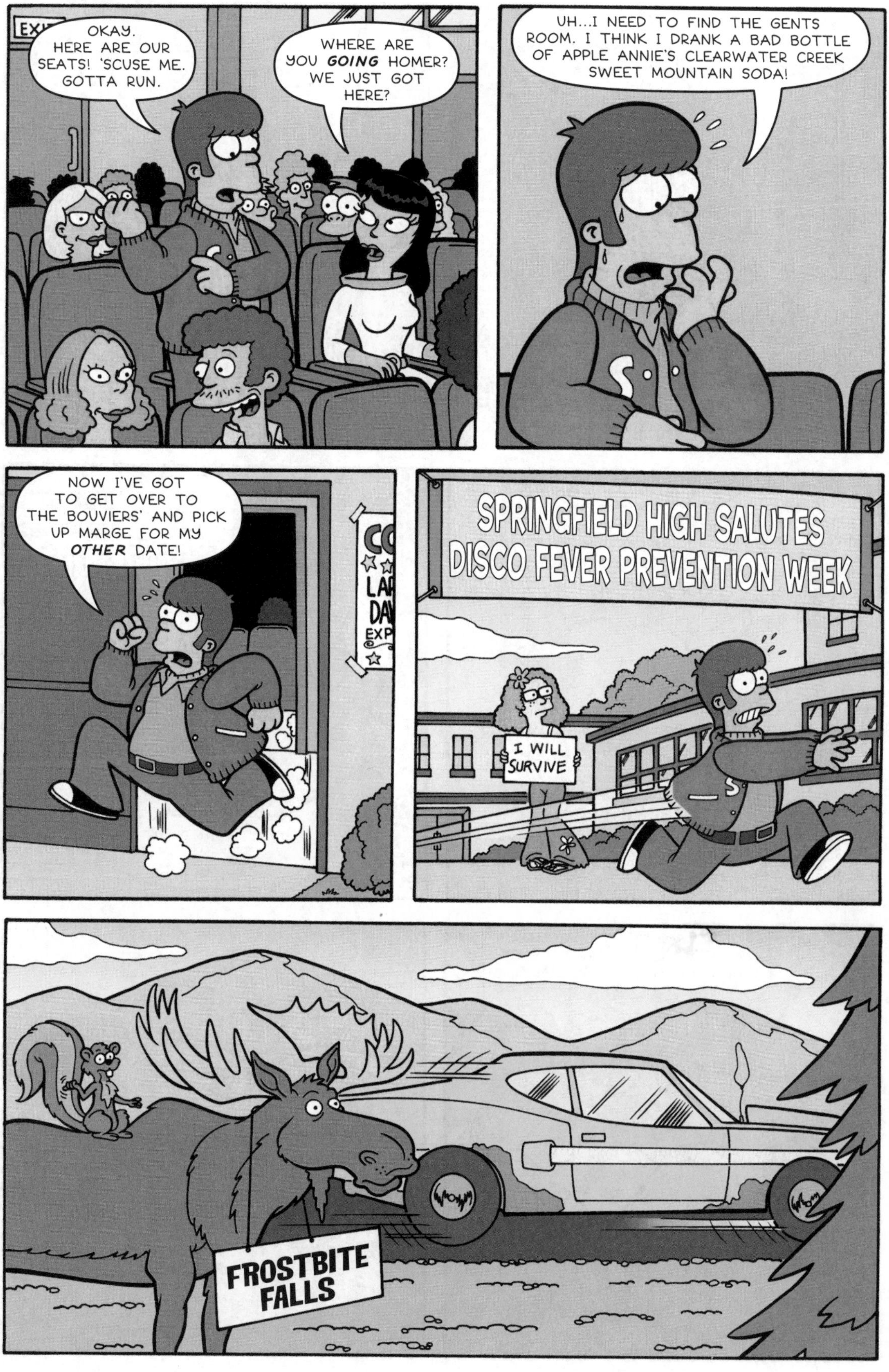
OKAY. HERE ARE OUR SEATS! 'SCUSE ME. GOTTA RUN.
WHERE ARE YOU GOING HOMER? WE JUST GOT HERE?
UH...I NEED TO FIND THE GENTS ROOM. I THINK I DRANK A BAD BOTTLE OF APPLE ANNIE'S CLEARWATER CREEK SWEET MOUNTAIN SODA!
NOW I'VE GOT TO GET OVER TO THE BOUVIERS' AND PICK UP MARGE FOR MY OTHER DATE!
SPRINGFIELD HIGH SALUTES DISCO FEVER PREVENTION WEEK
I WILL SURVIVE
FROSTBITE FALLS

MAN! I'M GETTING POOPED!

IS ⌐PANT⌐ MARGE ⌐PANT⌐ HOME?

CRIPES! GET A LOAD OF MARGE'S DREAM-BOAT!

HUFFING AND PUFFING LIKE THE BIG BAD WOLF!

HOMER! YOU LOOK EXHAUSTED! COME IN AND SIT DOWN.

SISTERHOOD PACKS A POWERFUL PUNCH

CAN'T ⌐PANT⌐ SIT. MUST ⌐PANT⌐ KEEP GOING...HURRY!

WHAT'S THE RUSH, ROMEO?

HE'S PROBABLY HOPPED UP ON GOOFBALLS.

SISTERHOOD POWERFUL PUNCH

DULLSVILLE

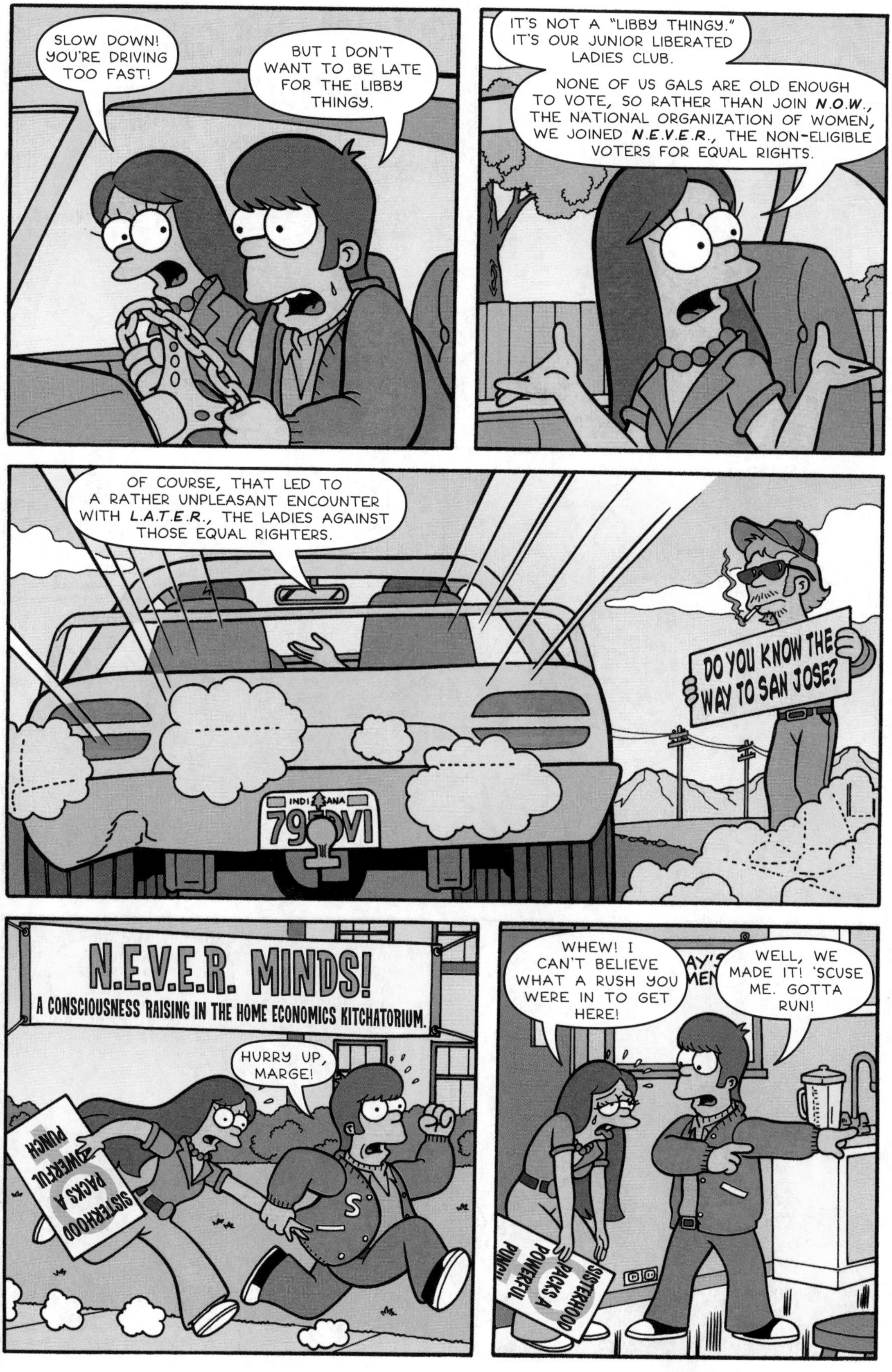

SLOW DOWN! YOU'RE DRIVING TOO FAST!
BUT I DON'T WANT TO BE LATE FOR THE LIBBY THINGY.
IT'S NOT A "LIBBY THINGY." IT'S OUR JUNIOR LIBERATED LADIES CLUB.
NONE OF US GALS ARE OLD ENOUGH TO VOTE, SO RATHER THAN JOIN N.O.W., THE NATIONAL ORGANIZATION OF WOMEN, WE JOINED N.E.V.E.R., THE NON-ELIGIBLE VOTERS FOR EQUAL RIGHTS.
OF COURSE, THAT LED TO A RATHER UNPLEASANT ENCOUNTER WITH L.A.T.E.R., THE LADIES AGAINST THOSE EQUAL RIGHTERS.
DO YOU KNOW THE WAY TO SAN JOSE?
N.E.V.E.R. MINDS!
A CONSCIOUSNESS RAISING IN THE HOME ECONOMICS KITCHATORIUM.
HURRY UP, MARGE!
SISTERHOOD PACKS A POWERFUL PUNCH
WHEW! I CAN'T BELIEVE WHAT A RUSH YOU WERE IN TO GET HERE!
WELL, WE MADE IT! 'SCUSE ME. GOTTA RUN!

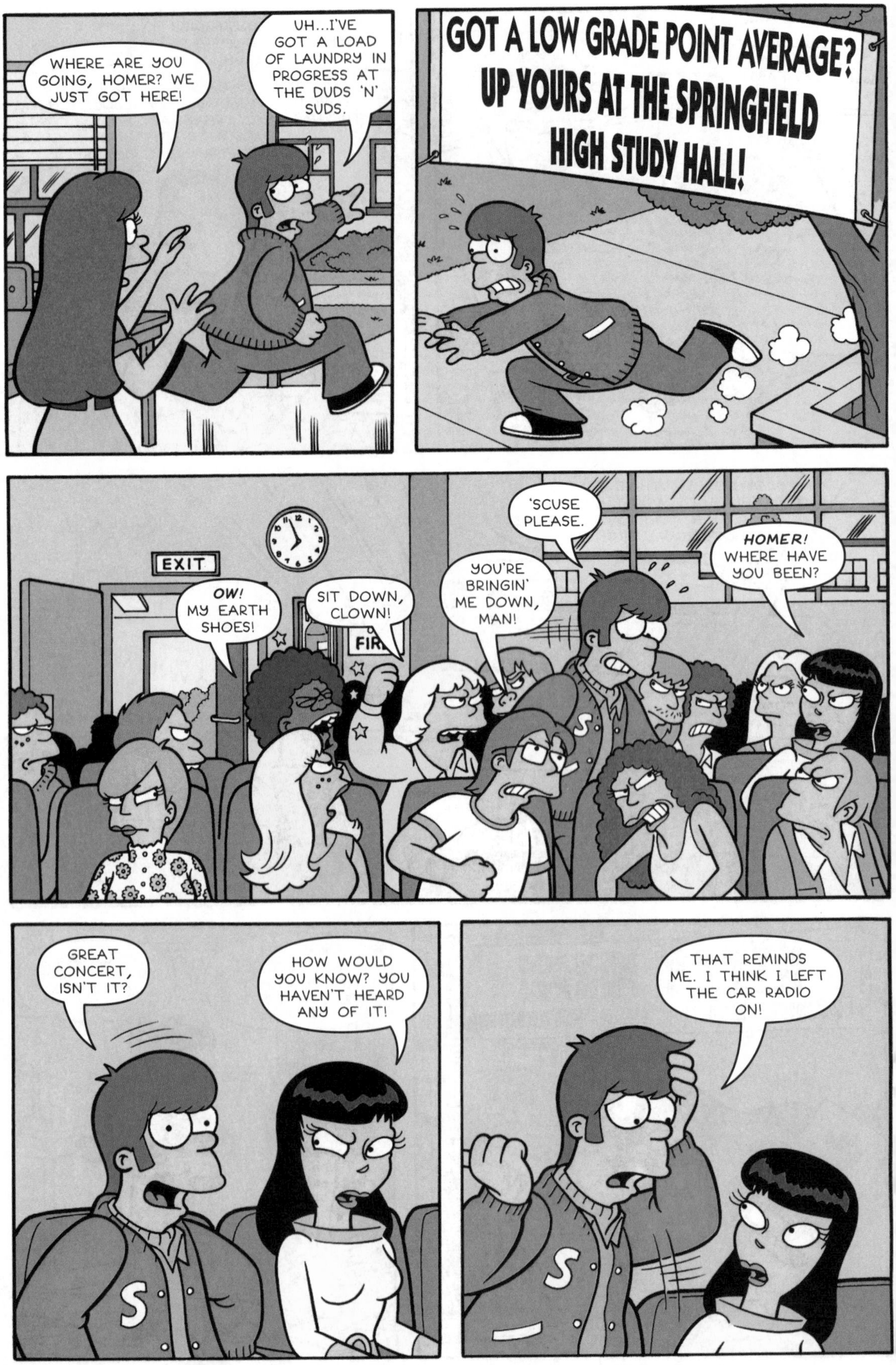
WHERE ARE YOU GOING, HOMER? WE JUST GOT HERE!
UH...I'VE GOT A LOAD OF LAUNDRY IN PROGRESS AT THE DUDS 'N' SUDS.
GOT A LOW GRADE POINT AVERAGE? UP YOURS AT THE SPRINGFIELD HIGH STUDY HALL!
EXIT
OW! MY EARTH SHOES!
SIT DOWN, CLOWN!
YOU'RE BRINGIN' ME DOWN, MAN!
'SCUSE PLEASE.
HOMER! WHERE HAVE YOU BEEN?
GREAT CONCERT, ISN'T IT?
HOW WOULD YOU KNOW? YOU HAVEN'T HEARD ANY OF IT!
THAT REMINDS ME. I THINK I LEFT THE CAR RADIO ON!

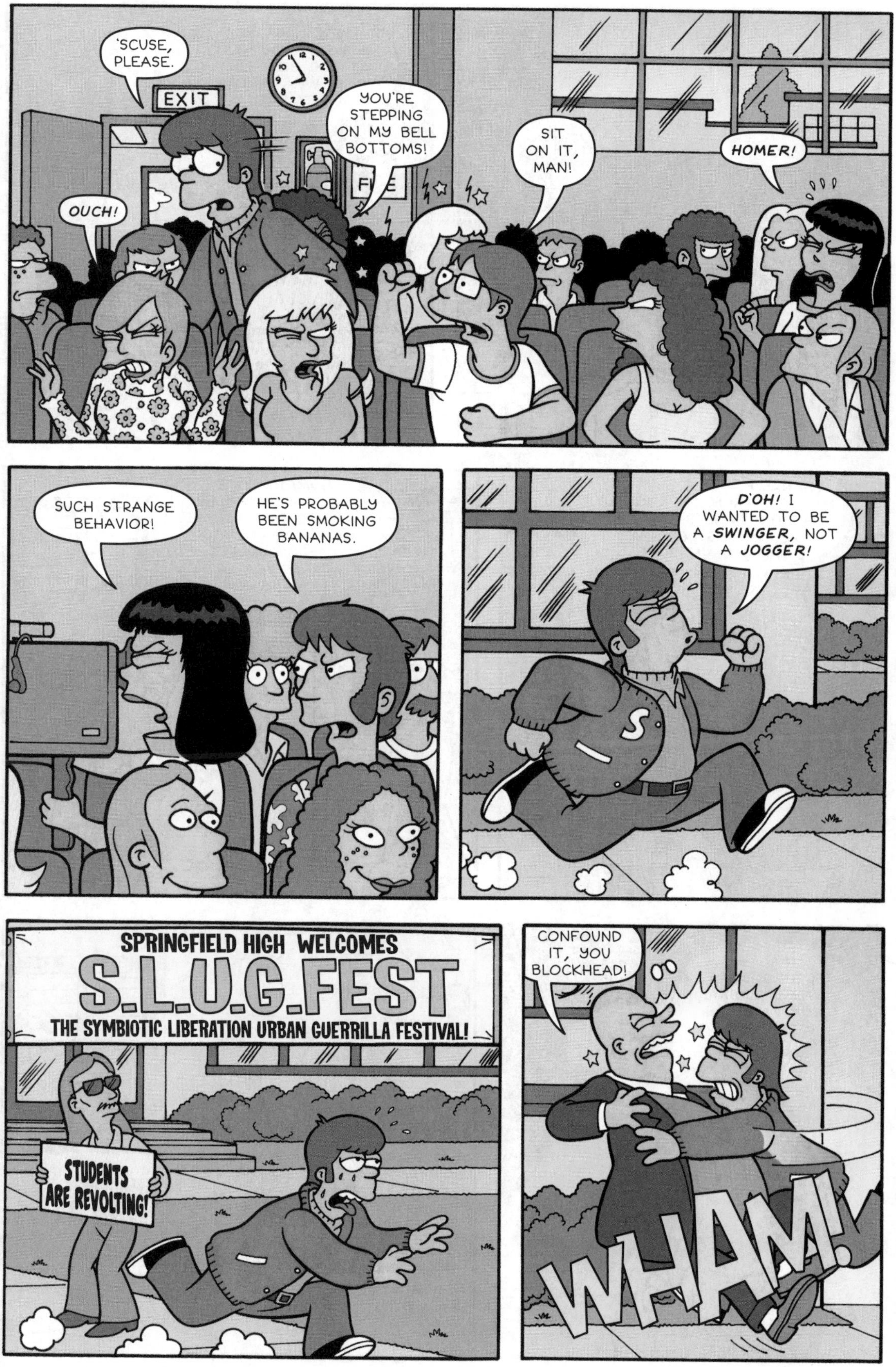
'SCUSE, PLEASE.
EXIT
YOU'RE STEPPING ON MY BELL BOTTOMS!
SIT ON IT, MAN!
HOMER!
OUCH!
SUCH STRANGE BEHAVIOR!
HE'S PROBABLY BEEN SMOKING BANANAS.
D'OH! I WANTED TO BE A SWINGER, NOT A JOGGER!
SPRINGFIELD HIGH WELCOMES
S.L.U.G.FEST
THE SYMBIOTIC LIBERATION URBAN GUERRILLA FESTIVAL!
STUDENTS ARE REVOLTING!
CONFOUND IT, YOU BLOCKHEAD!
WHAM!

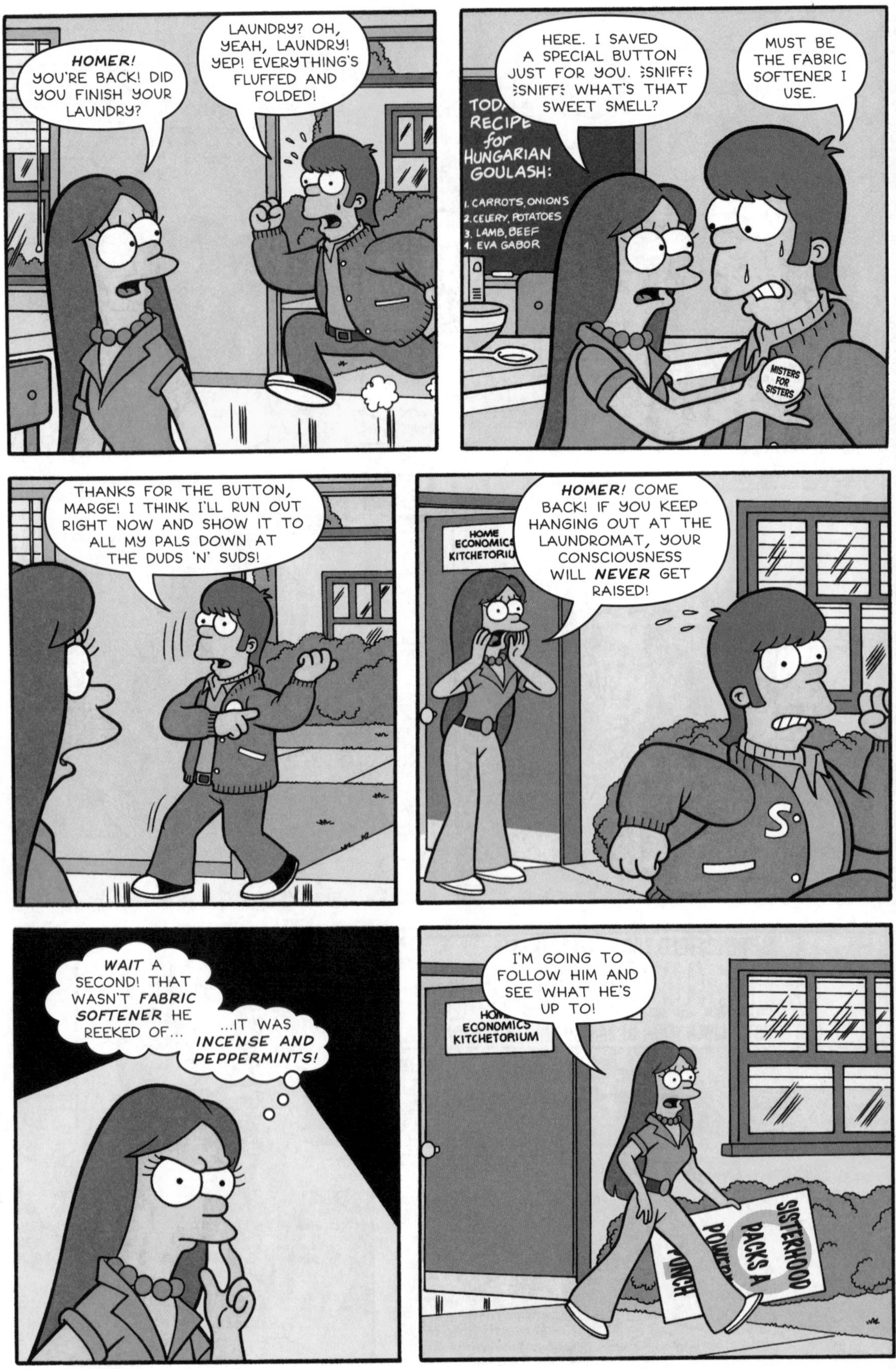

HOMER! YOU'RE BACK! DID YOU FINISH YOUR LAUNDRY?
LAUNDRY? OH, YEAH, LAUNDRY! YEP! EVERYTHING'S FLUFFED AND FOLDED!
TODA RECIPE for HUNGARIAN GOULASH:
1. CARROTS, ONIONS
2. CELERY, POTATOES
3. LAMB, BEEF
4. EVA GABOR
HERE. I SAVED A SPECIAL BUTTON JUST FOR YOU. ⁝SNIFF⁝ ⁝SNIFF⁝ WHAT'S THAT SWEET SMELL?
MUST BE THE FABRIC SOFTENER I USE.
MISTERS FOR SISTERS
THANKS FOR THE BUTTON, MARGE! I THINK I'LL RUN OUT RIGHT NOW AND SHOW IT TO ALL MY PALS DOWN AT THE DUDS 'N' SUDS!
HOME ECONOMICS KITCHETORIU
HOMER! COME BACK! IF YOU KEEP HANGING OUT AT THE LAUNDROMAT, YOUR CONSCIOUSNESS WILL NEVER GET RAISED!
S
WAIT A SECOND! THAT WASN'T FABRIC SOFTENER HE REEKED OF...
...IT WAS INCENSE AND PEPPERMINTS!
HOME ECONOMICS KITCHETORIUM
I'M GOING TO FOLLOW HIM AND SEE WHAT HE'S UP TO!
SISTERHOOD PACKS A
PUNCH

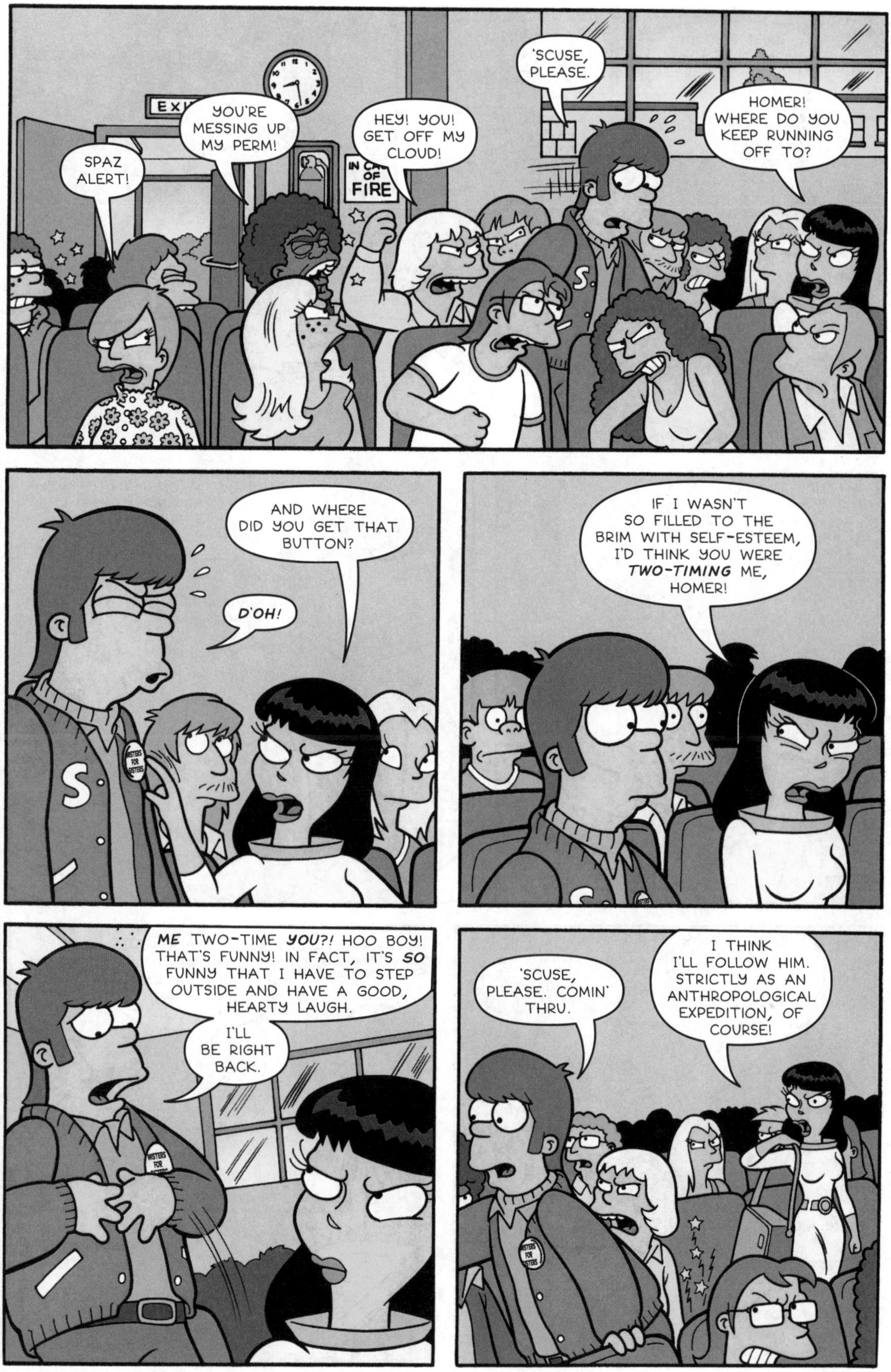

SPAZ ALERT!
YOU'RE MESSING UP MY PERM!
HEY! YOU! GET OFF MY CLOUD!
IN CASE OF FIRE
'SCUSE, PLEASE.
HOMER! WHERE DO YOU KEEP RUNNING OFF TO?
AND WHERE DID YOU GET THAT BUTTON?
D'OH!
IF I WASN'T SO FILLED TO THE BRIM WITH SELF-ESTEEM, I'D THINK YOU WERE TWO-TIMING ME, HOMER!
ME TWO-TIME YOU?! HOO BOY! THAT'S FUNNY! IN FACT, IT'S SO FUNNY THAT I HAVE TO STEP OUTSIDE AND HAVE A GOOD, HEARTY LAUGH.
I'LL BE RIGHT BACK.
'SCUSE, PLEASE. COMIN' THRU.
I THINK I'LL FOLLOW HIM. STRICTLY AS AN ANTHROPOLOGICAL EXPEDITION, OF COURSE!

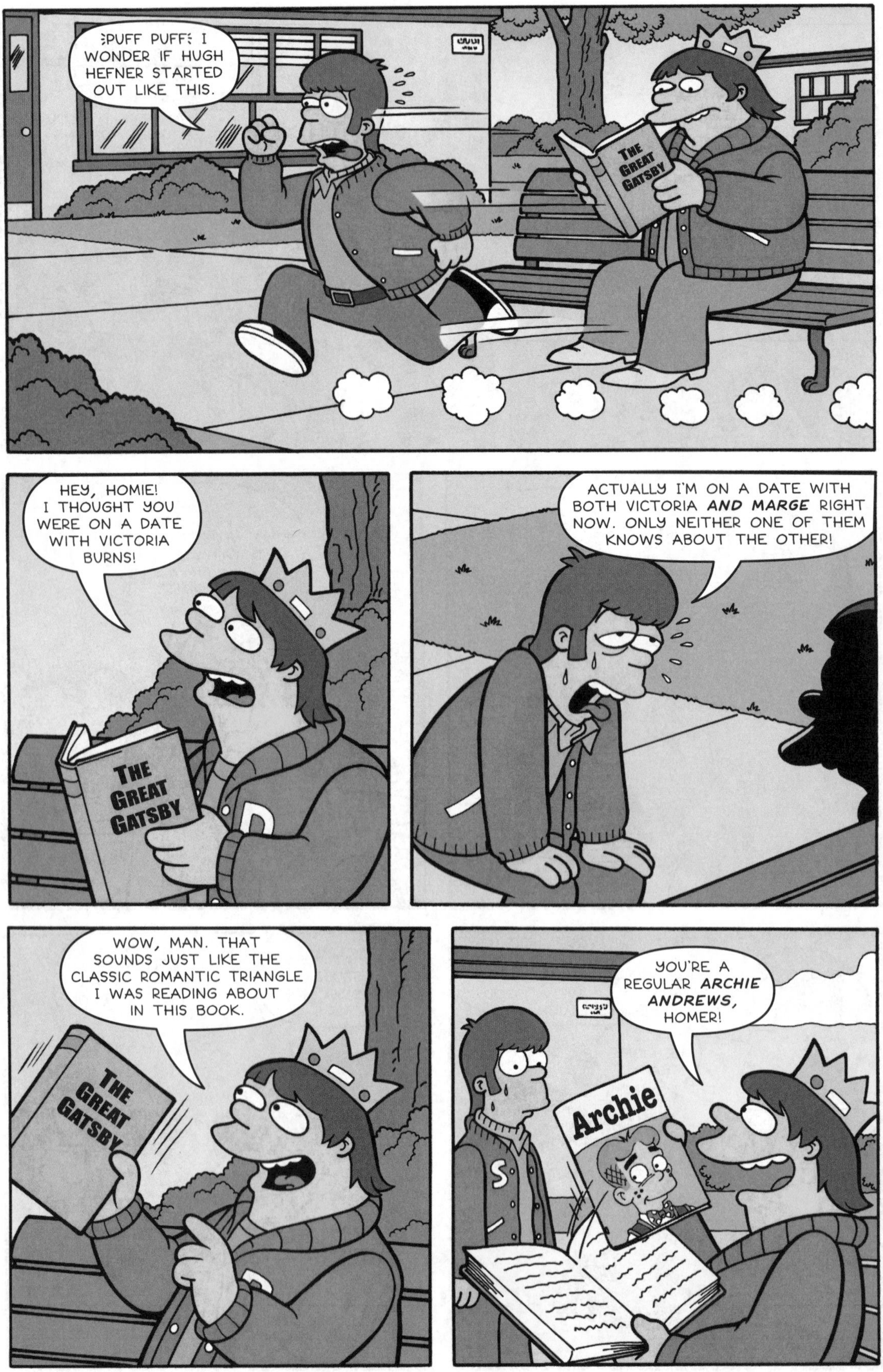

:PUFF PUFF: I WONDER IF HUGH HEFNER STARTED OUT LIKE THIS.
THE GREAT GATSBY
HEY, HOMIE! I THOUGHT YOU WERE ON A DATE WITH VICTORIA BURNS!
THE GREAT GATSBY
ACTUALLY I'M ON A DATE WITH BOTH VICTORIA **AND MARGE** RIGHT NOW. ONLY NEITHER ONE OF THEM KNOWS ABOUT THE OTHER!
WOW, MAN. THAT SOUNDS JUST LIKE THE CLASSIC ROMANTIC TRIANGLE I WAS READING ABOUT IN THIS BOOK.
THE GREAT GATSBY
YOU'RE A REGULAR **ARCHIE ANDREWS,** HOMER!
Archie

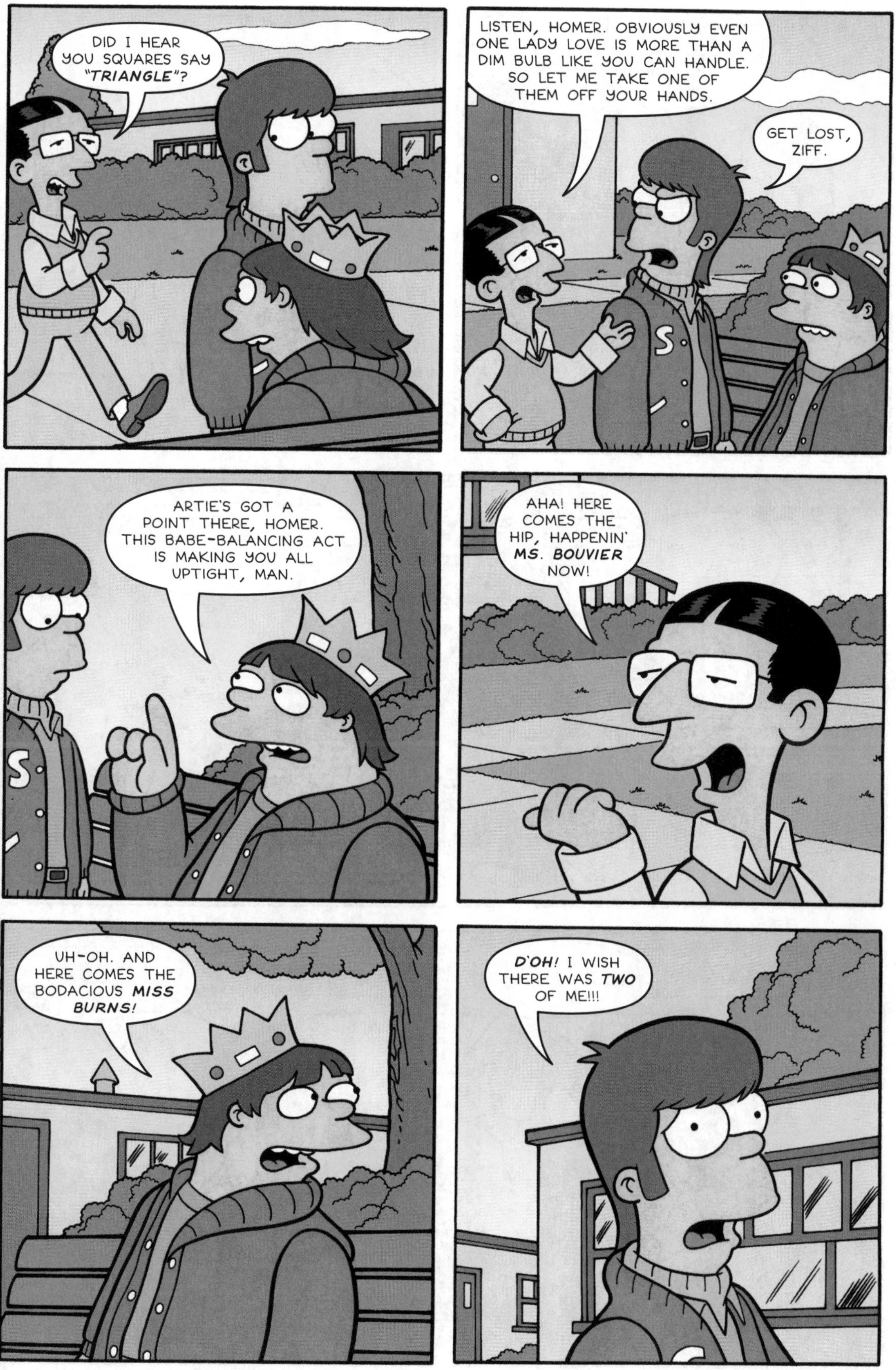
DID I HEAR YOU SQUARES SAY "TRIANGLE"?
LISTEN, HOMER. OBVIOUSLY EVEN ONE LADY LOVE IS MORE THAN A DIM BULB LIKE YOU CAN HANDLE. SO LET ME TAKE ONE OF THEM OFF YOUR HANDS.
GET LOST, ZIFF.
ARTIE'S GOT A POINT THERE, HOMER. THIS BABE-BALANCING ACT IS MAKING YOU ALL UPTIGHT, MAN.
AHA! HERE COMES THE HIP, HAPPENIN' MS. BOUVIER NOW!
UH-OH. AND HERE COMES THE BODACIOUS MISS BURNS!
D'OH! I WISH THERE WAS TWO OF ME!!!

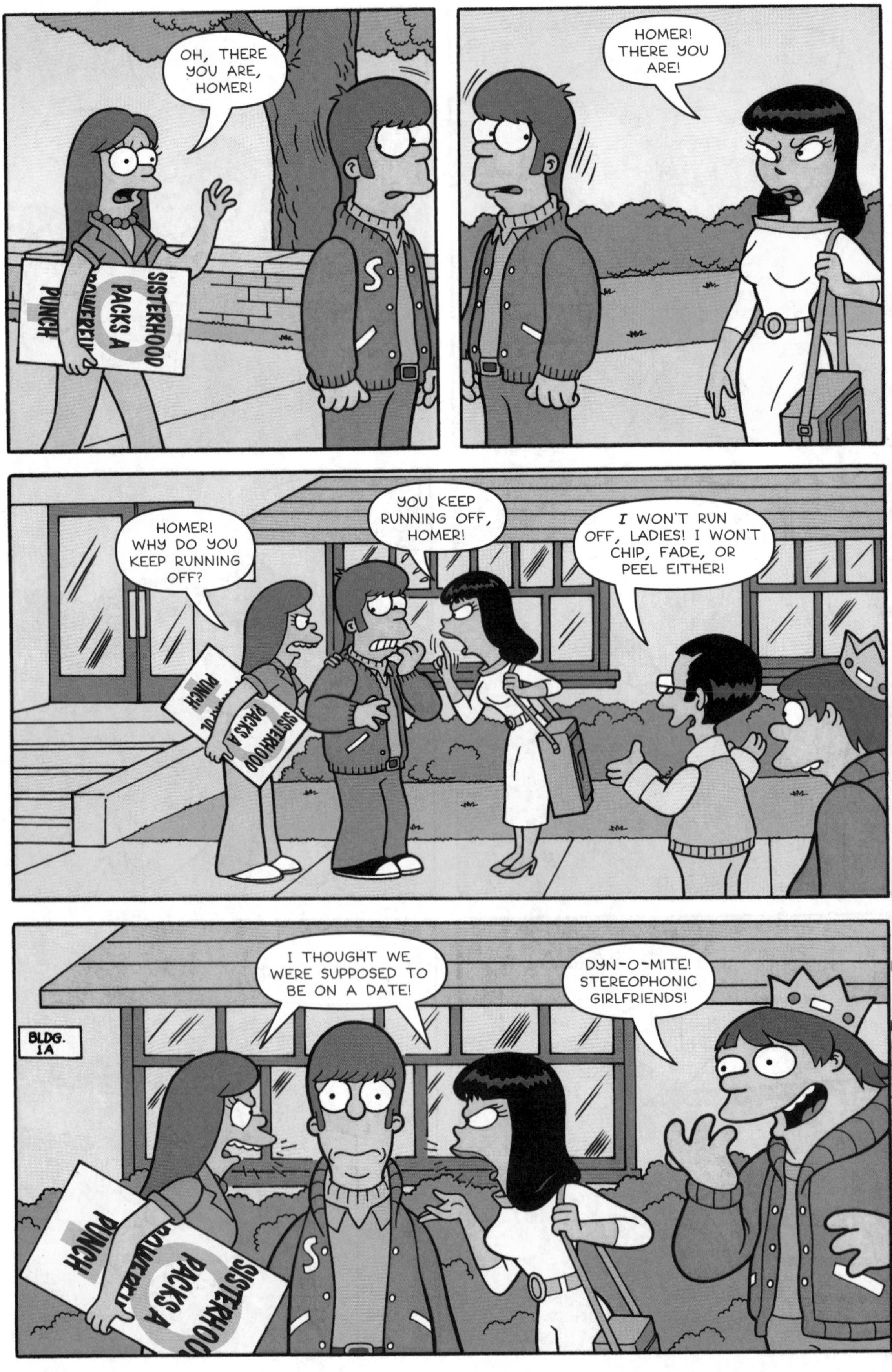
OH, THERE YOU ARE, HOMER!
SISTERHOOD PACKS A
PUNCH
HOMER! THERE YOU ARE!
HOMER! WHY DO YOU KEEP RUNNING OFF?
YOU KEEP RUNNING OFF, HOMER!
I WON'T RUN OFF, LADIES! I WON'T CHIP, FADE, OR PEEL EITHER!
BLDG. 1A
I THOUGHT WE WERE SUPPOSED TO BE ON A DATE!
DYN-O-MITE! STEREOPHONIC GIRLFRIENDS!

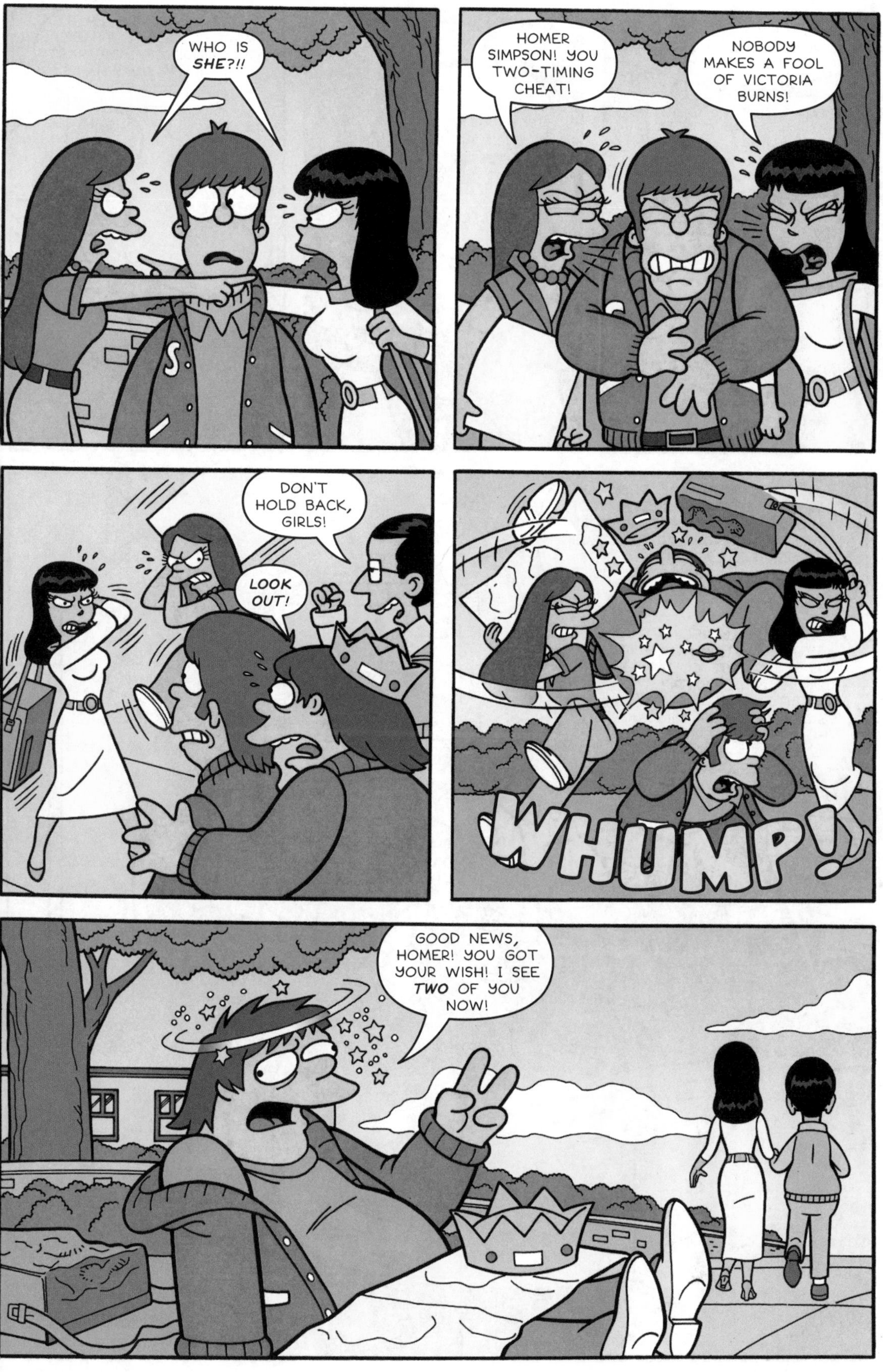
WHO IS *SHE*?!!
HOMER SIMPSON! YOU TWO-TIMING CHEAT!
NOBODY MAKES A FOOL OF VICTORIA BURNS!
DON'T HOLD BACK, GIRLS!
LOOK OUT!
WHUMP!
GOOD NEWS, HOMER! YOU GOT YOUR WISH! I SEE *TWO* OF YOU NOW!

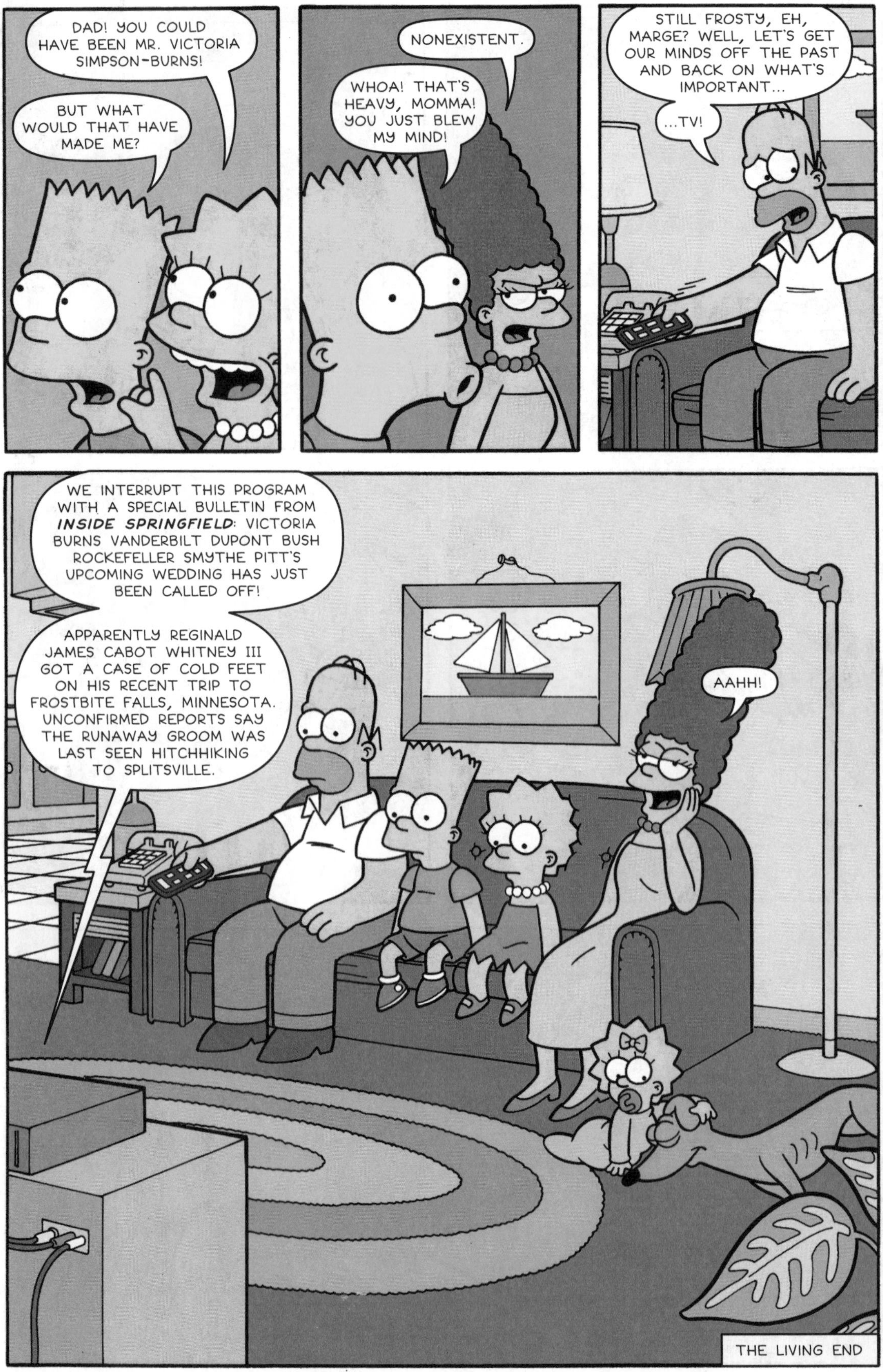
DAD! YOU COULD HAVE BEEN MR. VICTORIA SIMPSON-BURNS!
BUT WHAT WOULD THAT HAVE MADE ME?
NONEXISTENT.
WHOA! THAT'S HEAVY, MOMMA! YOU JUST BLEW MY MIND!
STILL FROSTY, EH, MARGE? WELL, LET'S GET OUR MINDS OFF THE PAST AND BACK ON WHAT'S IMPORTANT...
...TV!
WE INTERRUPT THIS PROGRAM WITH A SPECIAL BULLETIN FROM ***INSIDE SPRINGFIELD***: VICTORIA BURNS VANDERBILT DUPONT BUSH ROCKEFELLER SMYTHE PITT'S UPCOMING WEDDING HAS JUST BEEN CALLED OFF!
APPARENTLY REGINALD JAMES CABOT WHITNEY III GOT A CASE OF COLD FEET ON HIS RECENT TRIP TO FROSTBITE FALLS, MINNESOTA. UNCONFIRMED REPORTS SAY THE RUNAWAY GROOM WAS LAST SEEN HITCHHIKING TO SPLITSVILLE.
AAHH!
THE LIVING END